Praise for **15 STORIES, ONE BOB**

"Easy-to-read compilation of stories that will lift your spirits and inspire you. Inbal Hillel has brought together 16 stories about people from all walks of life; through carefully crafted interviews, we are taken on a journey with each individual and given tools to overcome our own challenges. The book is a very uplifting, spiritual journey of transformation and I highly recommend it."

> ~ Peggy McColl, The New York Times best-selling author, mentor, and expert speaker.

"Life is full of challenges and this book just proves that if you don't give up, great things can come. These 16 accounts are a testimony of strength, courage, and faith – each story will encourage you to never give up and keep working hard toward your purpose to fulfill your destiny! I highly recommend this book!"

> ~ Judy O'Beirn, international best-selling co-author of the Unwavering Strength series.

"15 Stories, One Bob is an amazing collection of inspirational stories by Inbal Hillel which will get you thinking about your own life and how you've gotten to where you are right now. As you read through the stories, you cannot help but wonder at the beauty of life and how there is perfection in what seem to be imperfections in life. Each story resonated with my personal experiences and I have come to the conclusion that we are here to grow and experience our lives the way we want to live them. When you look at your life from the perspective of being the creator of your own destiny, the universe delivers in miraculous ways. The question is, are you ready to receive it?"

> ~ Joanne Ong, international best-selling author of The Sun Within: Rediscover You.

"These are 16 stories of self-improvement, perseverance, courage, and faith. In this book, Inbal Hillel shows us how Bob Proctor's students found courage to face adversity and struggled to achieve their purpose by developing all their potential. These remarkable individuals achieved their dreams without surrender and worked until they found success, helping others with their positive attitudes and awareness of their beings. Their lives are examples to follow. I highly recommend this book."

> ~ Alberto Besga, interior architect, Spain

"*Inbal Hillel is a very passionate writer, committed to everything she does. In her new book, she shares how 16 people achieved their goals by following Bob Proctor's teachings and methods, and applying key principles in their lives. The results are amazing! I highly recommend this book, but be warned: you will be inspired to do the same!*"

~ Berenice Basvilbaso, *Thinking Into Results* consultant

"*As a business consultant who accompanies entrepreneurs through their success journeys, I have found that tasking budding entrepreneurs to learn from successful people who they admire is a valuable first step. The process involves interviewing people they hold in high regard in order to learn from their challenges, decisions, and ultimate successes. Inbal has done just this. She has gathered 16 stories which reveal a behind-the-scenes look at individuals who have succeeded as a result of their study with one master. The experiences of these featured individuals will inspire you and create a new awareness for your own journey. I believe every entrepreneur would do well to own this book; in fact, it might just be the pivotal piece that creates the desired results. Congratulations to Inbal for bringing this authentic, brilliant idea to life.*"

~ Racheli Orbach, coach and business adviser

"*Not everyone is fortunate enough to meet Bob Proctor in person. With her book, Inbal makes it possible for everybody to find out about the ways Bob can touch someone's life. By sharing her own and others' experiences, Inbal is imparting knowledge. Take Inbal's great gift, enjoy her beautiful writing, learn how to change your life, and DO IT!*"

~ Anca Dumitrescu, best-selling author of Journey – *An Outlined Path to Fulfillment*

"*In order to grow and maximize our true potentials, we need to change our paradigms – the ones we grew up with due to our cultural, social, and religious upbringings. Bob Proctor, the Master Thinker, through his teachings, books, and seminars has created experts who can take his legacy far and beyond. Inbal and her interviewees are a testimony to what an idea can do to our lives if people are willing to take the risk and walk the 'long green line.'*"

~ Aura Imbarus, Ph.D., author of Amazon bestseller *Out of the Transylvania Night* and founder and publisher of *See Beyond* magazine

15 STORIES ONE BOB

Plus a BONUS STORY

INBAL HILLEL

Published by:
Hasmark Publishing, judy@hasmarkservices.com

Copyright © 2017 Inbal Hillel
First Edition, 2017

No part of this book may be reproduced or transmitted in any form or by any means, electronic or mechanical, including photocopying, recording or by any information storage and retrieval system, without written permission from the author, except for the inclusion of brief quotations in a review.

Disclaimer

This book is designed to provide information and motivation to readers. It is sold with the understanding that the publisher is not engaged to render any type of psychological, legal, or any other kind of professional advice. The content of each article is the sole expression and opinion of its author and not necessarily that of the publisher. No warranties or guarantees are expressed or implied by the publisher's choice to include any of the content in this volume. Neither the publisher nor the individual author(s) shall be liable for any physical, psychological, emotional, financial, or commercial damages, including, but not limited to, special, incidental, consequential, or other damages. Our views and rights are the same: You are responsible for your own choices, actions, and results.

Editor:
Book Magic
bookmagic.biz

Cover Design:
Inbal Hillel
Inbal@inbalhillel.com

Layout Design:
Anne Karklins
annekarklins@gmail.com

ISBN-13: 978-1-988071-69-5
ISBN-10: 1988071690

Hasmark
PUBLISHING

Dedication

I grew up in a loving, caring home, thanks to my special parents Eli and Jenny Dahan; they raised me with the values of honesty, generosity, independence, and empathy.

It is thanks to them that I'm the person I am today: a contributing individual, with a positive influence in the world.

For that and so much more, I dedicate this special book to them.

With much love and appreciation,

Inbal

Acknowledgements

My first big thank you is to Bob Proctor* who has dedicated his life to teaching this important material to millions of people all over the world – including me. Thanks to him, all of us are growing in our awareness, changing our behaviors, and making significant contributions to the people in our environment. Bob has helped us to fight ignorance and gain understanding about how to think, act, react, and change our paradigms, so that we can have and become anything that we want.

Secondly, this book is special and inspiring because of the amazing people who shared their fascinated stories. I would like to say a huge 'thank you' to each and every one of them for their time, efforts, and willingness to help. They gave me motivation and many new tools. Their stories touched my heart deeply and will benefit my life forever.

Sending love to:

Lorrie A. MacGilvray and James La Trobe-Bateman: The love-at-first-sight couple who are living my dream of traveling all over the world and doing business from their motorhome.

Chaya Pamula: My great influencer with the biggest heart.

Valerio Caponetti: My inspiration to be myself and do what I love.

Austin Thomas: The man who opened my eyes

Mick Petersen: The writer who showed me how creativity can boost you to the top of the ladder.

Koby Benvenisti: The visionary who taught me to look for what I can't see in my life.

Barbara Daoust: The woman who taught me about the power of love.

Oddmund Berger: The leader who created success out of generosity.

Rodney Flowers: My hero of persistence and strength.

Eileen Bohr and Norman Petermann: The couple who inspire me with their excitement and radiant energy.

Ryan Pack: The individual who helped me to feel and understand what it is to be different.

Peter Hurley: The photographer who helped me to break old paradigms by proving that it is possible to earn money from art work.

Josh Thomas: The man who showed me the positive side to being radical.

Dr. Jussi Eerikäinen: The networking genius and my savior who taught me so much with his knowledge, kindness, and willingness to help. I appreciate Dr. Jussi for being there for me at all the critical moments.

Judy O'Beirn and Hasmark Publishing: The patient publisher who gave me great service and helped me to reach my goal.

Special Thanks:

I would like to extend a special 'thank you' to my mentor, Peggy McColl, who empowered me and led by example, teaching me how to manage tasks and successfully complete this project. She helped me – step by step – to transform a dream into realty.

Heartfelt Appreciation:

I would like to offer huge thanks to my loved ones, who make my life the best one I can have and who make me smile and laugh every day: Tom and Gil Hillel Wolff, Alberto Besga, Tamar Elias and family, Danit Shahaf and family, and all my good friends in Israel, Spain, and around the globe who have supported me and encouraged me.

---

*Bob Proctor is a world-renowned speaker, motivational life and business coach and mentor, and author of bestselling books. Bob Proctor, who came to international attention for his appearance in *The Secret*, has a reputation for getting the very best out of people and businesses.

What inspires us the most?

Real-life stories are our greatest inspiration to become better versions of ourselves; stories of struggle that we can identify with, stories in which we can see ourselves and that encourage us toward success.

This book presents sixteen journeys by students of Bob Proctor. Inbal Hillel skilfully interviews remarkable people who have revolutionized their lives by bringing change, balance, and Universal Laws to bear on their everyday existences.

Each one of these stories will excite you. The bravery of these heroes will encourage you. The wisdom of these mentors will help you find answers to life's most essential questions.

Table of Contents

1. *Old Self/New Self: The Battle Within* by Barbara Daoust   15

2. *Clear Vision* by Koby Benvenisti   35

3. *Live a Life You'd Want to Live Over* by Chaya Pamula   43

4. *The Businessman-Turned-Shaman* by Valerio Caponetti   55

5. *You Have the Power to Heal Yourself* by Eileen Bohr and Norman Petermann   69

6. *Dream Your Life, Then Live Your Dream* by Mick Petersen   83

7. *Everything Is Energy* by Dr. Jussi Eerikainen   95

8. *Be the Source* by Peggy McColl   111

9. *I Can Is More Important than IQ* by Inbal Hillel   127

10. *Who I Am in The World* by Ryan Pack   139

11. *Think and Grow Sober* by Austin Thomas   155

12. *Believe to Your Core and Live It* by Lorrie A. MacGilvray and James La Trobe-Bateman   171

13. *Think Beyond What You Know* by Oddmund Berger   191

14. *Follow Your Heart* by Peter Hurley   213

15. *Do it Anyway* by Rodney Flowers   223

16. *BONUS STORY* *Fight or Flight* by Josh Thomas   243

About the Author   255

Table of Contents

Foreword

I always find it interesting to read stories about how my father has influenced people from all around the world to live a better life. In this wonderful book that Inbal Hillel has put together, you will find stories written from the transcripts of interviews with some of Bob Proctor's students.

When reading these transcripts, let your imagination place you into the story, so that you can also take this information and apply it to your life in order to live the way you would like.

Inbal is a great example of someone who let go of the things she was not enjoying so that she could embrace the life she wanted to live. This book is an example of that. Whenever I have run into her at a seminar or event, she always has a smile on her face and you know that she is living the life she desires.

I know that I am fortunate to be Bob Proctor's son. I have lived all my life knowing this wonderful man and have seen first hand that he really lives the way of life that he teaches. Most mornings, my father and I will speak to each other on the phone before anyone else is up. The early morning conversations that we have will always be a blessing in my life. From these conversations I have learned so much and know that I am living a charmed life because of all that he has taught me – and, more importantly, by applying what he has taught me.

One of the first things we do everyday is to 'talk good' about people behind their backs. While most of the world seems to be focused on the negative, we have decided to focus on the positive. Imagine what a wonderful place this would be if, every day, we talked good about people, even when they are not listening. That one lesson in itself is worth its weight in gold. I have learned that when we stay in a positive way of thinking, we really do attract wonderful things and wonderful people into our lives. Yes, what we see in the world is really a reflection of how we are.

I know almost everyone that has contributed to this project. It is heartwarming for me to read how their lives have changed by implementing ideas that are usually right in front of us. Take to heart their messages and be sure to apply these valuable lessons to your own life. If you do, then you can also live a charmed life.

Brian Proctor
VP of Business Development
Proctor Gallagher Institute

1

Old Self/New Self: The Battle Within

Barbara Daoust

Barbara Daoust was born in Montréal, Quebec, and had a successful career in the entertainment industry in Los Angeles. After weathering a series of personal tragedies which made her lose her will to live, Barbara found inspiration and hope through her work as a consultant and business owner.

Can you please introduce yourself?

Barbara: I'm Barbara Daoust and I live in Los Angeles. I've been here for more than 25 years now. I majored in theater arts at university – that's where I met the love of my life, Patrick Joseph, an American born in Texas and raised in Chicago. The two of us decided to live in San Francisco. It was there that we founded a couple of theater companies: Phase One Productions and The Nova Theater. I started producing and directing in San Francisco for our theater company as well as for other theater companies in the Bay area. This lasted for about five to six years, before I decided to apply to The University of California, Los Angeles (UCLA), for a Master of Fine Arts (MFA) in directing.

I had some great success during that time in my career. I had a show that was selected to represent San Francisco at the Kennedy Center in Washington DC. I studied directing at UCLA and received my MFA. Then, I spent the next 10 years in TV and film, working with the Olsen twins – celebrity twins who work in the film and TV industry. I also founded an acting academy for young performers. Many of those young performers are now very successful TV and movie stars.

I eventually reached the end of my contract with the twins when they went to study at New York University. It was around that time that I began to question what I wanted to do next and if I wanted to continue in the entertainment industry. My desire was to direct for TV and film. I was very focused on that path, but it wasn't happening the way I expected.

In 2003, everything changed. In January, my husband and I made a short movie about a friend of ours who died of AIDS. It was called *Letting Go*. Three months later, my husband, Patrick, passed away – just two months before our 25th wedding anniversary. My husband was diagnosed with fourth stage lung cancer on May 5th and he was gone three weeks later, on May 31st.

I didn't really know what depression was until I was faced with this tragedy. That's when I discovered how much I didn't know how to love myself.

A year later, I found my husband's mother dead in her apartment. Then, my best friend of 25 years was diagnosed with liver cancer and, two months later, I was with her when she died. Soon after that, my father died of lung cancer within three months of his diagnosis.

Last but not least, my 40-year-old brother-in-law, PJ, died when he jumped out of a plane and his parachute didn't open. He was the instructor and he was diving with a young man who also died.

This was a two-year period where my whole support system – all my loved ones – left me. I was miserable and I decided to stay miserable. I didn't realize that I had such a dark shadow side. I always thought that I was a very positive, uplifting person. I was a teacher. I was somebody who supported people. I was somebody who helped a lot of people. I didn't realize that inside of me, this perfectionist – I like to call myself a recovering perfectionist – was constantly striving and seeking more. There were a lot of things in my way, because I was never perfect enough. As a result of my depression, I drank heavily for three years. I had never been a heavy drinker.

I risked my life in many very creative ways. I drank myself into a coma every night. Patrick and I didn't have any children. I would get up at one o'clock in the afternoon. I didn't have anything to wake up for. I had no purpose or reason to live, except for my 19-year-old cat, Honey, who also died.

It was a time of tremendous change. As Bob says, there are two ways that we change. One way is through a traumatic event where everything changes in an instant. The other way is through constant time-spaced repetition of a new idea.

Through Bob's work, I now understand that I was truly shedding my old self in order to create the new version of me – the newer self. One day, I took a kayak out to the middle of the ocean. I had never been in a kayak. I sat there for an hour and I prayed for sharks to come and attack me.

The funny thing is, after an hour, I looked at my watch and I thought, the sharks aren't here. I don't want to pay for another hour. I was too cheap to pay for extra time to wait for sharks. I guess, the human side of me was trying to be rational because I was disappointed in the outcome, but my spirit knew that there was still more left for me to do with my life.

Another crazy thing that I did was to sleep with all the doors of my house completely open, praying for a serial killer to take me out of my pain. I did some bizarre things. All I wanted was to be with my loved ones on the other side.

But, as you can see, that's not what happened. I spent two years traveling and drinking. I went back to every place that Patrick and I had ever traveled to in search of meaning. I scattered some of his ashes in all of these places.

After about two years of grieving, one day, I woke up and I made a decision. I remember the day vividly. I had kept flowers in my house from Patrick's memorial and they had been dead for two years. My living room curtains were shut. Life had become too overwhelming. I decided to open up my living room curtains and I said to myself, "I'm not going to be miserable anymore." From that time forward, I started to allow more and more people to help me and to love me.

It was a journey of understanding love at a much deeper level. At one time, I thought that love was just the love I experienced with my husband. I didn't understand that there was a lot more love that I could allow into my heart from many other people who were willing to be there for me. I could see that I didn't want people to think I was doing well because I was afraid they would think that I was no longer in love with Patrick. People say, "It's time to move on." But when it's not your time to move on, those are not comforting words.

I started to seek professional help. I attended a Master's program in Spiritual Psychology at the University of Santa Monica in Los Angeles. That's when I started to really heal and learn more about self-love. When I was there, I started to come alive again.

I had been very successful in my entertainment career and I thought that I was confident. I didn't realize that I didn't know how to love myself. I wasn't aware. I had been living my life from the outside in, instead of – as we know from Bob's work – from the inside out. I was constantly seeking approval outside of myself.

Today, I can look people straight in their eyes, but back then, I couldn't look anybody in the face. I was like a puddle of water, trying to drown in my own tears.

While studying at the University of Santa Monica, I had a project to design an affirmation vessel – a Buddhist spiritual prayer box – that you place around your neck to hold close to your heart. It was this affirmation process that helped me to realize that I was creating my outer world through my inner world.

After working on that project for a couple of years, I wanted to expand my business and continue my personal self-growth development. I signed up to the Quantum Success Coaching Academy to certify as a Law of Attraction coach through Christy Whitman. I had no intention of being a coach. I was there to heal myself and to study the Universal Laws. I wanted to understand how to live my life differently. As part of the certification process, I had to work with clients. I realized that my clients were getting results and getting them very quickly. Clients who had had 25 years of therapy were finally getting results in their lives because they weren't telling the same story over and over again. I believe therapy has its place, but I also strongly believe that work with the Universal Laws helps people move forward with their lives. Shortly after certifying and writing my book – *True Love True Self: A Journey to Self-Love* – I met Bob.

When did you first come across Bob Proctor's material and what was your situation in life at that time?

Barbara: I came across Bob Proctor's material at a 2012 event called *Making a Million Look Small*. Peggy McColl, Gay Hendricks, and Mary Manin Morrissey were also involved. At that time, I had started my practice as a Law of Attraction coach. I had also started to study neuroscience. I wanted to explore the difference between the brain and the mind.

I struggled to grow my business. I was very effective at helping others become successful; helping myself do the same now became my objective. Bob taught me how to grow a business, make more money, and combine a business mindset with spirituality. Bob is very focused on teaching success principles: having a success mindset, forming the habits of a highly successful person, and having the right kind of goals so that you continue to grow. It's not about achieving the goal that matters; it's who you're becoming along the way that matters most.

On stage, Bob shared concepts that I had never heard of before. I thought, "Why haven't I heard anything about paradigms, habits controlling your behavior, self-image, and the terror barrier before?"

I realized that I was stuck in a pattern of familiarity with what I already knew – even though I was experiencing some level of growth. I was having better results with my coaching, but I still struggled with sales conversation. Many consultants struggle with sales conversation: selling ourselves, selling our product, understanding enrollment, and understanding how to share with others the benefits of our work. Bob's material helped me to understand what I wasn't doing. That's the knowing/doing gap – the difference between what people know and what they do.

What happened from that moment and what did you start doing differently to change your results?

Barbara: I made a decision to become a *Thinking Into Results* consultant with the Proctor Gallagher Institute in 2013. My goal was to double my practice and triple my income. That's exactly what I did the first year I became a *Thinking Into Results* consultant. Bob told me to start some mastermind groups and study his book, *You Were Born Rich*. I hadn't read the book and I didn't think I was ready. Bob said, "Just do it."

A lot of people will tell you, when Bob says do it, you do it. I was screaming on the inside with doubt, fear, and worry, but within a couple of weeks, I had four mastermind groups with about 10 people in each group. The crazy thing is, I still hadn't read the book. I just decided to do it and focused on being prepared, one chapterat a time. I started to see changes happening inside of me. I feltconfident. I took risks and I started to enjoy myself. My attitude was changing.

I started selling the program; it started with a handful of people and I was happy to see they were getting results and having light-bulb moments. This inspired me, encouraged me, and motivated me. Their results allowed me to get out of my own way and trust that the material actually works.

I was surprised to see clients re-enrolling in *TIR*, over and over again. I have some clients who have repeated the program as many as 10 times. They keep investing in themselves and showing up for the next dream goal. Every time they come back to the program, they're a newer version of themselves. As Bob says, "You'll need a telescope to look back at who you were a year ago." That's been the case for me and many of my clients. I'm constantly surprised at who I used to be. I think, "Oh my God. Did I think that way two years ago?" What's more, I thought I was right. Now, I ask, who was I to think that way, be that way, or act that way? I'm now in a place where I can laugh because I understand the old behaviors, the limitations, and how my thinking was the cause of my paradigms. I'm grateful for the changes I've made in the way that I think.

I often apologize to my late husband, saying, "You may not be here in physical form for me to apologize to you, but please forgive me for the limited mindset I had at that time." I did the best that I knew how with what I had. I'm no longer beating myself up about it. I completely understand who I was, where I came from, and who I am now. There are still so many parts of me that I haven't met yet.

How did you meet your husband?

Barbara: I met Patrick in theater school in September, 1975. He sat in front of me in theater history class. I couldn't see his face, but I saw his hands. The way that he held his pencil intrigued me. I was attracted to his hands. When I looked at him, I was instantly attracted to him. He was so handsome. A month later, we went to a Halloween party together. We ended up dancing together under a disco ball. After our dance, I remember sitting at a table with all of our friends from the theater department. Patrick reached over and placed one of his hands on my lap. There was an instantaneous connection and I knew that we were meant to be together. We were married in 1978 in Las Vegas and we were together for 28 years.

Patrick's father, Jack, died when Patrick was two-and-a-half. Patrick carried a belief with him his whole life that he was going to die young. Every time he said that he was going to die young, I was very upset. He died at 47.

Maybe he knew. Perhaps I knew too. I had a dream in my twenties about him dying of cancer. A few months before he passed, I took an Artist's Way workshop where we had to present a monologue. The monologue that I chose was a 40-year-old woman talking to her husband who was diagnosed with cancer. I recorded the monologue on video and showed it to Patrick. He thought that I was overacting and too distraught. He was gone three months later.

What paradigm did you discover that you needed to change from the moment that you met Bob Proctor?

Barbara: I discovered a boredom paradigm. I didn't want to do the *Thinking Into Results* program again. I thought, "I already know it. It's time to look for another program." Bob talks about how it's illogical to read the same book over and over again. But, if you read a book once, you won't be able to tell somebody what the book was about. We think we know the information, but it's just on a conscious level. In truth, we really don't know the material at all. The idea is to repeat the information in order to have a deeper understanding and to apply the material. This is when you'll change your results and not be controlled by the old self which holds onto old paradigms. You can change your level of awareness and become a newer version of yourself.

I started to look for another program to help me, because I was bored (or so I thought). The paradigm that I identified was that I was always 'getting ready to get ready'. I have Masters' degrees. I have licenses. I have certificates. I have taught workshops and led seminars. But the real paradigm for me was, 'I'm not enough'. The big lie I had been telling myself was that I didn't know enough. I wasn't comfortable stepping out into the world as a professional businesswoman because I was attached to being an eternal student. This was my pattern and, therefore, I had limited results.

I'm an eternal student. I just have to be careful that when I go to a workshop that I leave with the information and apply it, live it, and share it. I must allow myself to become visible. Getting ready to get ready just kept me playing small. It kept me invisible. I was a good student, because I was constantly seeking approval outside of myself in order to find out if I was good enough. It was really interesting to see that in myself. Now, I do *Thinking Into Results* repeatedly; I've done it at least 20 times. With a deeper understanding of what was holding me back, I now focus on my business instead of spending all my time going to seminars.

It's difficult to discover these paradigms, but a coach can help you to see things that you cannot see in yourself.

Barbara: I believe that we all need help. I directed actors. Actors need a director. The actors who think that they can do it without a director usually end up not doing as well. The difference between myself and some other coaches is that I never stopped receiving coaching or having an accountability partner. I've had four or five accountability partners; if I'm not held accountable, my paradigms take over.

Can you explain what an accountability partner is?

Barbara: I know a coach, Marigrace Gleason, and every day for the last seven years, I've written out my goal-achieving, forward-moving action steps and emailed them to her. Every night, I've sent her my follow-up steps, highlighting the actions that I've completed. She does the same with me. I have another partner – a Dream Builder coach, Kevin Smith

– who checks in with me once a week. We hold each other accountable for what we want to accomplish and what next steps will help us achieve our dreams and goals. We call ourselves, 'Partners in Believing'.

I have another partner who is a *Thinking Into Results* consultant, Stephanie Hessler. In the beginning of my training, Bob encouraged us to read a chapter on persistence from *Think and Grow Rich* by Napoleon Hill. Stephanie and I talked every morning and read the chapter out loud for maybe three or five months. We still connect once a week and share our wins, our successes, our desires, and our needs. We support one another. It's a way to show up and acknowledge each other. I believe that a lot of my groups are successful because they show up for each other – if they're not showing up, they're not accountable. You'll never outperform your self-image. You'll never outperform what you already know. Sometimes, it takes other people's consciousnesses to expand your imagination. Otherwise we're limited by what we already know.

As Albert Gray says in his article, *The Common Denominator of Success*, "Highly successful people form the habits of doing things that failures don't like to do." As a result, I'm constantly talking to my clients about the things they don't like to do, but are willing to do. For example, I don't like to exercise. I don't wake up every morning saying, "I'm going to enjoy exercising today", but I'm willing to do it. I don't wake up every morning saying, "I like cold calling." It's that I'm willing to try.

How long did it take you to start seeing results?

Barbara: After about one month, I felt a change inside myself. It didn't show up in my bank account the way I expected it to at first, but I stayed consistent with the TIR program. I paid a lot of money for the program and expected to see that returned to me immediately, but I needed to do more internal work for that to happen. I needed to work on my commitment – being steady with the TIR homework and being consistent with the repetition. I also had to trust the process. When you start to understand more, it leads to faith. When you start to have faith, you relax more. When you relax more, you start to see all the opportunity that is already there, waiting for you to catch up to it. You start to feel it. You start to respond to it and change your outer reality.

Most people think that they have to keep going until they hit their goal. I like to tell people that as long as you are feeling your desire and continue to take baby steps toward your desire, there are going to be opportunities along the way. People, places, circumstances, and goals start to come to you as you move toward your desire.

What were the most difficult moment and the best moment in the process?

Barbara: The most difficult moment was when I paid the deposit to become a TIR consultant. I experienced buyer's remorse and anxiety. I felt that I was hitting the terror barrier, but I didn't know anything about it at the time. I didn't realize that investing in a higher priced program would motivate me and increase my desire to create change. That's why I don't buy cheap online programs, because I know I'm going to find excuses to not do them.

It was challenging. I invested a lot of money, which meant I invested a lot of money in myself. I told myself and my clients that the TIR program was a Cadillac program: you're going to need to put on your seatbelt, because you're in for a ride. At first, I noticed that the cost of TIR was scary for most of my clients. By the time they got to about lesson four, many wanted to quit because things were changing rapidly in their lives and their paradigms were resisting the change. Fortunately, they didn't quit, because they had invested a considerable amount of money in themselves. I could see that everything inside of them wanted to quit and run away. But, because they had invested the money, it kept them in the game.

You can count on fears, doubts, and worries immediately showing up to sabotage your dream, saying "Come back to what you know." I was stalled by my fears, doubts, and worries, but I had to figure it out for myself. Those are the kind of opportunities that help you to meet the parts of yourself that you never knew existed.

The best parts were the results I saw in my bank account and seeing the results that other people were also getting. Ironically, I still had doubts, even when I saw results for others as well. Now, I have more experience and evidence that the program really works. That's when faith takes over. I have to get my ego out of the way. I have to understand that I'm a messenger. I'm helping Bob deliver his message. I'm also asking other people to help me deliver these universal messages for the highest good of human evolution.

When you hear the words "Universal Laws", what do they mean to you?

Barbara: I believed in God until I witnessed an event that devastated me. When I was sixteen, I worked at a psychiatric institution and I saw something that I couldn't comprehend. I decided that it couldn't be possible for there to be a God, given what I had witnessed.

I always had an interest in discovering what life was all about; a search for meaning, so to speak. When I started understanding the Universal Laws, I felt more at peace and gained a new perspective on life. To me, the Laws are about co-creation and having infinite intelligence. The Universal Laws represent a higher power or source energy coming to and through me in order for me to breathe, to receive information and consciousness from others, to co-create, and to actively engage both the spiritual and physical realms.

The Laws really helped me to focus on having order in my mind. As Alexander Pope said, "Order is Heaven's first Law." When we understand the different Laws and can articulate what they mean, that helps to focus the conscious mind. When the conscious mind is focused, it impacts the subconscious mind and this helps us to relax and make better decisions. The Laws help me to live life by design instead of living life by default.

We need to consistently take steps that move us in the direction of our dreams. Our daily efforts keep adding up to the outcome. The Universal Laws are there to support that, to engage us, to inspire us, to motivate us, and to help us focus.

Can you talk about the effect of a specific Law on your life?

Barbara: When I was at the University of Santa Monica, I had a vision during a meditation. I saw my late husband and my late father holding me up under my feet; I was barefoot and they lifted me up to the sky. In the sky was a vessel – the piece of jewelry that I wanted to hold a note such as an affirmation. During my first month in the Spiritual Psychology program, we were taught how to design a personal affirmation: mine was, "I'm genuinely sharing loving kindness for myself and others as I revitalize hope and raise conscious living for the highest good of all." It helped me to heal my life.

When I started saying that affirmation repeatedly, bizarre things happened. People came up to me in grocery stores and said, "You look so kind. What's your name?" I would go to a store and the cashier would say, "I'm going to give you my employee discount because you look so kind." I thought, "What's this about?" I began to look people in the eye and not judge myself so critically. I moved out of self-loathing. I thought that I would create a vessel to hold my affirmation, so that I could hold it close to my heart.

I went on a journey to create my vessel. I kept visualizing it, talking about it, and speaking about creating something unique. Eventually, within three months, I was in production with a jewelry designer. I brought the designer my piece and he created a mold for me.

Once it was finished, I put my affirmation inside it and wore it close to my heart. I kept repeating my affirmation. People asked me if they could have one. That's why I began designing a line of affirmation vessels for self-love, serenity, abundance, empowerment, healing, and grief healing.

I wanted to make it more affordable for people to buy and to give as gifts to friends and family. I designed a package so that I could sell it on QVC, a TV shopping channel. I got cold feet. I didn't understand the Laws at the time, the way that I do now.

Next, I wrote my book, *True Love, True Self: A Journey to Self Love*. I tell people that I lost the love of my life in order to find out that I didn't know how to love myself. It was a journey of self-love and I helped other people to be true to themselves and to stop lying to themselves.

I also created a guided visualization CD. The butterfly image on all of my products represents the metamorphosis that I felt. It was like being in the cocoon; feeling lost, confused, frustrated, and not knowing what is next in life. When a caterpillar is in a cocoon, the old cells die (the old self), because the new cells (the new self) eat the old cells until they no longer exist. The new self – the butterfly – needs to build strength by pumping blood through its veins to reach the tip of its wings in order to break free and fly. The caterpillar can only see a few inches in front of itself; the butterfly has a much more magnificent view of the world as it travels the skies.

The other Law that I love to talk about is the Law of Attraction and Vibration. When I first started with Bob, one of the affirmations we were told to say daily was, "Bob Proctor, not only am I going to equal you in your achievements, I'm going to meet you at the post and pass you at the grandstand." We were told to say it in the mirror every day. I would say it, but I didn't believe it. As Bob says, you don't have to have 100% belief; you just need conviction. I kept saying it. I'd roll my eyes as I said it and think, that's impossible.

Shortly after, I was leading a mastermind group and somebody said to me, one day you're going to create your own program. I went to a fundraiser event where there was an auction for a week-long stay at a villa in the Dominican Republic. Everybody at my table said, "Barbara, bid on that villa. You can do a retreat there." I thought, No way. I just spent a whole lot of money on Bob's certification program. I have to focus on that right now. Before I knew it, the auctioneer said, "Sold to the man at the back." Archie Joel Tullos, a life coach with the Ford Institute, came running up to me, put his hands on my shoulders, and said, "This is my gift to you!" I didn't even know him very well. He was a member of my spiritual center. I had spoken with him maybe five times. He bought the week-long stay in the Dominican Republic and gifted it to me. I am forever grateful to him.

I had a week-long stay available to me at a luxurious resort in the Dominican Republic. The villa slept fifteen people. I suddenly realized that I had to do something, but what? At another mastermind group, I said, "I'm not sure what program I'm going to run." Within a week, a woman brought me thirty-five pages that she had compiled. She put the pages in front of me and said, "This is your program that you're going to do in the Dominican Republic. I've watched your videos and read your book. I've listened to your meditations. I've taken your classes. I've been in your workshops. Here's all your material, right here." I realized that I had to do it.

All my paradigms were saying, "You don't know what you're doing." I wasn't ready yet. The terror barrier* kicked into high gear. Then somebody came to another mastermind and said, "I made a flyer for you."

As a result, I led a retreat in the Dominican Republic in January 2014, with a handful of people who joined me. It seemed completely out-of-the-blue but, as I now know, there was a lot of power in repeating over and over again, "Bob Proctor, not only am I going to meet you at the post, but I'm going to pass you at the grandstand." I kept saying that affirmation in the mirror and I manifested something that was quite unexpected.

As Bob says, "Generously give and graciously receive." We can't do it alone. I've been saying my goal statement for the last four years. My intention was to attract more corporate work, but it's taken me four years to be in that frequency. Two years into my practice, I started working with lawyers and financial advisors. They're all having amazing results!

Today, I also work with producers, writers, coaches, consultants, therapists, CEOs, and Senior VPs who work in the corporate world. Now, I allow more. I'm acting more. I'm leaping more. That's what helps to create a different result; I'm not just getting ready to get ready.

Can you tell me a story about one specific goal that you managed to accomplish?

Barbara: I grew my coaching practice to the point where I could sustain myself and not give my services away for free because I wanted to help everyone. I wanted to honor and respect all my education – the years of experience, the learning, as well as my God-given gifts and talents. It was difficult for me, in the past, to place a dollar value on my worth.

People mostly look at goals in terms of concrete evidence – the physical outcome. Using the goal of wanting to double or triple my income allowed me to help more people. The more people I helped meant that I received more money for my worth. I believe that money is a reflection of self-worth and self-value. I started to recognize and accept that I had something to give and I could ask for my worth. It's my energy. You can't put a price tag on that.

My other goal is to keep moving toward bigger contracts, more people, and more presentations. I'm writing a keynote speech called, *Act Your Way to Success*. I'm starting to re-connect with my past. I want to combine the knowledge that I have from my experiences in entertainment with the Universal Laws to help people connect at a deeper level with their feelings. I'm really seeing that the missing link for a lot of people is that they're not taking their ideas and dreams from a conscious state to an emotional vibrational state which helps them move into action. To activate the feeling place is what helps spirit move into form. This is what causes results to manifest in the outer world.

I'm working with Dr. Jussi Eerikainen on a program called *Your Genius Code Unlocked*. We're taking the idea of a goal statement and helping people create a script which will include affirmations, statements, and presupposing questions. We're also applying neuro-science brainwave entrainment technology and adding brainwave frequencies that will bypass the conscious barriers preventing us from accepting new ideas and new beliefs.

With this scripting method and brainwave technology, we're seeing some great results. I'm feeling great results from it.

I've also developed a visualization course with Austin Thomas. I believe in the power of visualizing, but I believe that motor imaging** is more powerful. Motor imaging is when you are acting the part; it's called, 'the actor's technique'. Our visualization course is not just about guided visualizations, but also about how to activate the feeling place and how to act the part. It's about how to become the thing you say you want to be.

What were you prepared to give up, to sacrifice, to arrive at your goal?

Barbara: As I said earlier, my paradigm of getting ready to get ready had to go. What I was really ready to give up was my ego. I had to be willing to get out of my own way and stop playing small; part of me wanted to remain invisible. Even when you asked me to do this interview, part of me still wanted to say, "I'm not ready." I want to encourage myself and others to be messy. It's okay to be imperfect. As Bob says, "Our spiritual DNA is already perfect."

I was a great teacher. I knew how to tell everybody what to do. My students and clients had tremendous success. They were having more success than I was, because I wasn't doing for me what I was telling everybody else to do. Now, I really believe that to become a master of this material, you have to practice and do what you tell others to do. You've got to walk your talk. I was too scared to do the things that I wanted to do. Now, I understand that fear is important. Fear equals growth. It's what we do with it and how we respond to it that matters most. Conscious learning is all about awareness and choosing to change through practice and repetition. To become better and to have more, we must practice the change until it becomes a new behavior or new paradigm. Then, when something feels too comfortable, it's time to stretch and step out of the comfort zone once again. Bob says, "Highly successful people step outside their comfort zones every day".

I interview people even if I'm not feeling perfect, looking perfect, or if I'm feeling out of sync. I do it regardless of my imperfect English. This book and video package were created by stepping out of my comfort zone.

Barbara: If you climb a mountain, you won't always see the top in full view. Sometimes, you can only see so far in front of you or fog might block your view. The question is, are you willing to keep taking the steps? Are you willing to strategize a solution and work around the obstacles? When you take the steps and get to the top, you experience the result and the feelings that you wanted. You didn't just fly a helicopter and land on the top of the mountain to look at the view for a few minutes and fly away. You had to draw on resources that you never knew you had. You lived through experiences that you never knew you could survive. Solutions appeared as you said, "Yes, I can do this."

What is the one key lesson you can give to everyone who wants to reach their goal?

Barbara: The key lesson, for me, is about being clear on what you really want and then make a committed decision to go for it. When you make that decision, write it out in detail. Describe it like it's a scene in a movie. You're the star of your own movie. You only get one take, so why not give it your best shot? Write that movie as a story and hold it in your mind. More importantly, become it. You have to know that you already are who you want to become. Take the necessary actions to create what you want. Ask why you want it. What are the feelings you will feel as a result of achieving your dream goal? Is it confidence, joy, power, and/or security? Start activating those feelings daily. If you want more love, create more love every day. If you love gardening, be in the garden. If you love to bowl, go bowling. Let yourself feel the feelings of joy. From that place, you will be creating vibrations to match and attract more of those feelings. More joy will keep showing up.

Be grateful daily and let yourself be messy. Do illogical things. Do things differently to break up the old habits, the old paradigms. If you keep doing the same things over and over again, you're going to keep getting the same result. That's the definition of insanity.

Every day, wake up and say to yourself, "Who am I today? How should I behave as a million dollar-a-year earner? How should I think, feel, and dress? How should I speak and respond to situations, as if I had the success that I want and it's already here for me to experience?"

Sometimes, it's going to be uncomfortable. Plan for it. As soon as you go after something you really want, everything is going to try to stop you. Your fears, your doubts, and your worries rush right in. People around you, circumstances, and events will seem to conspire against you. Your refrigerator will break down, you'll get a flat tire, or you'll have to rush to the vet. The subconscious mind and ego do not like to change. They want to protect us. They're doing all these things to defend us from humiliation, fear, embarrassment, and danger. They're tied to our programming: our limiting beliefs, our DNA, our heritage, our parenting, and our education.

It's really hard to create from a place of expanded consciousness when you're stuck in old programs. The missing link for a lot of people is that they're not expanding their feelings to create inspired action. They're not dropping their ideas into the subconscious mind with emotion. It helps to start creating success habits. I ask myself every night, "Am I set up for success tomorrow?" I walk into my office and ask, "Am I set up for success today? Does this vibration feel good?" I believe that our number one responsibility is to feel good.

That also means looking at your negative self-talk; your inner critic and the devil within who wants to keep you the same. Sometimes,

I like to play with characters. I tell myself that my paradigms are like Darth Vader, but my new self is like Luke Skywalker. What's the conversation going to be? I recognize, all day long, that I'm in a battle with my old self and my new self. It's through expanded consciousness that I have the power to choose how to respond. What am I going to do in order to change? It takes consciousness and the will to do it.

What is your next goal?

Barbara: I'm designing an eight-week online workshop called *Your Genius Code Unlocked* with a two day in-person retreat called *Act Your Way to Success* to help people connect to the feeling place. My long-term goal is to create a reality TV show. It would involve a group of TIR consultants working with philanthropists who want to help people and communities achieve a big dream. It takes a village to raise a child and we need others' consciousnesses to create big results. As I lead my mastermind groups, I look at every single person as a philanthropist. I visualize them as highly successful people. Because their consciousness is growing, they are becoming more expansive, creative, and successful. One day, they will be a part of my reality TV show. They are already a part of my dream.

What would you like to accomplish in your life before you leave it?

Barbara: I would like to become a philanthropist myself. I'm growing the bandwidth and frequency right now. I'm nurturing my commitment to leadership. I'm developing trust and faith that I can build that kind of wealth for myself in order to give back. I'm practicing ways to give unconditionally. As Bob says, "Everything here is just on loan. We're just borrowing it while we're here."

If you had to choose one sentence that has a lot of meaning for you, what would it be?

Barbara: "You'll probably never know who you are until you uncover the parts of yourself that you don't yet know. You'll never outperform your self-image."

This concept comes from an experience that I had as a young actor. I had a challenging encounter with a director. He was very attracted to me, but I was already involved with my late husband. He tried everything he could to have a passionate relationship with me. I kept rejecting him and one day, he said to me, "Barbara, you don't know who you are and you probably never will." I was so struck by that comment that I decided to quit acting for a while. It was too painful to be that open and vulnerable. For many years, I resented that man and was angry about how mean he was, not only to me. I held on to that comment. Now, I have come full circle. I have a different understanding of that statement; it has become a powerful message for me. "You don't know who you are, and you probably never will, until you uncover the parts of yourself that you don't yet know." I use it as a reminder for myself when I'm stretching and I use it to inspire other people. To feel pain, to be vulnerable, and to be challenged to grow by someone else is extremely uncomfortable. I didn't have the tools to process my pain at the time. I didn't have a mentor. I understand differently now. He truly was one of my greatest teachers. I had to learn to forgive, forget, and let go.

Do you have something to add?

Barbara: Opportunity meets preparation. It starts with mindset. Take the time to acknowledge yourself every day, rather than punishing yourself for all the mistakes you made or all the problems that you have. Your subconscious mind is going to be working on whatever you put into it just before you go to sleep. You want to wake up with new, fresh ideas rather than the same old ideas repeating themselves throughout your day.

I've worked with a lot of successful people who come to me and don't feel successful. I was that person. I had success, but I didn't feel successful because I wasn't enough. Some people have three homes, three cars, five million dollars in their bank account, and they still don't feel successful. I believe it's because they are stuck in the past or they're focused on the future. We forget about the present moment. The present moment is where our power lies. What you give to this moment – right here, right now – is what's creating your future. Your thoughts, your feelings, your actions are pre-paving your future.

Most importantly, be grateful for what you have now. Acknowledge the good and value your gifts – your genius code. Appreciate all the education you have and all the belief that people have given you in this lifetime and value it. You will start to see the results in this present moment. It takes dedication, commitment, and persistence to create a new inner world.

As the psychologist, Abraham Maslow, says, "In any given moment, we have two options: to step forward into growth or to step back into safety."

The butterfly's view from up high is so much better than the caterpillar's view from below. Be aware of the paradigms that are going to keep you stuck in excuses. This is your old self. Get smarter than your brain: use your mind!

About Barbara Daoust

Barbara has an MFA in Theater Directing from UCLA. She spent most of her career in theater arts, film, and television as a director, acting coach, writer, and producer. She is a Certified Facilitator with the Proctor Gallagher Institute as well as a speaker, author, and speaking consultant.

Contact Barbara at:
barbara@barbaradaoust.com
www.barbaradaoust-tir.com

*"When you are taking action to break out of your comfort zone, there is this zone just before the breakthrough called the Terror Barrier. That's a zone where your subconscious mind does everything it can to keep you safe in what you know. Your subconscious mind generates fears, panics, and even creates external circumstances to give you every reason to step back. (Reprinted with permission from the Spiritual Self Transformation website: https://www.spiritualselftransformation.com/blog/tag/terror-barrier/)

**Motor imagery is a process where one rehearses or simulates a given action in order to investigate the unconscious processes which precede action.

2

Clear Vision

Koby Benvenisti

Koby Benvenisti resides in Jersey City, USA. After an accident left him half-blind, Koby transformed his life. In November 2016, Koby organized, produced, and hosted Carnegie Hall's biggest personal development event on the East Coast with Bob Proctor, Loral Langemeier, Michael Beckwith, and Bill Harris (The Secret), Peggy McColl, Mary Morrissey, and many others.

Can you, please, start by introducing yourself?

Koby: I moved to the United States in 1980 and for 24 out of the last 26 years, I have lived here as what society calls 'an illegal immigrant'. While living here, I attended college and worked in various jobs. I wasn't particularly happy with the work I was doing; I just knew there was more out there.

In 2009, I had an accident. Two of the transformational principles in life are through repeated affirmations or a trauma. Mine was the latter. It happened so quickly and this was when the answers to many of my questions started to flow.

What happened in the accident?

Koby: I was working in construction when a bungee cord broke and snapped, hitting me in the eye. I lost my vision in the left eye. I believe that everything we experience in life is designed to teach us. My mind was racing: *What didn't I SEE?* What direction did I need to look? The accident happened as I was loading toilets on a truck. Toilets, as we know, flush! What was I supposed to flush out of my life? Flush my behavior, my awareness, parts of my lifestyle, or flush my beliefs? At that very moment, it became clear to me: I needed to finally accept my calling to teach. I also knew that I'd have to get training that would help me structure my teachings. It was around that time that I met Mary Morrissey. I knew that my mentor had arrived.

When did you first come across Bob Proctor's material and what was your situation in life?

Koby: I met Bob in 2010. I was introduced to Bob by Mary during a seminar they ran together.

What happened from that moment? What did you start doing differently to change your results?

Koby: I seriously committed to studying. I went to study with Mary, because I had been studying Metaphysics, the Science of Mind, and Eastern philosophy for many years. I realized there was a way for me to utilize my knowledge in a specific and organized way

What paradigms did you discover that you needed to change?

Koby: I needed to *replace* my paradigms, not *change* them. As we try to 'fix' our lives, we dig ourselves deeper into the problem. A healthier way would be to adapt a new paradigm. I needed to learn to trust in myself and to have a mindset that allowed things to happen. You can't make things happen. You allow them to come in. Change occurs when we are ready to receive.

How long did it take you to start seeing results?

Koby: Immediately. It seems like when I accepted the decision, a new plateau was reached. When you change the way you look at things, the things you look at change. In order to get results, you need to envision them happening. Sometimes, the results may not be the ones that you want, but as long as you stay in the process, they will manifest. It takes a very deliberate and focused decision to do that. I truly believe that our life removes or adds circumstances needed for our growth.

What was the most difficult moment and what was the best moment in the process of changing and growing?

Koby: The most difficult moment was realizing that I wasn't living the life that was calling me and that my paradigms were the things that were holding me back from living life to its fullest. The most rewarding moment in the process of my change and growth was the *Modern Day Millionaire* event, where I took control of the stage at Carnegie Hall. It was the cumulation of the past eight years of study and all the time and money it took to do it. These were the results of investing in myself.

When you hear the words "Universal Laws", what do they mean to you?

Koby: For me, the Universal Laws mean that we are collaborators with life, whether we agree to it or not. When we familiarize ourselves with these Laws, we take control of our destinies. There are invisible laws that are at work and they are absolute – like the law of gravity or electricity. These laws, as Einstein said, "are not science but physics".

Can you give an example of the effect of one specific law on your life?

Koby: I would have to say the Law of Cause and Effect has had a great impact on my life. The cause of the accident, for instance, brought clarity and new beginnings to my life.

Can you tell me about this event and what was the process you used over the last one and a half years to create the Modern Day Millionaire event at Carnegie Hall?

Koby: I had a vision that I wanted to bring Bob Proctor to Carnegie Hall. There was no process because I'd never done it before. It was a process of exploration. Most of the process was revealed to me one step at the time.

We didn't know how things were going to turn out until the last minute. I was very fortunate to attract a lot of people who wanted to help and become part of the event. PJ Gaztanaga, who's been working with Bob Proctor for the past 10 years, upon hearing of the initiative to bring Bob to New York city, partnered up with me and was instrumental on many of the logistics. So were the 'Four Dames'*; one phone call to the Dames and they were in full support of us with their strategy and connections. Mary Morrissey** and Cynthia Kersey of the Unstoppable Foundation created and led a board of advisors. Dr. Michael Beckwith (*The Secret*) of the Agape Church and Berny Dohrmann of CEO Space International were also a part of the board, and a dream team was created. I just stuck with my vision. You stick to the vision in your imagination and revisit it over and over. I had rehearsed my event speech, night after night, in my head so many times that when I got on stage, for the first time in front of so many people, it was like second nature to me.

What was your goal?

Koby: My goal was to bring Bob to New York City and share the stage with him. However, as the phrase goes, "Sometimes, in life, we don't get what we ask for. What we get instead is the Good Stuff." I ended up in a two-day event, sharing the stage with 29 of the top speakers in the world.

How did you see yourself?

Koby: A part of the 'vision work' was to see myself getting on stage, with people clapping, screaming, and having a good time. I pictured myself being smooth, delivering the point. Peggy McColl told me in rehearsal, "Koby, you are opening the evening. You are the Energy Setter," and if I am excited, the people will be excited and raise the energy at the event.

Who else did you manage to bring to New York?

Koby: We had close to 30 speakers. Some of the other names included Dave Meltzer from Sport 1 Marketing, JP Maroney, Sandy Gallagher, Mike Long, Anik Singal, Abiola Abrams, Alena Chapman, Rodney Flowers, and JR Fenwick.

It was an amazing event. Everybody was so impressed and enjoyed it. There was such good energy.

Koby: A couple of months ago, I was reminded of a dream that I had three years ago. In my dream, I was on stage, standing at Stage Left. Somebody was playing piano. I woke up and I asked myself, "Why would I be on stage and who was playing piano? Who was this man on the stage? What was I doing on the stage and why?" I had so many questions. This dream was in my head for a few days, and then I forgot all about it. Now I know it was a premonition of this event. The man on the piano was my friend John Hardesty; he was playing the piano and introducing me on the Carnegie Hall stage.

On day two of the event, at the Pennsylvania Hotel, a lady came up to me and reminded me of the Future Memory Exercise I did with her at a seminar four years ago. In this exercise, you share with each other where you see yourself in the future, three years from now. She said, "You told me that you were going to be in front of thousands of people with the best speakers. You said you would touch thousands of people with Bob and with Mary. Congratulations. You did it!"

Did you remember that?

Koby: I didn't remember that specific incident, but it makes sense. We must dream and visualize. These emotions, feelings, and pictures activate the executing part of our brain. We certainly do not need the "How?" Why should we try to squeeze the infinite into our little heads? The level of speakers we had were the best line-up of speakers New York has ever seen. I'm so grateful for Bob and I'm grateful for Mary for teaching me these principles.

Carnegie Hall is a really impressive space.

Koby: It's Carnegie Hall. It's one of the most iconic halls in the world. I was so happy. It was a top-notch performance.

I had no idea how things were going to unfold and then, before I knew it, it was happening. I woke up on the day of the event, thinking, "It's today. It's today!" Five hours before the event, we had a rehearsal. Bob, Sandy, and their team; Mary and her husband, Joe Dickey (I owe them the biggest thanks in the world for their support); Peggy and other guests; everybody came into Carnegie Hall. No one had been there before. We opened the doors and everybody walked in. It was amazing to see Bob and Mary and everybody taking it all in, experiencing the grand tour, the spirit and the history of this place. The world's greatest speakers and performers walked this stage in the past.

Many people came up to me the next day and thanked me for making their dreams come true. I replied, "Thank you for making my dream come true." All I did was what I was taught to do. It's possible. As I said earlier, there are Laws at work. Study and apply them.

You were yourself, and that was special. It was so authentic.

Koby: I have to thank Mary, Bob, and Les Brown for teaching and preparing me. We are made of the finite and the infinite; our physical bodies and our mental ability to think and communicate; the human and the divine. Learn how to live on both planes.

Did you sacrifice something on the way? Did you give up something to achieve this goal?

Koby: I gave up fear. I spent a lot of sleepless nights. There were many hours when I did not feel worthy. However, it's never about the goal, but about who you become in the process.

Who did you become in the process?

Koby: I realized something about myself. If I hosted this event, I could host any event. My friend Carl said, "You just glided onto the stage." These are things I am not conscious of, but Bob teaches us to "Feed the mind with the right ingredients and the way will be revealed to you."

Did you learn the material every day? Do you have a routine?

Koby: I don't study as much as I would like. But I use 'Tunnel Vision.' Aim at the end of the tunnel, where you would like to end up. Focus and keep the end in mind. The way will reveal itself.

If you are too concerned about the details, you can't see the whole picture.

What is your next goal?

Koby: I learned what it takes to create an event. Will there be difficulties? Of course. Will it have challenges? Of course. But at least I know how to go about it a little bit differently.

My next goal will be stadiums – filling up a stadium with 25,000 people. Can you imagine? You see, this is the thing. You notice that as soon as you look at a goal, immediately, it feels right. It makes me happy. Life doesn't give you what you think you want. It gives you what you believe, what you feel. As soon as I said 25,000 people in a stadium, it was like, *YES! That's it!*

What would you like to accomplish in your life before you leave it?

Koby: What does Bob call success? He says success is constant pursuit of a worthy ideal, when you are constantly, diligently committed to pursuing a worthy ideal, you're on the right way. I remember at some point saying to myself, "What happens if I'm not going to make it? What if I die tomorrow?" My answer to myself was that I will die doing what I love, pursuing a worthy ideal.

If you had to choose one sentence that has a lot of meaning for you, what would it be?

Koby: Everything always, with no exception, works *for* you, not *to* you.

Do you want to add something?

Koby: I'm just so grateful. It was almost like it all happened to someone else. It was a year and a half of so much doubt, fear, and questions, but when I got off the stage, I was floating on air.

Even after losing part of my vision, I gained so much more from the Universe. Never give up, even when the odds seem insurmountable.

About Koby Benvenisti

Koby is the head of a performance coaching, goal expediting, and project building firm. He serves both corporate and private sectors, from initiating and goal-setting to developing a strategic way of achieving objectives.

Koby organized, produced, and hosted Carnegie Hall's biggest Personal Development event, with Bob Proctor and many other famous leaders and mentors.

Contact Koby at:
www.kobyben.com
koby@kobyben.com

---

*The 'Four Dames' are four dynamic certified Life Mastery Consultants and Result Experts: Patricia Barnett, Julie Hamilton, Lynn Kitchen, and Marilyn Macha.

**Mary Morrissey is a life coach, motivational speaker, and best-selling author.

3

Live a Life
You'd Want to Live Over

Chaya Pamula

Chaya Pamula lives in New Jersey, USA, with her husband Satya Mohan, her daughter Anusha, and their two dogs. Her husband works as an IT director at BNY Melon and her daughter attends Harvard Law School. Chaya owns a technology firm and is the founder of a not-for-profit organization to help underprivileged children in India.

Can you, please, start by introducing yourself?

Chaya: I was born and brought up in India. My education was completed in India. Even though I was a teenager when I lost my parents, I was very ambitious about my career and what I wanted to achieve in life. When you are a kid, your identity comes through your parents. I felt I was invisible and lost my identity after my parents passed away when I was in my teen years. I really wanted people to recognize thatI existed in this world and came from a very well-respected family. I remember during my school days, whenever someone inquired about my father and what he did, I used to say that he worked as a chief engineer in a sugar factory, but I would not say that he had died because I was never comfortable when people showed pity. As I was growing up, I didn't want to live a normal life. I wanted to make a difference. Although my teenage years were filled with adversity, they helped me become the strong woman I am today. I always saw my mother as a very strong and extremely compassionate woman. I grew up with my two older siblings, paternal uncles, aunts, and cousins. I watched my parents make so many sacrifices for the family and struggle to maintain the harmony of love and happiness.

After I lost my parents, I wanted to help children who had similar challenges in their lives; those without guidance or security and with no parents to take care of them. It is about having someone that you can trust and rely upon, someone that can give you moral support and guidance and be there for you whatever happens. I became ambitious to help children who did not have the support I had in the early stages of my life. This desire grew stronger and stronger over the years and when I came to this country, the opportunities that I received and the progress that I made in my career transformed my life. I succeeded in everything I put my mind to, mainly because of the promise I had made to my mother before she passed away that I would be successful in my career and be independent. This has a great influence on me even today; it's why I'm so determined to achieve my goals. I am also very fortunate that my family and friends were really supportive. My determination never left me. I always focused on my goal with positive exuberance and tried to realize my dream

As I was becoming more and more successful in my professional growth, I kept thinking, "What am I doing?" I wanted to help children, but I hadn't been doing anything about it. One day, it just hit me so hard that I realized I needed to do something about it. I resigned from my job at the pharmaceutical company where I had worked for eight years. I travelled to India to study institutions that support orphan and underprivileged children. With my uncle's support, I visited eight institutions, trying to understand what they do, how the work is done, and what challenges are involved in undertaking and executing such a project. During that process, I realized that there are many organizations that offer the basic amenities for children: food, shelter, medical attention, education, etc. What was really lacking was an institution that would give the children a happy and secure life, providing them with a family and the love that they craved. All this fuels them with tremendous positive energy and self-confidence. This further allows them to flourish in their lives, so that their hidden talents come out and they can be really successful not only in their lives but in the society around them.

I was looking for organizations that were giving that happiness to children. Everywhere I went, I looked for that exuberance in the faces of the children, but I was met with disappointment. I was about to lose hope, but then I came across an organization in Pune called Maher. In Marathi, that means 'Mother's Home'. It was founded by Sister Lucy Kurien. When I met those children, I saw all that I was looking for: happiness in those innocent faces. The moment we walked in, all the children came and gave me hugs. They were so happy. It was like a huge family. That project really attracted me and I felt that I should be able to create something like that. I wanted to create a home; I didn't want to simply adopt the children or help the institutions financially so that I could tell myself that I was helping somebody. Helping somebody means rolling up your sleeves and being part of their lives every day. It's giving them the mentorship, the guidance, the love, and, especially, the security they're looking for. If you can give that, you can make a tremendous transformation in their lives.

I spoke to Sister Lucy and I said, "This is my ambition. I want to do something for these children." She gave me moral support. She said, "Go ahead and start. I'm there with you. I'll be able to share my experiences with you and give you whatever moral support I can."

I came back to the US and I went back to my job. With the consent of my husband, I started supporting the project. We adopted a home in Maher and we started providing money from my personal funds. It gave me so much satisfaction, but something was still missing for me. I wanted to adopt the Maher model and start something on my own, where I could be with these children on a regular basis in their daily lives. After consulting with Sister Lucy, I felt that we could have a presence in my hometown, Hyderabad. Why not start something there? I founded SOFKIN (Support Organization for Kids in Need) in 2005. We adopted the model of Maher where we create caring homes with 20 to 25 children and two housemothers. The women and children come from dire situations; they are rehabilitated and receive medical attention. The women are trained to be house-mothers or caretakers for these children. This model works well because the housemothers and the children come from similar backgrounds and experiences, so they understand and share each other's pain.

Maher is a much bigger project. It's a community project making huge transformations in the lives of many women, men, and children in Pune. I got some help by bringing those women into SOFKIN in Hyderabad, initially to start as our caretakers. In the 12 years since its inception, SOFKIN has grown from strength to strength – from three children in the beginning to its present roster of more than 100 children: more than 50 children in Hyderabad and more than 50 children in Maher. The SOFKIN model is simple and easily expandable.

I get huge satisfaction from this project because I am involved in their daily lives. I speak to the children on a daily basis – in the morning and in the evening before I go to bed. I know every child by name, their likes, their dislikes, their strengths, and weaknesses. Each one of them has a unique story. I recognize their voices on the phone. It's like my extended family. We exchange emails. I correct their English grammar and spelling to improve their writing skills. I encourage them to speak in English. We exchange WhatsApp messages with the older children. The procedures that we incorporated in the organization make the children more and more responsible. Every December, the children have elections through a democratic secret ballot process to choose their group leaders. The older children become group leaders for the younger children. They learn how to be responsible for other children; they also learn how to report on the progress of the children. They are responsible not only for training these children, but they also take care of their hygiene, their food habits, and their overall behavior.

The children are monitored by these older children and the caretakers. I give a lot of credit to the housemothers for their dedication and commitment, without which we wouldn't have been able to run this organization with such high quality and integrity. Every week, on a Saturday morning, I have a Skype meeting with all the staff and children for 4 to 5 hours, where the group leaders report on the progress of their group. That is an opportunity for every child to talk to me and express their concerns, their happiness, and whatever's on their mind. Sometimes we just have silly conversations. We have established the technology in such a way that I can watch the children from anywhere and the children can call me anytime. Even if it's midnight, I'll pick up the call because I want these children to feel that I am there for them any time, without any reservations, to attend to their needs.

There is a strict routine every day. The children don't consider this a hostel; this is a true home, a family. This is what really makes a difference in their lives, because they go to regular schools. They have regular demands, just like our children. We treat them the same as our children. That's the goal and that's how the organization is growing.

Apart from SOFKIN, I'd like to mention my other passion: the for-profit organization that I co-founded about nine years ago, called PamTen. We are a technology solutions company operating in USA, Canada, and India. I am very passionate about conceptualizing and creating innovative software products that open doors into new marketplaces for PamTen and its clients. The reason I wanted to become an entrepreneur is that I wanted to make sure that I utilized my capabilities and skills to be able to influence and bring change in society; I can utilize the revenue from this for-profit organization to support SOFKIN and PamTen can be a learning platform for the children of SOFKIN to build their careers. Many children of SOFKIN and Maher are given internship and employment opportunities at PamTen. The co-founder, Prasad Tenjerla, also very much believes in the cause and extends his full support. PamTen offers a certain percentage of profits as a donation to the SOFKIN organization in addition to taking care of a few operational expenses. This allows us to maintain minimal or zero administrative costs at SOFKIN, which means every dollar raised is spent directly on the cause. We incorporated our passion to give back into our company's mission statement; we created our CSR activities to not only support SOFKIN, but to encourage active participation and interaction between PamTen employees and the children of SOFKIN. Both our employees and customers feel a strong purpose in working with PamTen. I am also able to mutually reinforce my leadership learning from both the for-profit and not-for-profit worlds, which helps me to be a better leader and a good role model for my children.

When did you first come across Bob Proctor's material? What was your situation in life?

Chaya: Six years ago, I first watched the movie *The Secret*. I watched it again before I went to an event on November 15th, 2016. When I watched Bob Proctor's movie, some of the principles – especially being positive and staying positive – made a huge impact on me. You ask yourself what you want and then focus on getting what you want.

If you determine what you want to do and are positive about it, Bob Proctor says that everything aligns and it happens. I think that was a revelation for me, because I've had several experiences in my life that really could be true testimonies to what Bob Proctor teaches.

What happened from that moment, and what did you start doing differently to change your results or to get the things that you wanted?

Chaya: When I wanted to establish the SOFKIN organization, everybody was skeptical. My family and my friends were not sure if this was the right move. My husband and my wonderful daughter have always been with me. I'm very fortunate to have a family that supports me. But when you speak to your friends and people in your outer circles, they would always say, "It's a huge responsibility. Are you sure you want to go that route?" This doubt made me hesitate a little bit, but the teachings say that we should listen to our inner call and jump into it. I asked myself, *Why am I hesitating?* When the gut tells you to move forward and do what you're passionate about, you should not hesitate, but just go for it. I think that's what Bob Proctor's teachings mean. The teachings give you the courage to make that bold step forward to do what you want to do. When I look back at my life, I feel so proud of myself for taking that bold step because I enjoy everything that I do. I'm so passionate about my organization. Now, many friends and family support my project.

Another incident in my life that proves Bob Proctor's teachings is that when I wanted to step into my own company, leaving a full-time job at a pharma company where I was drawing a six-figure salary, I challenged my family that I would earn that much money in three months by building my business. I did it, simply by being positive and focusing on my goals, and, of course, because of their support.

What paradigms did you discover that you needed to change to achieve your goals?

Chaya: I think I'm still working on some of those. I believe that every day you learn something new and experiences make you much stronger each day. I used to be very naïve and fearful – scared to talk to people. But, I learned from my experiences and every time I took a bold step, I became successful. That gave me more courage to do what I do today. I think one of the aspects – paradigms – that I would definitely want to continue improving is my self-confidence. I always tell people, be self-confident. Never lose confidence in yourself. Push the envelope to take those risks; sometimes you may fail, but you learn from the experiences. All that you need is to be positive. You need to ask yourself, what is it that you want to do? You need to really focus on it and make things happen. That's not easy, but I keep working on it and I keep seeing good results.

How long did it take you to start seeing results?

Chaya: I think that every time I made an attempt, the results were immediate or almost immediate. The desire was so strong each time I wanted to do something, it never took too long for me to achieve the results. Every time I have wanted to achieve something, so far, it has happened.

What was the most difficult moment and what was the best moment in the process?

Chaya: There were many such moments. What comes to my mind immediately is the experience that I had making that gut move to start this organization. It was difficult initially. I didn't have sufficient funds. No one had the knowledge or experience to advise me. I kept going back to Sister Lucy because she did this work and she took that bold step in her life. When you don't have other people's experience to learn from, you feel that everybody's watching you to see what's going to happen. Taking such a bold step makes you fearful sometimes and I think that was a difficult process for me, overcoming that. It took me almost a year to get the confidence to continue doing what I was doing.

I started by taking a little step. Sometimes you make a leap and then you think, *Oh my God. How am I going to continue this journey?* That's exactly what happened. I love every moment now and I think that process has changed me as a person. It has changed my daughter as a person as well. She's a lawyer and heavily involved in this work. I feel that this whole project has had a huge influence on her; it's helped her develop her character. I am fortunate to have some God-sent angels in my life who stood by my side, giving me both moral and financial support as SOFKIN grew over the years. I don't have any complaints about my life. I just love it.

When you hear the words "Universal Laws", what do they mean to you?

Chaya: People talk about spirituality. People talk about Universal Laws. People talk about the scientific approach to the universe; a lot of these different elements come into play in your life. There is nothing good or bad about anything. I am a big believer that, as humans, we all carry energy within us and it's up to us whether we use it as a positive energy or as a negative energy. I just wish that the entire universe was filled with positive energy. That's one part of Bob Proctor's teachings that I keep close to my heart: the Law of Attraction. The Law of Vibration and the Universal Laws have so much to do with people's daily lives. It depends on how you perceive that information. How you apply it to your own personal life can change everything about you.

I attended Bob Proctor's *Modern Day Millionaire* event on November 15th, 2016. I wasn't planning to go to that event, because I didn't even know about it. One of my friends, Joanna Black, introduced me to her friend, Bethney Ruggiero, and they felt that I should go to the event along with my other friend, Carol Gabel. We were both invited to the event and I thought, *why not?* I felt that I should go because I'm in this process of raising funds for constructing a building for my children at SOFKIN; there are more than fifty children living in one home with just two bathrooms. Every day is a challenge for them. They have to go to school. They have to go through their regular schedules and I can see that the house is not enough for them. I recently declined some new admissions because I didn't have any more living space. That was really heartbreaking for me. Fortunately, with the help of Siddharth & Mala Bhattacharji, who have been principal donors for the past 10 years and who donated a significant amount for the building project, and with the help of a few other sponsors and my personal funds, we were able to purchase the land. Now, we have to start the construction of two buildings; one for the boys, one for the girls. We estimated the budget to be $350,000 and we were able to raise almost $200,000. The remaining $150,000 had been lingering in my mind. Every single day, I wondered, how am I going to raise this money?

When I heard about Bob Proctor's event and my friends explained to me about Cynthia's story with the Unstoppable Foundation, I was hopeful and I believed that I should meet this man and his team. I needed this strong hope to go to people, to be able to get some funding for my construction project. Bob Proctor gave a short talk and then they opened it up to the floor for questions. As I was listening to others' questions, something in me told me to get up and ask. Bob Proctor also shared his story about the Unstoppable Foundation. I raised my hand and asked for the microphone. I shared my story in two minutes and I said, "Bob, I live with a purpose and I have a mission. I am truly inspired and motivated by your example of how to make a million dollars look smaller; now, I feel confident that I can reach my goal. I need to raise another $150,000. Please advise me how I can achieve this. Because I need this money." Everyone in the room started laughing – especially Bob Proctor – because they knew where I was going. Then, I said, "You helped Cynthia when she asked." Surprisingly, Bob Proctor said, "I admire your courage." He said, "If you can find 14 other people who can give you $10,000 each, I'll be the 15th person to give you $10,000." Right then, I wondered how I could get 14 other people to donate $10,000 each, when they didn't even know me. My conscious mind was telling me, I have the entire day. I can talk to people. Within seconds, Bob Proctor said, "This is how we're going to do it." He started asking the people in the room, "Who wants to help this lady?" It changed my life.

One by one, people raised their hands. Bob Proctor counted 12. He said, "I need two more." Two more hands were raised. He got me my 14 pledges and then he called me onto the dais, and he gave me a check for $10,000. He told everyone to contact me. That experience made me think that there is still hope. There are still great people out there who are generous, who believe in these kinds of causes. It totally boosted my hope for the whole project and gave me so much assurance and confidence that I could do anything I wanted. We were all in tears. In less than a minute, he had raised $150,000 for me! I was jumping with joy and pinching myself as I tried to believe what was happening in front of my eyes. This experience was so precious and a great lesson in today's world where we see divisions based on race, religion, color, and status. These people were total strangers. They didn't know anything about my project or me, but they trusted Bob Proctor and my story. I still become emotional whenever I think of this experience, which I will cherish until my last breath.

That was the Law of Attraction working for you.

Chaya: As I said, I'm still working on my self-confidence. That incident gave me so much confidence; I can ask for whatever I want, focus on it, and I will get it. This also resonates with the teachings of the saint Shirdi Sai Baba. He's a saint who lived in the 19th century. His teachings say that if you do good, it comes back to you threefold. He also says to ask for what you want when you pray to him. He said, "Don't just pray to me; demand. If you're a real disciple, you'll demand. I will give it to you." I believe that. My mother used to say, "You won't lose anything by asking, but you may lose a fortune by not asking." What happened to me was a true testimony to that.

What is the one key lesson that you can give to everyone who wants to reach their goal?

Chaya: Find your passion. We're all special humans. You're brought onto this earth for some purpose. We all can live a regular life. Everybody has that life. But what is special about you? What is it that you're very passionate about? I think it's important to find your passion, focus on it, be determined, and never lose hope. There will be ups and downs, but once you're determined and your goal is fixed, you will always be able to overcome those challenges and be successful.

What were you prepared to give up to arrive at your goal?

Chaya: My life revolves around my family, SOFKIN, and PamTen. Both the organizations are growing fast and demand my equal attention. I am so passionate about everything that I do, I keep thinking about what else I can do to become better. Sometimes, I give up my own time, my sleep. I give up my own personal commitments, family commitments, just to make sure I am doing justice to the goal that I want to reach. There is a lot of sacrifice required. But it's a sacrifice that you make out of love and out of happiness. I am able to achieve work-life balance with the support of my family and by continuously reprioritizing my work. I don't look back and worry about vacations that I missed or time I could have spent with my family. I can always get back to those things. I don't want to lose the focus on my goal. Everybody needs to make those sacrifices. That being said, I do celebrate my achievements and love to party and network with people.

What is your next goal?

Chaya: My next goal is to extend help to more needy children. I want to grow my business so that it becomes a strong channel to reach that goal. For me, at the end of the day, I'm happy just to sit with those children, play with them, work with them, help them to reach their goals, and make their dreams a reality. The happiest moment for me would be to see them all successful and settling down in their lives. Some of our children have grown up and they are settled with great jobs and professions. One of our children has a job at a Fortune 500 company and he comes back and supports the children in our organization. That's the full circle I want to see. That's my goal.

What would you like to accomplish in your life before you leave it?

Chaya: That's a difficult question, because I want to accomplish a lot in this life. I think it's important to be able to accomplish your primary goal. I would like to leave with the satisfaction that I made the world better for at least a few unfortunate children. If the world was better, we wouldn't require organizations like SOFKIN to help children. I want these children to grow up and for each one of them to extend this positive energy and helping hand to 10 other people. I am confident that they will do it. I want to see a world full of happiness, truthfulness, and honesty, with no difference between the poor and the rich. Everybody should have equal opportunities. We talk about globalization. I want to see globalization in the personal lives of people, where everybody's on the same plane, everybody is treated equally. That's my dream. I'm sure it won't happen before I die, but we are planting the seeds now through organizations like Maher and SOFKIN.

If you had to choose one sentence with a lot of meaning for you, what would it be?

Chaya: Martin Luther King once said: "Live a life that you want to live all over again." That really sits very well with me. When I lost my parents and I was going through tough times, I always thought, Why me? Why am I going through this? But I am here today because of the determination and the passion that I have about life. Today, I love my life so much. All my experiences were meant to happen, so that I could become stronger and stronger over time. If it had not happened, I wouldn't be who I am today. I have no complaints; I love my life so much. I would want to live it all over again!

Growing up as a teenager without parents influenced and drove me to succeed by myself; now I am able to create and support a real home for children at risk that provides them not just with food and shelter, but with love and a future.

About Chaya Pamula

Chaya Pamula is a visionary, philanthropist, mentor, technologist, entrepreneur, and, above all, a passionate human being. She holds an MBA, is a certified Business Process Management Professional, a Project Management Professional, and a Six Sigma Green Belt professional with an Executive Education Certification from Harvard University. Chaya has over 25 years of information technology experience.

Chaya is the President and CEO of PamTen Inc. and the founder of the not-for-profit organization SOFKIN. She has also founded the Global Women's League.

Chaya has spoken about diverse topics at many prestigious organizations such as the United Nations and Harvard University. She is also a trustee on the board of Maher (www.maherashram.org), a non-profit organization aimed at supporting destitute women and children, and Satyana Institute (www.satyana.org) which supports communities through gender reconciliation and inter-spiritual training and workshops. Chaya is currently serving as a board member on many professional and women-empowering associations.

Contact Chaya at:
https://www.chaya.pamten.com
chayapamula@gmail.com

4

The Businessman-Turned-Shaman

Valerio Caponetti

Valerio Caponetti is a business and mindset consultant living in the Canary Islands. Before setting up his business, he left a successful job at a multinational company and worked with a shaman in Peru. In his consultancy, he blends his experiences as both businessman and humanitarian to help others achieve positive results and lasting change.

Can you please introduce yourself?

Valerio: My name is Valerio Caponetti and I am 36 years old. I live in the Canary Islands. I was born in a little village with just 5,000 people, located in an Italian region called Marche. Since I was a young boy, I have always dreamt about traveling the world and visiting the best places.

I worked for many years at a large multinational company. However, one day, I decided to leave my job and travel for a year and a half, with the purpose of discovering and studying myself.

Today, I work as a business and mindset consultant. A big part of my methodology is based on Thinking Into Results by the Proctor Gallagher Institute. It's one of the things that I studied deeply and I'm able to teach to my clients.

Can you tell me a little bit about your life story up until the moment that you met Bob Proctor?

Valerio: I graduated from university with a degree in engineering. I went on to work for a company for 11 years. I worked in various departments: operations, consumer services, marketing, and sales. I really loved what I did, because it allowed me to travel. I worked in Italy and Spain.

By the age of 27, I was already managing a team of seven people in Italy. I loved managing people, leading them to action and developing their own abilities. I didn't like selling domestic appliances, which was the company business, but I was very involved in what I was doing because I was learning a lot and progressing inside the company.

When I was 29, I realized that there was a vacancy in Russia as a business unit director. This position was for an experienced senior director and my credentials didn't match that position. There were 90 people to be managed in Moscow. Russia is a very challenging country, but I dreamt so much about it! In fact, I would spend many moments during the day visualizing myself working in Moscow and leading that business unit. At that time, I had no idea about how my thought and emotions could create my reality. Since childhood, I fantasized about things. It made me feel good.

I wanted that challenge so much that after a month or two of dreaming about it, I decided to speak with the vice-president of the division. I can still remember entering his office with a mix of fear and excitement and telling him: "I'm the guy for the Russian position!" He looked very surprised. "Really?" he replied with a controlled smile. "I know that you are very talented, but you are too young. Do you know what you will face there? This would be very tough for you. It's a quantum leap. It's a double step. It's a huge stretch for you." I said, "I can do it." From that moment on, every week, I went to his office and I asked for an interview with the general manager of Russia. I probably annoyed him, but my attitude was very positive and I was constantly repeating that I could do it, that I wanted that promotion, and that I needed to grow.

After pressing him for a couple of months, he finally set up the interview for me. However, my English was very poor and I didn't speak any Russian. But, I wanted it very badly, so I began studying English every single day after work, for one or two hours with a private teacher. I did nothing else. I was obsessed by that chance. I just worked, went home, ate quickly, and spent all my spare time studying English and thinking about what I had to say in the interview. I had experienced that interview thousands of times in my imagination prior to the meeting. During the meeting, the executive told me: "Valerio, I like your energy, I like your passion, but you are very young. You are probably younger than almost all of the people you would have to manage. Why should I choose you? This is too much risk." I said, "You should choose me because I will give it everything. I would prefer to die than not succeed." I really meant it. This idea and my warrior approach were very strong. Now, I am a bit less extreme.

I got the job and spent four incredible years in Moscow. The first year, I had practically no life except for work. I just worked because that was what I wanted. I wanted to have success in that job and I did. I completely changed the department and my collaborators and leaders were very happy.

At that time, I was already studying personal development for maybe 10 or 15 years by myself. I started to have problems with my health, even before living in Russia. I was not looking after my health. I was taking care of my desires in an extreme way and not taking care of my body in a balanced way.

I faced huge challenges in the first two years. These took all my energy and I got very sick. I had gastritis and several other discomforts. My life was in a very critical moment. I was surrounded by success, I was living in a fantastic apartment, close to Red Square in Moscow, driving my dream car, being a young leader, and dating incredibly beautiful Russian women. People told me that I had an ideal life, but I didn't feel like that. I was struggling. I was apparently very successful by society's standards, but I was not happy. I was taking pills for gastritis. I was systematically going to visit different doctors for one thing or another, always keeping my focus on the business and believing in the results I wanted to achieve.

One day, I felt so bad that I went to my bed and I started praying. I was praying because I didn't know what else I could do. I asked,

"What I should do? I did everything I needed to do. I followed my passion. Now I'm here and I'm sick. I'm having great results, but my life is not what I want it to be. This is not what I thought success would be."

That night, something amazing happened that I still cannot explain. I remembered saying, "God, I give you my life, but in exchange, please give me direction, because I don't really know what to do next. I'm lost and I don't know anybody with whom I can speak about this." I saw myself from the outside, as if through the lens of a camera suspended from the ceiling placed in the center of the room. I saw myself lying and struggling on the bed. And then I fell asleep.

When I woke up the next morning, I was a different person. I didn't feel any pain. I didn't feel any struggle or confusion. I felt as if I was in the body of somebody else, living someone else's life. I suddenly became very calm. I was very present. My mind was still and I thought: "Now what? I'm working to sell domestic appliances? Come on!"

That was the beginning of a very long period of time during which I questioned who I was. I gave up on Moscow's nightlife, the models, and the parties; that no longer made sense to me. I was looking for something different. I started practicing different kinds of meditation. I painted and I did many creative things. I would envision myself having long hair, wearing a poncho, and helping people. One day in October, I decided to leave the company. By December, I had fulfilled my vision of becoming that long-haired, poncho-wearing servant to mankind.

Everybody at the company thought that I was completely crazy to leave this amazing position, but I thought that I had finally stopped being crazy. My father didn't speak to me for at least six months because of this decision. My friends thought that I was in a sect.

I knew already that I was no longer the same person. I never felt as normal as I did in that moment. I finally felt myself. I couldn't explain this to other people, because I didn't logically understand what was going on; I just felt it.

I started a period of discovery. I went backpacking to Peru with friends. In Peru, we participated in a shamanic retreat. At the retreat, they use a cactus called the San Pedro to open people's consciousnesses. I had never done anything like that. I had never had similar experiences with drugs. This is considered to be a secret medicine – not drugs – and for me it was something completely new.

This cactus is boiled for many hours to create a dark green juice which people drink. It is absolutely natural. When you drink it, your senses and your awareness are really heightened. You see colors in different ways. You feel connected with everything. For me, it was unbelievable. Something incredible happened to me. While most people were purging, crying, and releasing some emotional blockages, I laughed and cried with joy and gratitude to the point that the shaman came to me and asked, "How many times have you done this already?" I said, "This is the first time."

After drinking the juice, how long does its influence last? What did you see?

Valerio: It lasts eight or ten hours. You completely lose connection with time. You are focused on the present moment. The mind's activity is almost completely shut down and you start to see brighter colors and life in everything. You feel as if the clouds in the sky are alive. Your perception is sharpened. You have many insights.

I know that some other people saw past memories and faced some very challenging moments.

When the shaman came to me, something amazing happened. I realized that I was receiving a message for the shaman. I told her certain things as I received them and she started to cry. I don't know what I told her. In that moment, you feel as if you are an instrument. It was a very strange situation. It was like a movie.

She told me, "Valerio, I was waiting for you." I said, "Really?" She said, "You came into my dreams a few nights ago and I knew that you would come to teach me something." I thought, how can I teach her something? She was the shaman! She told me, "I want you to stay here. I have a few houses and you can choose one for yourself."

Two months before this, I was driving a BMW in Moscow, working for a big company. Now I was in Peru, living with a shaman, wearing a poncho, assisting and serving people for free by giving them chamomiles, helping them to purge, hugging them, or just listening to them.

I really started to listen to people. I didn't think I had a lot to say. I felt that I needed to unlearn and deprogram. That experience lasted for a few months. The people who thought I was crazy were now certain of it.

I learned many things from the shaman. Do you know that most shamans say that depression is a blessing? When you feel depressed, it is because there is something in you that wants to be expressed, but is blocked. The depression is a manifestation of the fact that you need to awaken. You need to do something differently. Bob would say that you are entertaining a new idea. The old, inferior condition and the new idea 'fight' and you experience anxiety. You must cross through the terror barrier to face freedom. If you stay in that confused state where anxiety is not expressed, but repressed, you enter depression. The shaman said that depression was the soul's way of expressing itself.

Can you explain a little bit about what a shaman is?

Valerio: A shaman is an expert on Peruvian spiritual culture. A shaman is somebody who works with energy. They move energy in, out, and through the bodies of people. They help them release old blockages or pain and to get more clarity in their lives.

The shaman and I lived at a big property with gardens and a kind of temple inside where people can go on retreat. There were three retreats every week. The retreat is for one day. You drink the San Pedro and you experience this transformation. If you want, you can do it more than once. People from everywhere in the world came to heal.

I saw things that I couldn't imagine I would ever see. There was a person who had facial paralysis for 10 years and who had lost her daughter. After drinking San Pedro, she cried for eight hours. I was worried. It was not light crying. She was desperate, crying from the heart. The next day, she woke up, had breakfast, and her face was okay. She didn't even realize it. Can you imagine? She could remember that she had been crying, but when you are under the San Pedro effect, you lose time perception. You float in your subconscious mind.

I also heard about people who were healed of very serious diseases. We know that the body is an instrument of the mind. Emotions that are blocked can generate a lot of trouble.

I stayed there for a few months. I was helping people with these retreats, but I was also facilitating family constellations as developed by Bert Hellinger – I think many people studying psychology and holisticism know this amazing technique. It is quite popular. I was practicing many different kinds of holistic practices; for example, Reiki.

One day, a person working there came to me and said, "I really appreciate you and I admire you, because you really help people feel better. I would love to do what you do." I asked, "Why can't you do the same? It's not difficult; just make the decision and do it." He replied that he served humanity for free at the weekend, but during the week, he drove a bus. When I heard this, I felt a bit annoyed. I said, "You are taking care of everybody except the most important person: yourself. How can you help yourself if you do a job that you don't love?" The guy looked at me and said, "I cannot make a living from this. I cannot charge somebody for something that I love doing."

This is a very common paradigm. This conversation made me think. I kept asking myself why it had such an impact on me. After a couple of days, I realized that I was doing many things for free and I was okay with that, because it was my decision. However, I knew I could help many more people – thousands of people. I could give much more than chamomile to people. I was not using my full potential. I was not doing all I could do. When I realized this, I decided to leave.

When I came back home, I realized that I had learned a lot from the business experience and from the spiritual experience. However, I also realized that I had to find a balance. There were many good things about the two experiences, but also many limiting beliefs in both. In the first experience, I was disconnected. In the second experience, I was connected, but in an environment with limited ideas about money and responsibility. People struggled to make decisions or they made decisions without being connected to their true natures.

One day, I was at home with my parents, with whom I have a wonderful relationship, and Bob came into my mind. A few months previously, somebody had told me about Bob Proctor for the first time. I searched for Bob Proctor on YouTube. A gentleman wearing a nice suit and a tie appeared. He was calm, strong, and energetic. He said that we are spiritual beings, we live in a physical body, and we have an intellect. I thought, wow, this is exactly what I feel. We are all spiritual.

I like how he speaks about the spirit being grounded. He is on Earth and speaking about responsibility, decisions, and making things happen. All my dots started to connect. Studying Bob's material, I realized how I had achieved my goal to get the promotion in Russia, how I had succeeded there, and how I had flourished as a little shaman in the course of a few months. On top of that, I started to become much more self-aware and have much more self-control.

What happened from that moment? What did you start doing differently to change your results?

Valerio: At first, I realized that we need repetition to change things. This really changed everything in my professional approach. Before, when I coached people, I was not happy that after the session my clients felt much better and more focused, but once back in their normal environments, they went back to their old paradigms. I struggled with that situation and I wanted my coaching to be much more effective. I would pray and ask, how can I help people to get these impactful and permanent results?

Then, Bob appeared and gave me the answer: constant spaced repetition. Before that moment, Bob's idea of reading the same book, *Think and Grow Rich*, over and over again for more than 50 years would have struck me as being completely crazy.

The second thing that I learned from him is about sales. You don't sell something to somebody, but for somebody. The main idea behind that is serving others. I love the idea of sales as a way to lead somebody into action. For example, now that I started facilitating *Thinking Into Results*, I never think about selling. Honestly, when I speak to a person, I really listen and I try to feel the person, to understand what the person really needs. Then, I try to give my best.

I don't even think about sales. Sales are a consequence of caring about and helping somebody. In society, we are always selling. We not only sell products, we sell ideas to our partners, children, and friends.

I also now understand the money issue much better. Bob is very clear about money. He says that money is energy and you need money to be more comfortable, more creative, and to spread your services far beyond your physical presence.

My ideas about self-image and self-confidence also changed. I really like studying Jung and I love one of his quotes. He said, "I don't aspire to be a good man. I aspire to be a whole man." This is the constant focus in my life. I want to express the integrity of the person that I want to become. I want to express integrity in myself. I don't want to be good, because love doesn't always mean being good. I know this because I've coached people for some time and I managed people in my previous company.

Loving and pleasing are two completely different things. Love can be expressed in all behaviors. It means that love sometimes can assume the appearance of toughness. For example, if a person following a pattern of self-sabotage comes to us for help, but doesn't want to take responsibility for his struggle (blaming circumstances or other people), being honest, direct, and tough could be the best option to follow in order to help. Kindness should always be the supervisor of the process, but kindness can be supported by strength and decision.

Obviously, you can lead others in an elegant and effective way only if you have first experienced their struggle, and faced and accepted their darkness in you.

Now I work with a lot of people who are lost in spirituality and need to come back to the physical world to be grounded. I also have other clients who come from the business world who are disconnected from their true natures and want to find their real purpose.

Did you discover more paradigms that you needed to change in yourself?

Valerio: I used to constantly improve my self-image in order to become a person in line with my goals. I think studying Bob's material made me become a more tolerant person. The more you know yourself, the stronger you become. The stronger you become, the less vulnerable you are, because you are not afraid anymore to go out and to speak with other people. You can say your truth without convincing anybody. You're just yourself.

If you tolerate yourself, you can tolerate others. If you do what you love, you can let others do what they love.

How long did it take you to start seeing results?

Valerio: I saw results immediately. When I watched Bob Proctor's first video, it really resonated with me. It immediately connected my dots and the results came very fast. Now, I connect the dots for my clients.

What were the most difficult moment and the best moment in the process?

Valerio: I cannot say which were the best or the most difficult, because we live in a process and the process is growth. We are here to grow. Either you grow or you go back and disintegrate, like nature.

If you want something, you must face your terror barrier and your fears; then you move a step forward. Fear is something that allows you to go to the next level. It cannot be bad or good. It is what it is.

When you hear the words "Universal Laws", what do they mean to you?

Valerio: For me, the Universal Laws mean God. I think that God is order, integrity, and law. The more you follow the Laws, the more you become a co-creator. The more powerful you become, the more contribution you give and the more compassion you get.

Can you talk about the effect of a specific Law on your life?

Valerio: When I got the position in Russia, without noticing, I used the Law of Perpetual Transmutation of Energy. We are always creating, even when we don't see the result of creation. We start to get emotionally involved with an idea and this idea starts to grow and it manifests.

When I wanted to be promoted for the Russian position, months beforehand, I had already achieved it in my mind. I imagined myself near Red Square, driving a nice car, and leading a big team. I could see myself delegating to others and growing as a leader. I realized that my persistence in applying for this position was automatically generated by the idea I had progressively engrained in myself. I created this image and I emotionalized it for a few months. I was like a faithful soldier and I obeyed this idea. Now, I'm also able to explain to others how to do it.

I also love The Law of Vibration. I realize that we live in perfect justice; justice surrounds us, even if sometimes it is tough to see it. Your vibration is creating your results in your life all the time. Anything that is happening depends on your vibration. If you want to change your reality, you need to shift your vibration. You need to first send out something different to get something different from the outside as a consequence. The more you understand this, the more you take responsibility and start responding and not reacting to circumstances.

Can you tell me about one specific goal that you managed to accomplish?

Valerio: I have an online business that I manage from the Canary Islands. When I moved here, I had a vision that I wanted to use my laptop and reach clients all over the world. Someone without awareness will tell you that that is impossible. I didn't have that awareness when I first started, but I had a vision.

On the one hand, I thought about the Law of Vibration and on the other hand, I worried that I didn't know how to find clients. I thought, I will follow the Law. I started sharing online what I was learning. The Law of Compensation came into action; it states that the more you give, the more you receive. If you are able to do something, give a lot; if there is a need for what you do, people will come to you spontaneously.

I started recording videos and sharing posts in English, although it would have been much easier to do it in Italian or Spanish. But my goal was to have clients from all over the world, and to be an expert and an international speaker. In order to achieve that, I need to publish in English and be consistent with my vision.

People started to respond. I knew that I needed to do what I love, to be myself, and everything would take care of itself.

I upload videos on Facebook and YouTube. I speak about what I love. I'm myself. To contact people and have clients, you need to give a bit of information about who you are or who you want to become. I don't know myself completely – that takes a lifetime of discovery and definition. But, if you are a person who is joyful, open, and authentic, people will love you because they want to be authentic as well.

What were you prepared to give up or to sacrifice to arrive at your goal?

Valerio: I gave up everything. I'm very good at sacrificing when I want something.

Napoleon Bonaparte said, "I see only my objective, the obstacles must give way." When I want something, I fuse with it. I become obsessed, because it's what gives me pleasure. I much prefer to study, to share, and to coach people than to have a beer with somebody without speaking about anything that I'm interested in. I study and coach for pleasure, so I do this all the time.

What is the one key lesson you can give to everyone who wants to reach their goal?

Valerio: Spend a lot of time with yourself. Study. The more you study, the more you understand and, for that, you need silence. You need time for yourself in nature. Connect with your true nature. I spent several months completely alone in nature, working on the beach, thinking, writing, and trying to understand what was happening to me. For me, silence is the best medicine.

What is your next goal?

Valerio: I want to speak in front of thousands of people. I know I will do this. That's what I love to do the most: to share and to speak about what I have learned.

What would you like to accomplish in your life before you leave it?

Valerio: I would like to write a book. Writing is a passion. I've always written. As I changed over the years, I found that the things I had written in the past didn't make sense to me anymore. I want to write about faith and belief.

I also want to help children. I don't know how, but every time I think about children, I feel touched. I will find some way to help them. I would love to help these amazing beings in their education and to help prevent struggles created by ignorance.

If you had to choose one sentence that has a lot of meaning for you, what would it be?

Valerio: I would quote William James: "Believe that life is worth living and your belief will help create the fact." Believing, for me, is always the key. Thank you for allowing me to be myself and listening to me. When somebody is listening to you, it's a huge gift.

If you do what you love, you can let others do what they love. If you are a person who is joyful, open, and authentic, people will love you because they want to be authentic as well.

About Valerio Caponetti

Valerio Caponetti is a Mindset and Business Consultant who helps people and organizations improve their performances by keeping a harmonious balance. As a former sales and marketing executive, he was recognized as one of the most effective young leaders in the multinational company that he worked for.

He spent the last three years traveling and coaching hundreds of people in different countries: Australia, Peru, Russia, Italy, and Spain. His current mentoring system is based on a process which develops the *Thinking Into Results* program inside a holistic framework of non-duality.

Contact Valerio at:
valeriocaponetti.com
info@valeriocaponetti.com

5

You Have The Power To Heal Yourself

Eileen Bohr and Norman Petermann

Eileen Bohr and Norman Petermann are a young, enthusiastic couple who live in Bremen, Germany. One step from giving up on life, Eileen saw the movie The Secret, *and from there, everything changed. Norman left his architecture studies. Together, the couple discovered their real lives' purpose. They have both recently become PGI Thinking Into Results consultants.*

Can you, please, start by introducing yourself?

Eileen: Norman and I are Bob Proctor's personal development consultants. We love to travel around the world, seeing new places. I love going to another country or another town and seeing how the people live there. I'm also passionate about Thai boxing. I love watching movies with Bruce Lee, Jackie Chan, and all the famous fighters – I started watching them when I was three years old.

Norman: She's dangerous – that's the reason why we are together! I enjoy many different types of sports. I used to play ice hockey, but I stopped a few years ago. I love to travel. Now we have the opportunity to work from wherever we are. We began the process of becoming consultants last year; you can do this kind of work from anywhere – Germany, Canada, or Denmark.

When did you first come across Bob Proctor's material and what was your situation in life then?

Eileen: I watched the movie *The Secret* in 2013. I was sick at the time. I had tumors in my head, behind my face. The doctors told me that I would need many operations throughout my lifetime to deal with my condition. I spent seven months in bed. It was hard for us. Norman did everything for me. He fed me, he washed me – everything. I couldn't stand unaided for even 10 seconds. I had a lot of time to think about myself and my life. I was very depressed all the time for many years. Eventually, the doctors told me that they couldn't help me anymore and they didn't know how long I had to live. They had operated on me several times, but the tumors kept coming back, big and fast. They said that they could repeat the operation several times, but my body wouldn't respond to the surgery after a while and I wouldn't be able to walk because I would be on so much medication. I couldn't talk to Norman about this. I didn't want to talk to anybody, because I wanted to die right then. Norman was with me 24 hours a day. I wondered how I could make a plan to die without him knowing about it. Of course, he sensed what I wanted to do.

Norman called my friends. They came here, but I refused to see them and avoided them; I didn't want to talk to anyone. One of my best friends called me 50 times. Eventually, I answered the phone, crying, and she said, "Eileen, I know you've given up on life, but I want you to do just one thing and promise that you will do it this evening. I want you to watch the movie *The Secret*." I agreed and my friend gave me the number of an 85-year-old woman who she promised would be able to explain the movie to me.

I watched *The Secret*, and I realized that I had this disease because of my negative thoughts, which I had held for many months and years. The old woman explained this to me and told me that in four days I would be healthy. I would no longer have any tumors in my head. I thought, I can believe that she is crazy or I can believe her, trust her, and do everything she tells me. I chose the second option. I trusted her, I believed her, and I did everything she said. She gave me an affirmation and said, "You will drink a lot of water during the next four days." As I looked at the water and then drank it, I said, "Thank you for my health." I did this for four days before I had my operation.

The doctor had screened my head a week beforehand and he had said, "You have so many tumors; they are so big." Then, they operated on me and were completely shocked at what they saw; they couldn't find any tumors at all. Everything was healthy.

The doctors said it was a miracle. They couldn't figure out what happened. I didn't tell them what had happened, because I thought they would think that I was crazy. I only shared the story with Norman, my family, my friends, and his family. I realized that if I can heal my body, I can heal everything – my environment, my life – with this knowledge. I approached Bob, the first speaker in *The Secret*. I liked how he acted and how he talked. I read his biography and all his books. The journey was wonderful. Once you know you will be healthy, you forget your pain; I had my normal life back.

I was a bank consultant and a make-up artist. I worked seven days a week for many months. In 2016, on the first of January, I realized that I was miserable. I thought, why do I work so much? Why am I always ill? There were no tumors, but I was still sick all the time. I watched *The Secret* and watched Bob speak again, and I decided that from that day on, I would do only the things I loved to do. So, Norman and I became consultants. We started to visualize it in April, 2016, and we made the decision together to become consultants.

Norman: I first saw Bob Proctor in the movie *The Secret*. I was interested in the material, but I thought, I'm not good enough to become a consultant, because I used to be very shy when I was young. However, I made a very big shift to work on learning to believe in myself. I started to read books about personal growth and I started to become a consultant. All of us have so much potential and most of us don't realize it. When you really start to learn something about yourself and about what you are capable of doing, it's a great journey.

We met Bob last year for the first time in Austria. Since then, we've seen him several times in Toronto, Germany, Frankfurt, and also New York.

Norman, how did you react when you saw Eileen's dramatic recovery?

Norman: If you spend time with yourself and think about what's holding you back in life, you realize that paradigms hold you back.

If you understand these paradigms – if you recognize that you can change negative habits into positive habits, and that we are only limited by weakness of attention and poverty of imagination – you will realize that you can do so much more if you change your old paradigms. That was exactly what Eileen and I did. We changed our negative habits and negative paradigms, and in their place, we developed good paradigms and good habits. Now we are getting results like we have never gotten before. The results you get in life are always a reflection of what's going on inside of you.

Eileen: I remember calling Norman and telling him the doctors said that I had no tumors in my head. He said, "You're a miracle." I felt Norman's astonishment through the telephone. He was at the hospital 10 minutes later. He said, "I can't believe it. It's magic."

What happened from that moment? What did you start doing differently to change your results?

Norman: You start to think differently and you focus on wanting positive things, not on the things you don't want. In the past, Eileen always focused on what she didn't want and the result was that she became very sick. One of the biggest shifts you can make in your life, as we found out, is to concentrate instead on what you really want.

Eileen: For the first time in my life, I was thankful for everything I had, every day. I began to write a list every day of 10 things that I'm grateful for. This was a small change in my life, but it was a big shift for me. I prayed and gave thanks for my health every day. I had never done that before, I had never prayed before, but I now knew I had to be thankful for everything. I was grateful for my legs, that I could walk. I hadn't walked in seven months, so everything was a gift for me. I was so grateful to wake up every day without pain or without a headache. I still give thanks every day.

When you decided to be a consultant, you didn't have the money. How did you get around this problem?

Eileen: It was a wonderful journey. On January 1st, 2016, I promised Norman that from that day on, I would do only what I loved. In February, we were in Denmark, holidaying in a very small house near the sea. We had no TV, no radio. It was just us and our dog.

One day, I was down by the sea. I looked up at the sky and I said to the clouds, "Please, Universe, tell me. What is my purpose? Give me a sign." I did this for five days, more than 100 times a day. I said, "Please tell me. I know I am good at one thing. Please give me a sign and tell me what I should do right now."

Five days later, I was sitting alone in the living room with the computer, watching Bob's videos on YouTube. I came across a video called *Make Your Mark*. I thought, oh my God. I started to shake. I laughed and I cried. The video was about becoming a consultant at the Proctor Gallagher Institute. I watched it over and over again. I was crying and shaking, and I was afraid. But I was also happy because I knew that it was my purpose to become a consultant.

Norman came into the living room and said, "What happened? Should I call the doctor?" I couldn't speak because I was so shocked and so happy. I could only cry with happiness. Norman watched the video with me and then he said, "You should be a consultant with Bob Proctor." We drove home to Germany; I had this burning desire in me because of this message from the universe. Two days later, I called them and they said, "Of course you can become a consultant; it will cost $18,500."

Norman came into the room and I told him about the $18,500 cost. I started to cry. We didn't have the money, but the burning desire was still in us both. Two weeks later, we attended an online seminar with Bob. It was a live stream from Los Angeles called *The Classic Seminar* and it cost $147; that was still a lot of money to us at the time.

In addition, everything in the seminar was in English and we were concerned we wouldn't be able to understand the content. Norman said to me, "It doesn't matter. Let's buy it. We will get the money together for the three days." We bought the live stream. The first day I watched it alone because it was Norman's brother's birthday. Norman came back from the birthday and found me close to the television, my notebook in hand, writing and writing. I had written a whole book after three days. I was fascinated. I only understood about 20% of what was being said, but I was fascinated by Bob and Sandy and the material they shared with their audience.

After the three days were over, Norman came to me in our living room. He put his hands on my shoulders and said, "Eileen, I know what I have to do now. I will drop out of my architecture studies and I will also become a consultant, like you. Let's do it together." That had been my biggest wish – for Norman and I to do it together – but I hadn't told him that. I had only visualized it; my dream came true.

Norman: I decided to become a consultant, but my plan was to start in April or June of 2017. Then, we met Bob in Austria last year and he said, unexpectedly, "You have to come next month to Toronto." It was a sign. I decided to cancel everything, burn all our bridges, and start this journey.

Eileen: We had a burning desire to see Bob live, just one time. I saw an advertisement on Facebook saying that Bob would be in Austria, 10 hours away from our town in Germany. I wrote to a friend of Bob Proctor's and asked him how much one ticket for the six-day event would cost. He said that it would cost €3,000 per person. At first, I was so sad to hear this. But in the middle of the night, lying awake, I thought, I will not give up on seeing Bob. I wrote to my contact again and asked, "Is there any option to see Bob for just one hour?" He said to come on the last day for the Winspiration day, which was a charity day.

I asked how much one ticket for that day would cost, and he replied that it would be just €50. I couldn't sleep because I was so excited to see Bob. I wanted to tell him that I wanted to be a consultant, but my English was so bad that I wasn't sure I could get my message across. I thought, I will write him a letter. It took me five days to write the letter using Google Translate. I visualized, I practiced, and I acted like Norman was Bob. I said to him, "Please stand here and I will read this letter to you." We drove to Austria, we saw Bob. There were so many people there and I wanted to give him this letter, but I was still afraid to, because my English wasn't good.

There was an old paradigm inside me which said, Who do you think you are? You are not good enough to become a consultant. Bob will not talk to you because your English is so bad. But I said to myself, I want to talk to him anyway. I tried to approach him five times, but each time I turned back, afraid. On the sixth attempt, I pulled myself together and went up to Bob. I said, "Hi Bob, I'm Eileen from Germany. Last night I drove 10 hours to come here to meet you and to tell you that I want to do what you are doing." He said, "You remind me of myself when I was your age."

We talked for about five minutes. I introduced Bob to Norman, and the first question he asked was, "Are you two married?" He asked us to come to Toronto the next month. "We will train you to become consultants," he promised. We told Bob that we wanted to be there, but we didn't have the money. We asked him what we should do.

Bob told us that the most important thing was get to Toronto. He told us to read the chapter called '333' in his book, *You Were Born Rich*, and to figure out how to get the money.

Norman: Bob always says, "Don't spend even five seconds thinking why you can't do something. We should only think about why we can do something, not why we can't."

Eileen: We drove the 10 hours home. We sat up until 4 a.m. with this burning desire to get the money together. In three days, we sold everything that we had in the house: furniture, jewelry, shoes, bags, everything. It was crazy. Our friends would visit and ask, "Where is your furniture?" We got money from that. We sold everything at the flea market or on eBay.

Norman: When Eileen was on a trip to Paris with her mother, I went to my grandma. I had worked for her for a few years in the past. I cleaned her flat every week and I bought some food for her. I asked her to lend me some money to start my own business. She said, "Norman, in the past few years, every time I needed help, you came to me and you helped me. I want to give you the money as a present." This helped us so much. I also went to my parents and they gave us some money.

Eileen: Norman's mother's parents had passed away. Norman's parents had received an inheritance from them, and they said, "We have three sons and we want to give you each some money to help you." That was the same day.

Norman: They helped us so much. Without their help, I don't know when we would have started; perhaps it would only have been this year. We are so grateful to everyone who helped us.

Eileen: It was magical. It was like a miracle. In three days, we had the money. I'll never forget it. I had bought a new mobile phone number for €10 for our new business. Many people would say that's crazy. We hadn't started the business and yet we bought a new mobile phone number! But I did it and Bob was the first person to text me on that number. He told us to send him an email when we had finished the exercise of reading the book he recommended to us. It took three days – just like the story in Bob's book – to get the money and to begin the journey of becoming a consultant in Toronto.

To have a burning desire is very important.

Eileen: It feels like you're falling in love with something or somebody. You are so excited and afraid. You can't sleep because you love this idea and you are determined to make it happen.

What paradigms did you discover that you needed to change?

Norman: The biggest paradigm for me was thinking that I'm not good enough to be successful and that other people are better than me. We had never worked for ourselves, so we thought we wouldn't be able to. We thought our English wasn't good enough.

Eileen: We had no business experience. We had no money. We had no savings. We said, it doesn't matter, the money will come. But there's that feeling of who do you think you are that you would quit your job? You have no security. You're not good enough to succeed.

Norman: We needed to believe in ourselves.

How long did it take you to start seeing results?

Eileen: The first result was getting the money in three days.

Norman: After a few days, we noticed that we had made a very big shift in ourselves and in our personalities. This happened very quickly, when we really started to study the material, every day, every morning, and every evening. We felt so much better. We felt self-confident and knew exactly what we could do.

Eileen: We changed how we dressed, for example. We look different.

Norman: We felt different. The biggest change in ourselves is that we developed ourselves so much. Our personal growth has been our biggest win in the past month.

Eileen: All our neighbors say we look different. They say, "You look relaxed, you look happy. You are so confident." I used to always be in a hurry. Now, we smile at our neighbors and say, "How are you? How are your kids?"

What was the most difficult moment and what was the best moment in the process?

Norman: The most difficult moment came after we became consultants; we spent a lot of time with many clients who worked for a particular company. The clients wanted to start the program with us, but the company they worked for went with another coach from Germany. We had invested a lot of time and we really trusted that they would start with us. We had spent a lot of money visiting them, but they finally told us, "We don't need you anymore, because we managed to get a coach for free."

Eileen: We were so sad. I cried. I knew I shouldn't cry, because it would attract more bad things, but we had spent so many days and weeks with this company. We were very down.

Norman: However, we learned a lot from the situation.

Eileen: The best moment for me was when Norman said, "I will work with you as a PGI consultant." That was a dream come true for me. We were going to travel around the world together.

Norman: That was also the best moment for me.

When you hear the words "Universal Laws", what do they mean to you?

Norman: There are so many different Laws and we have to know how to use them. If we understand that, it will make life so much easier for us.

Eileen: I heard about the Law of Attraction when I watched *The Secret*. You think about something and then you will get it. It sounds so easy, when you understand it. But the Law of Attraction is the secondary Law. The first Law is the Law of Vibration. I tried to attract things and I succeeded, I attracted all these things. Bob always tells us – and this is my favorite quote – "If you can see it in your mind, you will hold it in your hand." I love that.

Can you talk about the effect of a specific Law on your life?

Norman: The Law of Cause and Effect is very important.

The Law of Cause and Effect says that whatever you send into the universe comes back.

Norman: We teach this as part of our program. The Law of Cause and Effect says that when you are always friendly and helpful to other people, you will get it back – maybe not from that specific person, but from another person. You leave everyone better than you found them. People call us – people who we have never met before – who have seen us on the Internet and they want to work with us. This is the key to our success: leave everybody with an impression of increase. That is exactly the Law of Cause and Effect.

Eileen: It doesn't matter how short the time is that you spend talking with somebody. What we say comes from the heart. We're very honest. We thank people for everything they do for us. For example, take the woman from our local bakery. We thanked her one day for the bread we buy every Sunday from her bakery. It took just twenty seconds, but tears of happiness welled up in her eyes. She said, "Thank you. You have made my Sunday."

Take another example. If you meet an unfriendly person, that person is only the mirror image of you. My mother used to always think negative thoughts. I learned it was better to be positive with her; I interact with her differently and compliment her expertise in cooking. Once I did that, her vibration – her energy – changed. She would say, "Really? You like it? Of course, I will make it for you." In one or two seconds, she'd change. I could make her feel better.

You know that if somebody is angry with you, you can change that. You need to understand the person and understand why he is angry. When someone is angry, people normally say nasty things, but that is not the solution. The solution is to be friendly.

Norman: Leave everybody with an impression of increase.

Can you talk about one more Law and how you use it in your life?

Norman: Take the Law of Opposites. We have to decide what we want to focus on all the time. We can focus on good things or bad things. Everything has an opposite, and most people are always focused on the bad things first and foremost, instinctively. If they focus on what they don't want, that is what they will get. For example, they say "I don't want to become sick," and then they become sick. If we just focus on what we want, on the positive side, we will get positive things.

Eileen: For example, I lost my pen. I had the option to be angry and sad. I also had an opportunity to say "That's great. I can buy a new one that I really like." In every situation in life, it's up to you whether you see a positive or a negative. Sometimes, I put my makeup on in a hurry. I find that if I don't have enough time and I'm in a rush, all my makeup will often fall down on my white carpet. I could think, "I'm so stupid!" Instead, I choose to think, "Thank you, Universe. I know now that I have to relax." Don't be in a hurry. It won't help anything.

Can you tell me about one specific goal that you managed to accomplish?

Eileen: The biggest goal we have is to give all this information to people in companies worldwide. We will accomplish this step by step. We have attracted more people who want to start. People call us who we've never met and, after 10 minutes, they agree to start the six month Thinking Into Results program with us. Our goal is to give this knowledge to companies, people, and even to children.

Norman: One specific goal that we achieved is that we became consultants and we started our own business. That was a very big goal for us. We are very grateful and happy that we accomplished this goal and that we do what we love to do. Every day, we wake up and feel good because we know we can do exactly what we want to do.

What were you prepared to give up or to sacrifice to arrive at your goal?

Norman: In the beginning, we focused on becoming consultants and on building up our company. We didn't take any vacations. We traveled a lot, but it was only to build up our business. I love playing sports, but I had to cut back so that we could focus on getting our business off the ground.

Eileen: For me, it was seeing my best friends. They would say, "Where are you right now? We are meeting here in town, we want to see you." I would have to say, "I am not in Germany. I don't have time." That used to make me sad, but it has gotten better and better. Now we make time to see my friends on weekends. But, at first, I gave up time with them.

What is the one key lesson you can give to everyone who wants to reach their goal?

Eileen: The most important lesson is to study diligently. Invest as much time and money as you can; invest in yourself. This is the best investment you can make, because if you study yourself every day, you will one day become the person you want to be. You will have the things you want to have and do the things you want to do. If you don't study yourself or develop personally, you will not grow. Study every day and attain personal development.

Norman: You should have a very clear picture of what you want to become, of your goals. You have to see it clearly in your mind. Vincent van Gogh said, "I dream my painting and then I paint my dream." You have to see your goals clearly.

What is your next goal?

Eileen: Some weeks ago, we attracted many good account managers and salespeople to our company. We said, "We want to work with big companies in Germany." Our goal is to enable employees and companies to understand themselves and to have a better feeling for the world. For me, as an employee, I was afraid to go to work. I was stressed and I was under pressure to make sales targets. I felt bad. I don't want that for anyone else; I want all these people in these companies to feel good. I want them to understand themselves. For example, I met a salesperson who was not good at selling. He had a paradigm, he understood it, he worked with his paradigm, and we helped him to improve his approach to sales over the course of three months.

Norman: One of our major goals is to develop our whole potential so that we become the best possible versions of ourselves and achieve personal growth.

What would you like to accomplish in your life before you leave it?

Eileen: I want to become the person I want to be. We've come a long way, but I know it could be even better. I will leave the world with the feeling that I helped many people and that they lived life with this wonderful material from Bob. Some of our clients call us crying and say, "Eileen and Norman, thank you so much for your support. You changed my life so dramatically." It's the best feeling and I'm so thankful. This is the biggest fulfillment for me. We've experienced it already, but I know it can be bigger; I am sure that we will help people not only in Germany, but worldwide.

Norman: It is the best feeling when somebody calls you or writes you an e-mail and tells you that you changed their life in just one or two days.

Eileen: We received a letter from one client. It was six handwritten pages, written with so much love. It said, "You are my second parents. You are the only people in my life who trust me and believe in me." This is the best feeling in the world and I want to have it every day.

To do what you love and get positive feedback is one of the most powerful things that you can get back. It might be just one word or one sentence or letter, but it gives you power to continue.

Norman: I think that the most important thing is to help other people to live the life they really want to live, so that they start learning about themselves. The people that we are privileged to work with have so much potential and so many good qualities; we help them to bring these qualities to the surface.

If you had to choose one sentence that has a lot of meaning for you, what would it be?

Eileen: Before, I would have said, *"If you can see it in your mind, you can hold it in your hands."* But I found another inspiring sentence in Bob's program. I think about it every day. *"If we are praying, we are talking to God. But if we are using our intuition, God is talking to us."* It struck a chord with me because it is so true. If you think about something or if you have to make a decision, your intuition is the thing that hits you in the first few seconds. After that, the paradigms kick in. This helped me in many difficult situations; now I only listen to my intuition.

Norman: For me, the sentence that means the most to me is the one telling you to walk away from anything that no longer serves you, develops you, or makes you happy. I think many people walk through life and do things that they don't want to do. They don't respect themselves. If you really respect yourself and walk away from anything that no longer serves you, helps you grow, or makes you happy, you will have a much better life. You will be happy, you will be healthy, and you will definitely become wealthy if you do what you really love to do.

We changed our paradigms and promised ourselves we'd follow our dreams. It feels wonderful to effect positive change in other people's lives, while getting back happiness and fulfillment in our own.

About Eileen Bohr and Norman Petermann

Eileen Bohr and Norman Petermann are the founders of Eileen & Norman Superior Mind and certified Consultants at the Proctor Gallagher Institute.

Contact Eileen & Norman at:
support@eileennorman-superiormind.com
www.eileennorman-superiormind.com

6

Dream Your Life,
Then Live Your Dream

Mick Petersen

Mick Petersen grew up on a ranch in New Mexico. He is the author of the Amazon bestseller Stella and the Timekeepers *and has been approached by an Oscar-winning producer to make it into a movie. He has moved to Hollywood to fulfill his dream.*

Can you please introduce yourself?

Mick: My name is Michael, but as a kid I was Mickey. When I was about 18, I changed my name to Mick. I'm 50 years old this year. I'm not even halfway done with my life because my goal is to live to 120.

I was born in Oregon, which is on the west coast of America. It's the state above California. There's lots of rain. If you've been to England, it's kind of like that, except there's a lot more mountains and volcanoes. There are big waves in the ocean and lots of forests.

Later, as a child, I lived in Arizona and New Mexico on a ranch. When I lived in New Mexico, I was between the ages of seven and eleven. I think that's where my imagination really expanded, because I had two brothers and not much supervision; we roamed the desert together. We would swim in the Rio Grande River. There was a big hill right behind our home. My mother decided that instead of spanking us, she would punish us by making us run to the top of the hill and back down again repeatedly.

We called it Punishment Hill, but soon, our mother realized it wasn't much of a punishment because we enjoyed it so much. We would run through the desert and play in the bluffs and have a good time. At the back of the property, there were these bluffs. Rain erodes a mountainside over hundreds of years and wears it down into a sort of cliff – that's a bluff. It's not a cave because it's open, but there were these walkways within the spaces that you could shimmy into. There were tons of them; some were deep, some were small. You could squeeze into some of them – some were like big rooms, and others were narrower, but we would pretend to be prospectors mining for gold and we just played.

That play really helped to evolve and grow my imagination. That environment and the images and places I created in my mind became a landscape that I would return to again and again. That's why I became a writer – to create those worlds and paint those images with words.

Peggy McColl is my writing mentor. I met her two and a half years ago and we have become very good friends. When I met her, I had written the first draft of a book, but I didn't really know what to do with it. I signed up for her program and I couldn't get enough. I did everything she recommended. I watched the videos she showed me over and over again. I was always hungry for more. I was a very good student because I really wanted to be a writer. I wrote and studied and promoted my book. My book, which is called *Stella and the Timekeepers*, became a best-selling book on Amazon. After that, lots of people who were interested in the book contacted me. The most exciting connection was with Phil Goldfine, an Oscar-winning producer. He asked me to come to Hollywood, to Universal Studios, where he said he wanted to partner with me to bring this to the world, by making it into a franchise on a par with *Harry Potter* or *Twilight*.

I moved to Los Angeles – in fact, tomorrow, I'm going to look at a new home. It's a 10-minute drive to Universal Studios. It's in the Hollywood Hills. It's just beautiful. I have an office there, and I work there. It's so exciting that I had this idea that is now growing into something monstrous; it's enormous and exciting. I think of all the people who will get to read my books and watch the images that I've created in my mind on the screen. It is exciting to get to bring that to life. All of us are creators, but not all of us break through the 'terror barrier'. We don't dare to do what we think we can do or what we think we can't do. We're conditioned to hold ourselves back.

When did you first come across Bob Proctor's material? What was your situation in life?

Mick: I first saw the movie *The Secret* in 2006. I was captivated by Bob Proctor, but also by the entire concept. I watched the movie over and over. I started doing the things that it suggested, not really understanding that the Law of Attraction is one of the many Laws of the Universe. It got me started and my life started to change. The 15-year relationship that I was in ended. These sorts of shifts began to happen; it was because I had hope and a dream of doing something bigger and better than what I was doing. At that time, I owned a whole bunch of rental properties and I was a flight attendant. Once, while working, I was stuck in Mexico City for four days during a hurricane. The hurricane was battering Galveston Island, which is where I lived and owned a whole bunch of rental property. My intention was to get to Mexico City and then back to Galveston Island to board everything up.

However, the flights changed because of the weather and I couldn't get back. It was a rock bottom moment for me. All the conditions I had created in my life were coming to a head and everything I had was going to be wiped out. In hindsight, I can see that I needed my life to be wiped clean, but at the time, it felt terrible. I wrote in my journal, "All is lost." That was a little dramatic, right?

That night, in the hotel, I had a dream about a character called Stella. Stella lives between three worlds: the Earth Realm, the Water Realm, and the Sky Realm. Each realm is a metaphor. The Sky Realm represents our imagination or our subconscious mind. The Water Realm represents the fluidity of life. The Earth Realm represents the physical domain, that which grounds us. These are the three fluid states that became clear to me, which I discovered over the course of the next three years while I rebuilt my life.

My life wasn't so great and my world wasn't so great, but the world in which Stella resided was fabulous. I went there at night in my dreams and in the day during my thoughts and my daydreams, I would just wander off as I rebuilt my rental properties. At that time, my father came to live with me and helped me to rebuild. It was really great to have that bonding period with my dad, because we had grown apart. This brought us back together. Bob Proctor had a lot to do with that.

My book lived within me for three years before I wrote anything down; then, it took another three years to get it onto the computer. It was still generating ideas in my mind. Someone said to me, "If you want something different in your life, you have to make space for it. Get rid of the old stuff."

I sold all my rental property. I took the check to the bank, deposited it, walked out to my truck, and I looked at my phone. There was an email from Bob Proctor waiting for me. It was a video. I didn't know how he'd gotten my email address. It seemed like magic. I now know that it was Internet marketing. It was one of those 'wake up' kind of videos, so I paid careful attention. He was offering a seminar in Dallas in mid-May 2014. I went and that's where I met Peggy, and my life began to change. It changed so much that now I have an office at Universal Studios. I can't believe it.

Tell me a little bit about what happened since that moment. You started studying Bob's material, but what did you start doing differently to change your results?

Mick: I learned that the conditions on the outside are a reflection of how you are living on the inside; everything comes from the inside out. Of course, there are actions I have to take, but my thoughts are the most important things. It's the same for all of us; we all live from the inside out. We are the center of the divine operation. We are the center of our own worlds and our own creation. In the Bible, it says that God made us in His image and He is a creator. We are creators of ourselves; we create our lives. Vincent van Gogh once said, "Dream your painting and then paint your dream." I've adapted this phrase for book signings. It's my little moniker. I write, "Dream your life, then live your dream."

What paradigms did you discover that you needed to change?

Mick: We get so comfortable living the way we are. When we get comfortable, we're in trouble. I think it's very important for us to try to stay in a state of discomfort so that we stretch ourselves and do things differently.

My parents had terrible ideas about money – money doesn't grow on trees, all those sayings. I've changed that paradigm for myself, because life is easy and we live in an abundant universe. We can have an abundant life. We can have whatever we want, whatever we can dream up. We just have to hold that in our mind.

Then there's the paradigm about our self-worth and self-value. There's the paradigm about saying 'yes' too much. Learning to say 'no' is important, but it's also important to surrender to 'yes' if something presents itself to you. It may not feel right, but if you lean into it, it'll be a roadmap. It could be the beginning of the roadmap taking you somewhere else. I had this idea about Stella. I wrote it down, but I didn't know what to do with it. One thing led to another, which led to another. I'm in the middle of my own personal quantum leap. I am not going to get stuck worrying about where I am now; I worry about where I'm going to land. I have this big vision of where I'm going.

How long did it take you to start seeing results?

Mick: I recently went to a Bob Proctor seminar and he said that people underestimate how much time it will take for them to reach their goals. Oftentimes, when the results aren't immediate, they quit. My goals haven't all been realized. At the *Total Author Immersion* event last year, I wrote myself a note – a thank-you note to the universe. It read: "I'm so happy and grateful now that one year later, all these things have happened." I wrote five things down. Of those five, two of them have solidly come about. Three of them are in their infancy. It's like standing in front of a mirror after you've taken a shower. The image is all foggy, but you stand there with a blow-dryer, and the image starts to open up. That's what is happening with my other three goals. I keep thinking about where I'm going and wait for the evidence to come. But absence of evidence is not evidence of its absence. My vision is becoming clearer.

What was the most difficult moment and what was the best moment in the process?

Mick: Life is never about one particular moment or one occurrence or one event or one time. There's always the yin and the yang, the good and the bad. Something amazing can happen at the same time that something not so good happens. There is a balance – each side of the Law of Polarity. I think the most exciting period for me was when I got the phone call from Phil Goldfine and he said, "This is going to be huge. It's going to be great." He told me in the executive dining room of Universal Studios, "Welcome to Hollywood royalty. I'm making you the next J.K. Rowling."

Afterward, we had very little contact for six months. Then, he called me and said, "Are you done having me torture you?" I replied, "What are you talking about?" He said, "I haven't responded to your emails. I haven't taken your calls. I've done this intentionally." I was confused and asked him why he had done this. He said, "I don't want to go to the heads of the studios and get a $100 million or $200 million or $300 million budget for a blockbuster film and then find out I've partnered with a quitter."

I said, "Phil, I'm not a quitter. I'm holding the vision that you cast for me and I believe that this can still happen." He said, "I'm holding the vision too." That was a really great time in my life as an author – to have somebody of his stature, an Oscar winner, say that to me at Universal Studios. It's easy to be seduced by that whole idea of Hollywood, but in truth, it's run by people like you and me. You have crests and troughs. That's how life is.

Life is ebb and flow. It comes in and out like the tide; it's yin and yang. It's constant. I went from thinking *This is great* to *Why isn't he calling me?* Now I understand that he wanted to see what type of person I was. I kept showing up, holding the vision of what I wanted to create. He's part of my vision, and I'm part of his vision too.

When you hear the words "Universal Laws", what do they mean to you?

Mick: There are natural Laws, like gravity. You're not going to jump off a building and start flying; we don't have wings. Stella could, because she's an angel. She can manifest wings and fly, and then they disappear and she can be a human. The Universal Laws are a set of laws that run the world. We plant an idea in the soil of our minds, a seed that grows like an acorn. An acorn has the blueprint of a giant oak, but it could take a century for it to reach its full potential. It isn't trying; it's just growing into itself, into the blueprint of itself. These thoughts, if we focus on these thoughts, can do the same.

Can you talk about the effect of a specific Law on your life?

Mick: The Law of Cause and Effect says that whatever you send into the universe comes back to you. I see it all the time, where people do something and it causes the effect of the outcome, the results that they want. When they do it, they think they can, somehow, defy these Laws. Well, you can't. You can stomp your feet and act like a little baby, but the truth is you can't change these Laws, so it's better to go with the rhythm of the Law, understand it, and use it to work to your advantage. By just starting this whole ripple effect of events, my life is changing exponentially. It's just growing and changing. I don't want to say that I'm scared. It's more like I have a lot of 'holy shit' moments. I think, *I can't believe I'm about to do this, but I'm going to do it anyway,* because I understand that when I do this it's going to be the cause of the effect and give me the outcome that I'm thinking of. I am beginning to understand the kind of power that I have and that all of us have the same power. We are magicians. We just don't understand our power.

Can you tell me about one specific goal that you managed to accomplish?

Mick: Tomorrow, I'm going to LA to look at a house. The price tag is way higher than I can afford. That's what my paradigms are saying. It's a magnificent home and I deserve that home. I'm a responsible person. When I sign on the dotted line, I know what will happen. What happens is that I have these flair-ups of my paradigms telling me, "Who do you think you are? You can't afford that. You've never made that much money." I will have all these doubts, these fears. I understand that's just the functioning of our brains, our limited thinking. But I have to attune myself to the unlimited; I have to remind myself of my track record and what I've done in the past.

I mentioned that I owned rental property before. There was a time when I wanted to buy an apartment complex. I didn't have the money to do it. How did I think I could do that? However, I made the decision to do it and every time an obstacle came in my way, I told myself, *I'm going to close this deal. I'm going to get to the finish line.* I went around the obstacle or over it or under it or through it. I think Napoleon Bonaparte said, "I only focus on the outcome and all obstacles give way." It took a lot of effort for me to do that, but once that goal happened, I was on the top of the mountain. I was jumping up and down. It was as if I had won an Olympic gold medal and I was on the podium. I felt like that.

Now, I'm stretching myself to do something even bigger. I have no idea how it's all going to happen, and I don't have to know. I know that there are invisible, unseen forces that work either in our subconscious or in our mental imagery. We're partnering with these forces and they're working to bring about what we're thinking about.

I'm going to visit this home tomorrow and I have all kinds of ideas about how to make this happen. I've already envisioned myself living there. I've already decorated it. I can see myself sunbathing there; it's gorgeous. I'll get on my bike and I'll ride through the Hollywood Hills to Universal Studios.

People say terrible things about Los Angeles because of the traffic. It's true. If you look at the top 10 worst bottlenecks in freeways in the United States, seven of them are probably in Los Angeles. I want to avoid that. The new location is beautiful. The weather is perfect. You can have your windows open all the time. It's the ideal climate, like Spain.

This house is nestled right on the border of Griffith Park, which is covered with bike trails. There are pathways and roads that go around Lake Hollywood to Universal. It's optimal. It's the best house in the best neighborhood on the way to the best office to make the best movie.

We all deserve the best. This is a great example of what we can do. When I was a kid, I lived in a trailer. Our trailer burned down. I lived in terrible conditions, but I didn't even know that, because I have always been an optimist. I've always looked on the sunny side of everything. That's why I'm here. I attracted this into my life and I'm so glad. We have to work at it constantly; work on it and advance.

What were you prepared to give up or to sacrifice in order to arrive at your goal?

Mick: I gave up my old thinking. I'm willing to give up my old self, my old life, so that I can lean into and bring to fruition the goal and the dream that I have. I'm willing to give up everything to do that as I advance forward.

What is the one key lesson that you can give to everyone who wants to reach their goal?

Mick: Decide what your goal is. I think that's the hardest thing for most people. Most people have a really vague image of what they want. In the book *Your Invisible Power* by Genevieve Behrend, she says that we should create our picture, and then examine that picture and continue to examine that picture. Focus on it, pay attention to it, look at it, dream about it, think about it, write about it, talk to yourself in the mirror about it. When you do all these things, all things requisite to the fulfillment of your desire begin to come to you, thanks to the Law of Attraction.

What is your next goal?

Mick: My ultimate goal is to have a franchise of blockbuster movies, a best-selling book series, and a huge following of people who want to read about Stella. Stella teaches all these principles that are in the books and the concepts behind them. This book is for any age group, because it's about magic. It's like *Harry Potter*, except the magic isn't in a wand. It's in the mind, as all of us have this power. We're all wizards; wizards of our own lives. I go to Universal all the time, but I don't have a permanent pass to get in; one of my goals is to have that. That would be a physical manifestation of validation that I'm moving ahead with my reality show concept.

Tell me about this reality show.

Mick: It's called *Masters of Possibility* and it will feature Bob Proctor, Peggy McColl, Mary Morrissey, Les Brown, and Blaine Bartlett. I've got a whole wish list of other people, including Marie Forleo, Tim Ferris, and Brendon Burchard. We have a 12-episode season laid out. There would be auditions, like on *American Idol* or on X Factor. People would talk about their dreams to our panel of experts. We're looking for people who have a compelling story. Then a camera crew will follow them, twelve hours a day, every day, all the way through to the fulfillment of their dreams. In the meantime, our experts team – the *masters of possibility* – will let them understand that it is possible for them to attain their dreams.

The coaches will mentor, guide, and help them to identify their paradigms and the things that are holding them back. Meanwhile, they will keep working toward their dreams. One thing that I find so compelling about shows like *The Voice* or *X Factor* is that people love to watch others succeed. This concept isn't only for singers. It could be an ice-skater who is competing for a title. It could be somebody with a business who wants to get out of that business and start a different business. The mentors are the masters of possibility, but the contestants will go through a process that will cause them to realize that they can be a master of possibility if they live in the possible, as the impossible doesn't exist. "Impossible" also spells "I'm possible."

The audience will see that and, hopefully, that will be the catalyst to make them wake up and realize that they don't have to do this dead-end job that they don't like. They don't have to be miserable in the life that they have. They can change that. They can shoot for something bigger. That's what I want to do. I want people to understand that they can go after their dreams and they can live their dreams. That's what the show is really about. We're working on the budget right now; it's in development. It's going ahead.

In the first season, we'll follow six people and we'll have five masters. The masters will teach the contestants about themselves, so they will be masters of self-development. We'll also bring other people in. If somebody wants to be successful in business, we're going to bring in business experts. If somebody wants to be an actress, we're going to bring in acting coaches and agents. We'll be able to help them to bring their dreams about faster.

What would you like to accomplish in your life before you leave it?

Mick: I want to leave a legacy that lives on. I read the autobiography of Benjamin Franklin and it gave me the idea, years ago, to write a 30-year plan. Thirty years from now, I'll be 80 and I'm going to live beyond that. As an 80-year-old man, of course, I'll be slowing down. I'm not going to be as active. Benjamin Franklin said it would be great to be able to look back on a life well-lived and leave a legacy that shows that. I've said that I would love to be the author of a beloved series – a fiction series that millions of people around the world enjoy, that would continue past my death. It will grow legs of its own. I'm already doing that.

If you had to choose one sentence that has a lot of meaning for you, what would it be?

Mick: Dream your life, then live your dream.

I recently received an outstanding achievement award from Peggy McColl. I don't necessarily feel that what I've done is outstanding, but I posted it on Facebook and the outpouring of comments and congratulations humbled me. Apparently, I'm an ordinary person doing extraordinary things. It also made me realize that people want to follow what I'm doing.

I have a masterminding meeting in Hollywood on Tuesday and Wednesday with an amazing Internet marketer. He's one of the members of my team and we're building a platform. You can't think of *Harry Potter* without thinking of J.K. Rowling. You can't think of *Twilight* without thinking of Stephanie Meyer. Soon, you won't be able to think of Stella without thinking of Mick Petersen. I'll be posting videos of my progress on my YouTube channel, because people are interested in that. I hope that people can understand that I don't come from a place where I feel that I'm better than other people. I'm coming from a place where I think, *look what's happening. Isn't this cool?* And you can do it too. We can all do whatever it is we want to do.

I'm a normal person. I'm very grounded. Yesterday, somebody came up to me, and he said, "I wanted to come up to you so many times yesterday, but you intimidate me." Me! There is nothing intimidating about me. He learned that very quickly when I started joking with him.

It's so important to dream your life, then live your dream. We all have that capability. We have to be very clear about what we want and, then, remember that it takes the time it's going to take to fulfill our dreams. We have to hold onto that dream. Too many people give up because it hasn't materialized when they want it to. We need to remember that we're not in charge and just let it grow.

I've dreamt my life and I'm living my dream. I don't know exactly where this path will lead me, but with the help of Stella and my journey through writing, I'm excited to take this quantum leap.

About Mick Petersen

Mick Petersen is the Amazon International Best-selling Author of *Stella and the Timekeepers*.

Contact Mick at:
mick@mickpetersen.com
http://www.mickpetersen.com

7

Everything Is Energy

Dr. Jussi Eerikäinen

Dr. Jussi Eerikäinen is a cardiologist and mathematician, as well as the survivor of a deadly attack by Columbian guerillas. He lives in Tenerife, in the Canary Islands, where he is pursuing his second career as an author and online program creator. His book, Transforming Vibes, Transforming Lives, *recently became an international Amazon bestseller.*

Can you please introduce yourself?

Dr. Jussi: Most people know me as a cardiologist. I have practiced my profession for more than 30 years, sometimes using unorthodox methods. I use more natural remedies and a good lifestyle to help people, instead of using drugs and pills. I am also a mathematician.

I was born into a Finnish family that was very energy-oriented. My father was hired as an engineer by the Pacific Mining Company in the western part of Colombia and so I lived in Bogotá, Colombia's capital city, from the time I was five or six years old.

When I was 10 years old, we were kidnapped by communist guerrillas. In those days, there were many groups that were trying to overturn the government: these were so-called liberated Colombians. Many of these groups had Russian ties – this was before the Cuban missile crisis – but it was also the dawn of that movement of guerrillas around all of South America. We were taken by the guerrillas and my

95

parents were killed, shot in front of my eyes. That day I lost everything I had, everything I knew.

After they were killed, the other hostages and I had to walk for many hours. I was trembling and it was dark and very humid. It was raining. I don't know if I was shaking because I was fearful or because it was so cold. I was taken to a camp. Luckily, in the camp, a woman who was a cook there always gave me extra portions of food. She smiled every time she gave food to me. I was a skinny little fellow with glasses, but she took a liking to me. We had a connection. One day, she said, "I am going to help you escape. You have to trust in me and I will help you out." It turned out that one of the guerillas was in love with her. He was in charge of both the sentinels in the camp and the security of the camp. He knew the schedules of when they moved the groups around. In order to gain her love, she made him help me escape. She said to me, "You have to trust me completely and when I tell you to do something, you have to follow it to the letter." On a walk during the day, she showed me a special tree I had to climb into and hide in for a while during my escape. She gave me specific instructions.

One night, about 10 days later, she said, "The time has come right now. "You have to leave tonight. I will tell you exactly when to go and what to do. Remember my instructions." I was terrified, but I repeated the instructions to her and she corrected certain things. I was afraid, but excited about what was going to happen that night.

It was raining. She came in the middle of the night and said, "It's time. *Ahora. Corre. Corre.*" ["Now. Run. Run."] I heard some shots because her would-be lover was creating a diversion in another corner of the camp. Everyone's attention was over there and it was clear for me to run and climb into the tree. It was a dead tree with a hollowed-out trunk and, because it was raining, there was water inside. She told me to stay put there for many hours. I stayed there for probably more than 24 hours, until the hour before dawn of the following day.

When it was silent, I pushed the bark of the tree and it opened slowly, revealing a hole. I climbed down and, at that moment, I knew I was going to escape. The guerillas were still looking for me, of course. I had been told to wait in certain kinds of bushes and stay put, even if my pursuers passed very near to me.

In one of those bushes, I saw a little creature, a colorful toad. The toad jumped on my shoulder, and I was disgusted and frightened. I tried to shake it away, but it jumped on my hand and then it jumped on my shoulder. At that moment, I realized that I was fearful inside. Fear was inside me but not outside me. I thought, *I have fear within me, but the little toad is not afraid of me*. It was an 'aha' moment. The fear was inside me and thus within my control. I said to the fear, "You have 10 seconds to leave my body." After 10 seconds, it was like a switch turned off and that changed my life completely. I was released from the heavy burden of fear in that moment. From then on, I had that assurance; I knew in that moment that I was going to escape and that I was going to be okay.

I arrived at a small, scattered village – just one house here and another house there – and I sneaked into one home. The family who lived there knew who I was because word had spread quickly and the guerrillas had already been there looking for me. The woman of the house said, "I know that you are escaping. Come with us." They fed me. They gave me water. They gave me some juice with sugar cane, called *agua de panela*. The food gave me energy. She had a brother, a bus driver, whose route was from that place to the capital city. She talked with him and he agreed to take me back to Bogotá.

The long bus ride was made longer by the possibility of encountering the guerrillas again. With every bump in the road or pump of the brakes, I feared being recaptured and taken back to their camp or worse, killed. When my thoughts wandered to this dark place, I redirected them to the frog and the 'aha' moment I had in the bushes and the fear passed.

At the main bus station in downtown Bogotá, the driver made everyone disembark. He informed me that he would take me back to the only safe place I knew – my school. It was located in the far northern suburbs of the city. It was not on a bus line and it was a long way from the bus station, but he chauffeured me there anyway. With profound gratitude, I shook his hand as I stepped onto the sidewalk. A cloud of black exhaust churned from the exhaust pipe as the bus disappeared down the road.

The next morning, the headmistress found me curled up at the front door of my school. She cried tears of compassion as I recounted my story. She and the other staff members felt sorry for me and introduced me to a wonderful German family who took me in and raised me as their own.

This was the dawn of a new era for me. This was in the '60s. I was with that German family for four years. The family had some records by Earl Nightingale and one especially caught my attention. It was called *The Strangest Secret in the World*. I played it over and over again. It was about setting goals and how important it is to have goals to guide your life. Everything changed in my life because of this record.

My grades improved. Before, I had been very shy and introverted. Thanks to the record, I had an objective. I was passionate about energy and I was amazed by the power of energy, the power of water, and the power of wind. I idolized Albert Einstein. There was one quote from Einstein that really inspired me. He said, "Everything is energy and that's all there is to it. Match the frequency of the reality you want." You cannot help but get that reality. There can be no other way. This is not philosophy; this is physics." That sentence was like fuel to my mind.

I wanted to become a nuclear physicist. I went to Switzerland for a while, but I came back to study mathematics at the University of Los Andes in Colombia. I was able to support myself and to study, but my health was not good. I decided to study medicine to learn about my condition – I grew up with a problem in my left carotid artery. Five times in my life, my right side had become completely paralyzed, including my face. The affliction would last between one or two hours, and every time it happened, it would get worse and worse.

The first time I had an attack, everything went back to normal within a few minutes. The second time, it took two hours to recover. The third time, I was incapacitated for half a day. My condition was progressively worsening. After an arteriography, they discovered that I had an aneurysm that was pressing on certain areas. I had a nearly completely blocked blood supply in that area. Back then, surgery was risky, and diagnoses were unreliable, so I was refused any surgical procedure. I was told by my doctors, for example, to watch my blood pressure. That answer never satisfied me, so I went to study medicine to find the answers by myself.

I became a cardiologist, but I taught and shared my knowledge as well. I consider that a true physician is an educator. I became a little bit discouraged because I discovered that, even as trained physicians, my colleagues and I in the medical profession would rely more on drugs and pills than anything else and we would focus very little on lifestyle and health. In fact, medical training is more geared toward finding and discovering new diseases, diagnosing symptoms instead of concentrating our attention on health.

I became a rebel against that idea. I thought we needed to concentrate not just on sickness, but on health. Health is not the absence of disease. Health is internal balance. Everything in our bodies should be balanced. Everything should be in equilibrium. That quotation from Einstein was vivid in my mind: everything is energy and we must match that frequency to attract that reality and to attract those events, good events. For example, people who have failed marriages tend to have the same pattern, the same fate in all their marriages, because they attract the same kind of people or they attract the same sort of conditions.

I worked in Venezuela as a physician for 30 years. I gave my patients natural treatments and advocated good nutrition; I told my patients to eat more fruits and vegetables. In Venezuela and many parts of the world, there is a tendency to rely more on refined carbohydrates. That's why so many people are overweight and obese. Obesity is one of the biggest health problems in medicine, leading to diabetes, arthritis, and all kinds of diseases. Now, science is discovering that even diseases such as Parkinson's, dementia, and Alzheimer's don't begin in the mind; instead, they begin in the gut.

Nutrition is very important. If we have a leaky gut, or the gut is permeable, there are a lot of toxins that will seep into the main bloodstream and trigger autoimmune diseases. That's the main reason that I became involved in changing the lifestyles of my patients. I have a database of more than 42,000 patients; I became famous in my area and many people – many physicians – referred hopeless cases to me. I was able to help those people. I was happy doing that, but I also felt that something was missing. I wanted to use my capacity for creativity.

In Venezuela, starting in 2007 through to 2010, the political situation and the quality of life deteriorated. Crime was on the rise, and food and supplies were scarce. I thought that the universe was telling me to move away from there. Years before, I had bought a small property in Tenerife because I had an uncle whose heart belonged to the Canary Islands. He was a golfer and he used to tell me all about the Canary Islands. I also had some patients from the Canary Islands in Venezuela. When they left Venezuela, before Chavez came to power, I contacted them and they suggested that I come to Tenerife. I thought, *Why not?*

I visited Tenerife for the first time in 2007; in 2012, I bought a small property there, in case I decided to move to Tenerife for good. Since I'm a Finnish citizen, it's easy for me to live there. Tenerife is a paradise for me where I can write books and do many things I love to do.

When I moved away from Venezuela, I left all my patients there. It was hard to see the tears in their eyes. Many of them really loved me. I still get hundreds of messages daily from them. They say things like, "We miss you; please come back."

I discovered Bob Proctor in August of 2015. In Venezuela, there were a lot of blackouts because of poor energy and electricity supply maintenance. One day, I was working on my computer and, suddenly, the lights went out. The computer died. I still had my iPhone, so I began surfing the Internet. I was searching on YouTube for *The Strangest Secret in the World* by Earl Nightingale, the record that had influenced me so much in my youth, and I came across a video about it by Bob Proctor.

It was like traveling back in time 50 years. It made such an impression on my mind again that I immediately called the Proctor Gallagher Institute. I subscribed to *The Matrixx program*. Meanwhile, I moved to Tenerife for good in November of 2015. Then, I traveled to Toronto in December of the same year and met Bob Proctor. At one of the meetings, there was a huge round table with 12 people sitting around. I was talking about my life with someone there. A blonde woman overheard what I was saying and she said, "You have to write about that." We started to chat a little bit more and she told me that she was helping people to write bestsellers; her name was Peggy McColl. Then, that same day, I saw her on the stage as a speaker. She said that everyone has a story to tell and that we should share this story with the world, because as human beings we have infinite potential and our gifts and talents should be shared with the rest of the world. She said, "Take Jussi here, for example. He lives in the Canary Islands." She remembered everything from our conversation and she introduced me. There, in the spotlight, at that moment, I felt the need to become a writer and to do something about my passion.

What happened because of that moment? What did you start doing differently to change your results?

Dr. Jussi: When I met Peggy McColl, that night I woke up at three o'clock in the morning and the name of my book came into my mind: *Transforming Lives*. I was particularly influenced by the Law of Vibration. I signed up for Peggy's program; she became very dear to me because she was extremely supportive and she understood my background. She said, "You are going to be famous. You have a huge story to tell."

I remember when I told Bob Proctor my story. He said to me, "This story is not for a book. It's for a film. You have to make a film of that story." The main subject of my book is not the story of my life. My book is about my passion, which is something we all have. If everything is energy, then each one of us is like a radio station. A radio station broadcasts energy on a certain frequency. That frequency – which I call the signature frequency – is what we attract. We match the synergy and that's why we get the friends we have, or why we experience certain situations or events. We attract certain tragedies into our lives, certain good or bad situations. We attract opportunities. It's this energy that we have that created my inspiration to write *Transforming Vibes, Transforming Lives*.

Everything changed in my life. I became passionate about the book's subject and I created a course based on that book called *Upgrading Your Signature Frequency*. What I mean by that is, to improve, you have to upgrade the kind of energy, the kind of vibration, and the kind of frequency you broadcast to the world. Sometimes, we feel that our normal life is up and down. Sometimes, it's a feast; sometimes, it's a famine. We have to discover that happiness is a choice.

Society sells the idea that to be happy we have to achieve a certain type of status, along with the symbols of that status. We need money or success to be happy. However, once we achieve success, our goals change completely, so happiness is postponed.

On the contrary, I believe that happiness is something we can choose now and that it's a mindset. People need to know that. For example, I can choose to be happy today and by choosing to be happy, my vibration will be different. If we realized how our thoughts produce effects in the outside world, we would be more careful about how we think, because negativity is something that kills opportunities, friendships, and everything good in our lives. If we focus on positive things like happiness or enthusiasm – if we pursue our precise objective with that attitude – we can completely change our reality for the better and even change our health.

Despite my age – I am 70 years old now – I still feel full of life. I can produce more and I can create more. I never knew that I could produce videos, MP3s, and music, but now I'm an expert in the field. I work with energy and use vibration to make media with gamma and delta waves; this induces changes in your personal frequency, which helps improve your mind.

I have had so many testimonials about how my program has improved people's lives. Because of these, I feel that I have something to share, something that can change the lives of many people for the better, using simple remedies, simple nutrients, and simple habits. If you form good habits, you can change your life completely for the better. For example, there was one woman who came to me who had a number of diseases; she had shaking hands that trembled so badly that she couldn't write or sign a check. She began using my program and using what I call the 'tools of wonder'. Now, she can write with confidence and her hand is not shaky.

My life has changed immensely in just one year. In November 2015, I was working in Puerto Ordaz in Venezuela. I worked there as a normal physician. Now, I am writing books and creating programs. Bob Proctor says that if you look back on your life, you should need a telescope, because where you are now should be so far away from where you began. My life has changed completely.

What paradigms did you discover that you needed to change?

Dr. Jussi: Because of the loss of my parents, I felt somehow abandoned, even though they weren't to blame. I had a tendency not to finish things. I have now begun to finish every single idea that I start. This year, for example, I took a lot of courses to prepare myself for the online business. However, I noticed that I was starting many things and not finishing some of them. I recognized that as a paradigm and now I know the reason: because I felt abandoned, I had the tendency to abandon my own work. I changed that vibration and I became very reliable. Now, people hire me because they know that I am very reliable, fast, and produce good quality work. I create quality media with good content. I am overcoming that paradigm.

How long, after you changed this paradigm, did it take you to start seeing results?

Dr. Jussi: Before *The Matrixx*, I had tunnel vision. During that event, something happened and my compass was turned in a different direction. I was able to see more clearly what I was supposed to do. When you write a book, you have to study and research many things. I discovered many things while I was doing this work. My goals became clearer. I recognized, for example, that life is not like a ladder with rungs; rather, it is like a tree with different branches – you have to jump to this one here and then you have to jump there. But, in the end, you are still climbing that tree.

I began to see results immediately. I was living in a different country and nobody knew me except for a handful of people. Still, through the Internet, Skype, and other different kinds of technology, I was able to communicate with different people or groups. They were my family at that moment. I tried to connect with them every single day using letters or messages. I can see perfectly now where I am heading, which is toward sharing my gifts. We are all interconnected in the world with one mind. We can change the world for the better.

Is your family – the German family – still in Colombia?

Dr. Jussi: They moved back to Germany. I lost contact with many friends from my childhood because in those days, we didn't have the Internet. Now, I am beginning to connect with them again. I found my father's family in Finland in 2000. I discovered that I had two living uncles. In July 2000, 63 members of our family met at a hotel in Turku, in the east of Finland. That was the beginning of a different journey.

We can only see a fraction of the universe. There are many unseen things around us; this is energy. By paying attention to positive things, we can change not only ourselves for the better, but we can change our family and we can change our relatives.

Everything is energy. We are vibrational beings and, by changing that vibration, we change that being, that persona. It is wrong to say, "I am this way." We can be this way in a temporary state, but we can change. We have infinite potential inside and if we tap into that infinite potential – which is God – we become channels of the universe and we can change everything for good. That's my message.

What was the most difficult moment in the process?

Dr. Jussi: The most difficult change was living with a reduced income. I had been earning a nice income, but I had to start living on my savings with zero income. That was difficult and would have caused many other people to be negative or have doubts. However, I was prepared. I felt that everything had to be positive. I could not see the end from the beginning, but I knew that it would be better. There is a saying that if you are afraid to enter the cave, that cave probably houses the pressures that you fear.

I believe that. I can see my future changing. Now, my income is increasing and it more than covers my expenses. Peggy McColl called me one day and asked, "What motivates you?" I told her, "I don't need motivation because I feel inspired. I jump out of bed in the morning because I know there is something new that I am going to create; that sense of creativity is my fuel. It gives me enthusiasm, it gives me energy, it makes me think positively, and allows me to reach my peak."

What was the best moment in the process?

Dr. Jussi: My best moment was probably when I went to *The Matrixx* program, where I met Peggy McColl. I feel that was my best moment because I felt very connected with her. She can discover and unearth the many talents you have. When I was 12 years old, I used to create comics and films about Vikings. There were no computers back then. I drew and painted each celluloid by hand. I made 27,000 hand-painted celluloids. I also created music; I was an accordionist as a child. Music and videos now enlighten my life. I can produce many things with music, vibration, videos, and media that can change lives. That's my goal at this moment.

When you hear the words "Universal Laws," what do they mean to you?

Dr. Jussi: As long as we learn to live by the Universal Laws, we are going to be guided. If we understand the meaning of the different Laws, we're going to see that the universe is not against us. It's in favor of us. It's like God. It's inviting us to improve our lives. We see religions that rely too much on rites and doctrines. God is not interested in religion. God is interested in uplifting you. You have to upgrade your spiritual life to become a better human being and to become more sensitive. We need to learn that we are all connected, and we have to respect everyone, no matter what they believe or the pigment of their skin. There's no difference in race; there's no difference in gender. It's all nature.

Flowers come in all kinds of colors. It is the same with human beings. Roses are not superior to daisies. They are different and they are connected. Human beings are also connected. We learn that it's okay to have love for our country. It's okay to have love for our family. But why does love have to stop at the border? Love should go out to more people. We are all connected. We are all living on the same planet and in the same universe, so we have to learn to love each other, to see that every human being has a gift to share with the rest of the world. We help people to discover what their gifts are.

What specific goal have you managed to accomplish?

Dr. Jussi: The book was a major goal for me. English is not my native language, so that was hard for me. But the more I wrote, the easier it became. When you have passion, writing becomes easier. Everything fell into place. When I gave the manuscript to the editor, she said to me, "This book is unique. I have read many books, but I am very impressed with your book." She said, "I have to know you." That was a very nice compliment that I received from the editor. I began to realize that my book could make a difference.

Now, the goal is to go a little bit deeper. I've built a course about upgrading your signature frequency, which I'm going to launch next year. I recently ran a focus group to test the course. This course uses methods that I have used for nearly 20 years with my patients to change their health. I thought, Why not use the same methods with healthy people, to improve their lives? I don't solicit testimonials. There is a message board for participants in this course where people can write whatever they want. Many people have written that it's an amazing course and that it's changing their lives. They say it's improving their health and that they feel the effects immediately.

This course helps people to improve the way we broadcast our frequency, our energy: the signature frequency. We have a default frequency that we have as natural beings. Unconsciously, we broadcast our default signature frequency. Science has proven that we can inherit certain traits and beliefs that came from our ancestors, even as far as six generations before us. Sometimes our ancestors experienced wars or displacement; look at the people in Syria right now or years ago in Chechnya – there were families who were destroyed. Cities were destroyed. People were forced to move. That affected the lives of the offspring – the children and the grandchildren. We can inherit these things. That's why we are prone to failure, prone to having certain tendencies and forming certain paradigms easily.

If we discover that we are broadcasting a particular kind of frequency and we discover how to change that frequency, it's easier for us to design our lives with a sense of purpose, to decide to choose a different direction. We can find a different perspective in our lives and change and bend our reality. By changing the vibration, we can change reality completely. Reality is what we perceive. People might choose to blame the economy or their husband or wife, but if we learn that we are responsible for our lives – 100% responsible – we can change that, and we can be free. People don't know that they are in a jail produced by society, by religious beliefs, and by paradigms: cultural paradigms, semiotic paradigms.

Five hundred years ago, people thought that the Earth was flat. That was a paradigm. Changing a paradigm isn't easy. Right now, medicine is suffering from a similar type of paradigm. For example, medicine encourages people to battle cholesterol. Yet, our brains are made of cholesterol. Cholesterol is very important for the neural transmission of the synapses; it is a key component of the makeup of our brains and supports the development of neurons. We prescribe drugs to lower cholesterol, because we blame cholesterol for sickness, but cholesterol is here to protect us. The problem happens when that protection becomes too much; it's like inflammation. Inflammation is triggered in the body to protect it when there are too many problems that can cause damage. The problem isn't cholesterol; it's the buildup of excess cholesterol.

Likewise, up until quite recently, people bought into flawed science about the low-fat diet. Everybody thought we had to eat fewer fats, no cholesterol, and no eggs because it was too dangerous. There were commercials on TV insisting that this was true. People were misguided. They became completely brainwashed. They now expect that pharmaceutical companies will suddenly discover a magic pill for diseases like Parkinson's or Alzheimer's. There are already many drugs for these conditions, but none of these have proven effective at all.

Instead, I recommend changing the way we eat. For example, we may have genes that predispose us to breast cancer or prostate cancer, but we don't have to activate these genes. By changing our habits, we can maintain our health. We can 'turn off' those genes and, as a result of this work, the tendencies of our bodies and the trajectories of our lives will change completely. The media tells us what to eat and how to dress, and we listen without questioning it. We have to change that paradigm. We have to learn to live by the Laws of the Universe, by the laws of nature. Then we can improve our quality of life.

What is the one key lesson that you can give to everyone who wants to reach their goal?

Dr. Jussi: First of all, we need to define the correct goals. Many people set goals that are really about seeking the approval of society. For example, in certain cultures, if you get a university degree and become a doctor or an engineer, you are considered to be successful. Or you are successful if you marry a certain kind of person. These are goals defined by society, not personal goals. We need to differentiate personal goals from societal goals. We need to reject everybody else's goals: the expectations of our parents, the expectations of society, and even the expectations of our own teachers. We have to learn that we, human beings, have enormous potential inside us, but we also have blurred vision. By acknowledging the Laws of the Universe, our vision will be clearer. We will become focused. Once we discover how to move toward our mission, we see the way we need to go. Once we decide which way our life is oriented, then we can set our personal goals. But don't wait for that precise moment. You can set a personal goal right now and know that you risk changing everything, even your friends. I changed everything. The environment around me has changed completely; I even changed my profession.

I now experience more fulfillment in my professional life because of the way I see the universe. It's completely different. It's a broader experience. It's a vision. Set a temporary goal, shoot for that; once your vision begins to clear, set another goal that is a little harder to achieve. Commit to that goal and tell yourself that this goal will change your life. Remember that you will never fail unless you give up completely. You may make a lot of mistakes. Learn from them and keep going. That's the idea.

What is your next goal, Dr. Jussi?

Dr. Jussi: Right now, my goal is to complete the program that I am creating. It will make it easier to reach people so that I can transform lives for the better in the areas of relationships and communications, health and abundance. We sometimes complain about being poor and blame the economy, but the truth is that we can make our own economy. We don't have to depend on the country's economy or the prevalence of employment; we are greater than that. My mission is to give people the tools to improve their lives for the better, in health, in ambition, and in spirituality.

What would you like to accomplish in this life before you leave it?

Dr. Jussi: I want to make a difference in the universe. I see that we can change the world for the better. I want to be that difference. Mahatma Gandhi said, "Be the change you wish to see in the world."

If you had to choose one sentence that has a lot of meaning for you, what would it be?

Dr. Jussi: Everything is energy. We all have a frequency and, if we match that frequency, all our reality will change completely. It's not theory, it's not philosophy – it's physics, according to Albert Einstein.

Because everything is energy, I can change my frequency to no longer feel abandoned. Now, I am able to harness my personal energy to help others, both as a doctor, a creator of media, and as an author.

About Dr. Jussi Eerikäinen

Dr. Jussi is the author of *Transforming Vibes, Transforming Lives*. He is also an International Special Programs builder and consultant for UNEG (Universidad Nacional Experimental de Guayana), founder and former president of Fundación Educativa Bonanza, and a former approved consultant at the Colombian Association of Clinical Hypnosis.

NeuroplasticWork is an initiative created by Dr. Jussi Eerikäinen, who has combined his mathematical expertise with more than 35 years' experience working as a cardiologist and naturopathic doctor in Venezuela.

Contact Dr. Jussi at:
http://neuroplasticwork.website/
info@VibrantResults.com

8

Be the Source

Peggy McColl

Peggy McColl is a New York Times *bestselling author, Millionaire Author mentor and has written 13 books. She has run a personal development business for the last 22 years.*

Can you, please, start by introducing yourself?

Peggy: I am a mother, a grandmother, and a wife. Those are the most important parts of my life. Even though I have a phenomenal career and a wonderfully successful business, and even though I'm blessed to serve many others in the world, I have always kept my family as my priority.

I've run my business for 22 years. I've been studying personal development for 37 years. I will study personal development and professional development until the day I die. I love what I do, and I do what I love. I have written 13 books, which have been translated into 37 different languages. I've been on *The New York Times'* bestsellers list. I've helped many other authors write their books and I've made their books international bestsellers. I help authors bring their passion, expertise, and knowledge to the world in a way that can serve others, and I see that they are compensated in wonderful ways.

When did you first come across Bob Proctor's material? What was your situation in life?

Peggy: I was 19 years old – I'm 57 now, so that was a long time ago. I was working for a company in Toronto, Canada. The company had hired Bob Proctor to do an event called the *Kickoff Event*. It took place in January and involved helping employees of a particular company to develop a mindset that would allow them to collectively create more success for the business. I was an employee at this company. At the time, my life was what some people might call a bit of a mess. As an employee of this company, attendance at this session with Bob was mandatory. It was in the evening, and I remember that I didn't want to go and listen to somebody for several hours after work.

I showed up at this event and the room was already full of people. There were no empty seats, so I turned around to leave, but somebody grabbed me by the shoulders and said, "There's a seat right in the front, in the center. You can sit there." I didn't want to be front and center, but that's where I found myself. Bob Proctor came on stage and he started speaking. If you've ever had an opportunity to hear Bob speak, he captivates you. It's like he's hypnotizing you and drawing you in with his voice and his messages. He said so many things that evening that just shook me up; he rocked me to the core.

Bob quoted Vernon Howard, saying, "You cannot escape from a prison unless you know you are in one." In that moment, I realized that all the misery that I was experiencing in my life, everything that was lacking – lack of results, lack of money, lack of healthy relationships, lack of a healthy body – was something that I had self-created. Until then, I had honestly thought that it was my parents' fault or it was my employer's fault. It certainly wasn't mine. I wasn't taking any responsibility for it. I thought that I was destined to live this miserable life. Bob woke me up that night. I'm so thankful that I was open to his ideas. I took a lot of notes, and I paid careful attention. I found myself sitting on the edge of my seat, absorbing all this information.

Bob said, "If you want your life to change, you must change. The only way that you can do that is through study. You have to seek a level of understanding, and then you have to apply it." I knew there was work to be done. That evening, I decided that I would dedicate my life to this, not knowing where it would lead me; not knowing that one day, I'd be doing the work that I'd be doing in the world. However, my initial desire was to clean up my life. I knew once I cleaned up my life, then I could help other people. That was my eye-opening, wonderful, life-changing experience, which got me into the work that I'm doing today.

You're so lucky to have met him when you were so young. What happened from that moment on? What did you do differently to change your results?

Peggy: Some people believe that there's some kind of magic that's going to happen and that if you read one book or go to one seminar or listen to one audio tape – bam! – it's all going to happen; but the truth is, it doesn't work like that. I started to study and I kept studying. I never stopped. It became an everyday experience and I still do it today. Last night, I sat in my family room, reading. Yesterday, I had out-of-office appointments and I was in my car for probably an hour and a half, listening to audio programs. I listen to my life script. I listen to Dr. Joseph Murphy. Quite often, I listen to Bob Proctor. I saturated my mind and my consciousness with new material so that it would infiltrate the dense stuff that was within me – the destructive paradigms.

At a very young age, our minds are very open and receptive to all ideas. I had been conditioned in a certain way. I knew that what I needed to do was to make this a daily study. I started studying every single day. I would create techniques of how I could apply these ideas and knowledge to my life so that I wasn't just reading the material for the sake of reading the material. I would internalize the feeling of knowing that this was true. Everything that I was studying was absolutely true. There was scientific proof. There were people in the world who had applied this and enjoyed wonderful success. There were many resources to study and learn and understand even more. Bob Proctor was one such resource.

When I began studying, Bob would recommend books. For example, he recommended *Think and Grow Rich*, a book that at the time he had been studying for many years. If Bob said to read *Think and Grow Rich*, I would read *Think and Grow Rich*. If Bob said to read *Psycho-Cybernetics* by Dr. Maxwell Maltz, I would read *Psycho-*

Cybernetics by Dr. Maxwell Maltz. If Bob said to read *Your Erroneous Zones* by Dr. Wayne Dyer, I would read it. I wouldn't just read it; I would devour it. I would take that book, I would underline passages, I would highlight words, I would dog-ear the pages, and then I'd go back and review it again. At the time, Bob had these cassette tapes that he would sell in packages. I bought all of his packages and I would listen to them in my car. I listened to them so much, they would wear out, and I would have to buy them again. I was thrilled to invest in another Bob Proctor program or another book or another audio program, because I knew it would change my life.

It wasn't the material that was changing my life; it was *me* that was changing my life. It was a conscious choice that I made – one that anyone can make – to make a change in my life. But, it takes time. We don't know how much time. We set goals. We set objectives for ourselves. It's like you, Inbal, and everything that you're doing with your interview series and your book. We set the objectives.

I remember hearing Bob Proctor say that quite often people will set a date for a goal to show up, and it doesn't show up on that date. There's a Law of Gestation that dictates that there's a period of time that must elapse before all things will manifest themselves. We need to accept that we don't necessarily know when it's going to happen. We set the objective; we get on with the work. If something happens, we can be so easily knocked off course; you need to put yourself back on track again. If you arrive at the date that you've set for yourself for a particular goal and you don't achieve it, set a new date. Don't give up on it.

These were the things that I learned as I moved along, and I had to continually re-correct my own thinking and put myself back on track because I would often get off track. I would go back to the old way of thinking. I would engage in the old beliefs. I had to really pay attention to that.

Another valuable lesson that I learned from Bob is that it only takes a little bit of poison to kill. He's talking about poisonous, destructive thoughts. As soon as you think, "What am I doing this for? This isn't going to work. I'm not getting the results," you start getting angry, and you contaminate your results. It's like pouring poison on top of a plant. You're killing it. You're killing your ideas.

When you get on an airplane – say, from Spain to Canada – it's going to be off course most of the time, but the autopilot puts it back on track. Autopilot is a steering mechanism and it knows there's a destination in mind. That's what happened to me. I know there's a destination in mind. The ultimate destination is to leave this earthly planet, but I've many destinations or milestones that I'm working toward in my life. I know with absolute certainty that I must continue to study. I must be consciously aware of what I'm allowing into my mind and choose the thoughts that will serve me, allowing me to serve the greater good.

It sounds so easy to do, but few people study every day. People who study get results.

Peggy: We get to choose if it's easy or not. We're conditioned, habitual beings. We do the same things over and over again. Until we mold our study into a habit, it's definitely a challenge. That's why, now, I couldn't imagine waking up and not writing in my gratitude journal, doing my affirmations, looking at my goal card, listening to my life script, or listening to somebody else throughout the day.

I do this every day, but that took time. I call this the good news and the bad news. The good news is that we're habitual beings, so we can develop new habits and patterns that will serve us. The bad news is that we're habitual beings, and we're typically going to do the same things that we've always done, making it difficult to create some new patterns. The idea is to get into some new disciplines.

What paradigms did you discover that you needed to change in the process?

Peggy: We're always going to have paradigms. Bob has paradigms, Peggy has paradigms, you have paradigms. Everyone reading this has paradigms. I had a big paradigm that I needed to change, which was that I wasn't deserving. I wasn't worthy. I didn't deserve success. I didn't deserve to live in abundance or opulence. I didn't deserve love. That was a big paradigm for me which came from my upbringing.

My parents did the best they could with what they knew. I'm not blaming my parents. I loved my parents. They're both deceased now. They only did what they knew best. We weren't poor, but we weren't well off. We certainly weren't even middle class. Both my parents worked. I had two brothers. One of my brothers died of cancer. There were six of us: two brothers, a sister, me, and my parents. We lived in a tiny two-bedroom home. I slept in a bedroom that was the size of my walk-in closet today. My brothers slept in two bunk beds and, on the other side, there was a small three-quarters-sized bed that my sister and I shared. You had to walk sideways between the two beds. It was like a closet.

If I wanted something, my parents would get angry. It's very natural for us to want. Children will ask for things because they don't know any better. I would ask for something and they would refuse. They would be angry and shout, "Who do you think you are?" That had a connotation of *you're not worthy* or *you don't deserve that*. "Who do you think you are? Money doesn't grow on trees." Many people heard these things growing up.

Also, we weren't shown love – not like the way I treat my son and my grandson. I was never told, "I love you." I never heard my parents utter those words. I tell my son I love him multiple times a day. Once, when my son was young, a girlfriend of mine asked me, "Why do you tell him you love him all the time?" I said, "Because I do." She was kind of frustrated and she said, "I think he knows." I said, "When I was a little girl, nobody told me, 'I love you.'" Nowadays, it's pretty common. I tell my grandson that all the time; "I love you, I love you, I love you." You tell your friends you love them. I don't know if it was a generational thing, but we weren't told we were loved. We weren't hugged and kissed good night. They said, "Get to bed." That's how I was raised. That paradigm was very strong. I interpreted it as *you're not worthy; you don't deserve good things*. This was a big paradigm in all areas of my life. I had to reprogram my consciousness.

I had to put new ideas into my conscious mind through repetition that I was deserving and worthy of everything that I desired, including success and prosperity and abundance and love. As a result, I attracted those things into my life. That paradigm spilled into self-confidence issues; I couldn't even look in the mirror. I'd be walking down the street and I'd catch a glimpse of my reflection in a window, and I'd think, "Ew." That's not a nice way to treat your being, something that you should love.

In the 1980s, I discovered Louise Hay. This was after I'd been studying Bob Proctor. Louise Hay had started doing a lot of work with cancer patients and AIDS patients and helped people to love themselves. At the time, my father had been diagnosed with cancer, and that's what led me to Louise Hay. He survived cancer. He died of a stroke 25 years later, 30 years after he had been diagnosed with cancer. I was led to Louise Hay's work in the mid-'80s. One of the things that Louise suggests that you do is to look at yourself in the mirror and say, "I love you." That was very difficult for me at first.

Bob also talks about the value of loving yourself. You'll sometimes see Bob Proctor on stage and he'll say, "I love me." Loving myself was something I had to learn, but if you work on it, it can significantly change your life.

I see many parents who cannot say these three simple words – "I love you" – to their children.

Peggy: I'll tell you what the reason is. They don't love themselves. It's easy to express love when you feel love. I studied Neale Donald Walsch in the '90s. He's the author of *Conversations with God* and he sold millions of copies of that book. He's a wonderful communicator. I remember him talking about saying the words, "I love you." He said that if you want to experience love in your life, cause another to experience love in theirs. In other words, if I share love with you or if I give you love, I'm the source of love. In order for me to give you love, I have to be feeling love. It's a wonderful exchange. It's like a circular motion. If I help you succeed, I succeed. Whatever it is that you want for yourself – I remember hearing Neale say this – cause another person to have it. That's why I created my morning money classes. If you want to have prosperity in your life, give prosperous thoughts. Give prosperous ideas. Give abundance. Give easily and freely. When you do, it will come back to you. That's not why you do it. You don't do it because you want to receive something back. It's about what I can give that's of value to the world. When we do that, good comes back to us.

He sums up that concept with three words: be the source. Be the source of whatever it is you want to have in your life, and you will have it. If you want to have fun, be the source of fun. If you want to experience laughter, be the source of laughter. If you want to experience romance, be the source of romance. Many women complain that their partners aren't romantic. Be the source and you will experience romance. Light some candles, prepare a romantic dinner, put on music. Draw the curtains and wear something sexy. Whatever it is that you want, be the source of it. You'll experience it and you'll cause another to experience it as well.

Recently, my son had a birthday and I bought him a new truck. He had been driving a vehicle that was not in the greatest shape and, because my family is so important to me, I wanted my son and my grandson to be safe on the road. I bought him a new vehicle for his birthday. I am quite certain I received the most joy in the experience of giving it to him. I love giving. It fuels me. It excites me. It's almost like an addiction. I have found that the more you give, the more you get. It's not why you do it, but the more you give, the more you get.

We have to wake up every day and think about what it is that I could give today. Right now, Inbal, you're doing an interview and you have no idea if it will return anything to you. There's no guarantee that you're going to be compensated with a single dollar. You're doing what you're doing unconditionally. You're doing it for the greater good. I have absolute certainty that good will come back to you. We don't always know how or when or where, but our responsibility is to get up every day and do the best we can. If we find ways to add more value to the world, we're going to be compensated.

How long did it take you to start seeing results?

Peggy: I saw an immediate change in me. I looked at myself differently. It was a realization that occurred because of the study. As far as evidence of results that were occurring in my life, it took a period of time. It could have been years, but it was very likely weeks or months that I started to see different results. I run an annual program called the *Elite Circle of Influence*. I've been working with this group and talking to them about what they've accomplished during the last year. Where have they seen positive change in their lives? It may not be a monetary return. It might pertain to how you're feeling. It might have to do with how you're expressing yourself. It may be in who you're hanging out with now, who your friends are. It may be some other more tangible results like money or home or relationship or something specific that you can actually put your finger on. But there will always be positive return when you make that investment.

When I take my money and I put it in the bank or invest it, I don't know if I'm going to have a positive return. I hope I'll have a positive return, but I don't know for sure. When we make an investment in ourselves – by which I mean studying these materials, studying the books, taking the programs, watching the interviews – I know with absolute certainty there is a positive return. How much time, energy, and effort you invest in it will determine what your rate of return is. When we talk about return, it's not studying the stuff that makes the difference; it's how you feel. Your feelings are the language of your soul. Your feelings create something called vibrations, energy. It's an energetic exchange. When we're feeling certain things, we draw similar things to us, using the Law of Attraction. The Law of Vibration is a subsidiary Law of the Law of Attraction. When we're feeling good, when we're feeling successful, when we're feeling vibrant and alive, when we're feeling energetic, when we're feeling loving, when we're feeling abundant – and we're really, genuinely feeling it – we will attract these things to us like results. But we must be feeling it.

I remember hearing Wayne Dyer say, "Infinite patience produces immediate results." I wrote about this in my book called *21 Distinctions of Wealth*. Patience is about knowing that the desire that you've set for yourself – seeing your book on *The New York Times*' bestsellers list, having the abundance in your life that you desire, being recognized as one of the best in the world in the field that you're in – is already done, then you are in the experience of it. That produces immediate results. How long it takes shouldn't be a matter of sitting there, waiting, thinking, "Is it coming? Is it here yet?" You have to know it's here now. It's yours. If you had the thought and if you had the idea in your mind, you've got the ability to hold it in your hand. You've heard Bob say, it's yours right now. If you get nothing else from this interview, understand that, because that will change your life.

What was the most difficult moment and what was the best moment in your process?

Peggy: They were the same. The most difficult experience that I've ever had in my life was going through my divorce. It wasn't because

I wasn't going to be married to Charles anymore. He's a wonderful man and a great human being. I thank God that I married him because, if I didn't, I wouldn't have my son. It was difficult for me because I thought marriage was forever; I took those vows seriously. The fact that it was no longer going to be a marriage – it was going to be a divorce – felt like a failure to me. It felt like a failure because I thought, where did I go wrong? I realized later that the relationship was what it was.

I remember seeing a movie with Ted Danson and Whoopi Goldberg. In this movie, they were in a relationship and they were in love. They're very different people. But there was a line in that movie that summarized it well for me: *A bird and a fish can fall in love, but where do they live?* Charles and I were very different and we weren't good together. There was no synergy. It's not that being different is not a good thing. I'm different from my current husband, Denny, to whom I will be married forever, and we work well together. Charles and I are very different, but we didn't work well together. It was like a square peg in a round hole; it wasn't working. The relationship was changing form, but the bigger challenge for me was that we had a young son. My son Michel was barely two at the time that we split up. Being a mom is the most important priority in my life; now I wasn't going to have Michel with me all the time. He was going to be spending part of his time at his dad's. I found that hard. That was really difficult for me. That was 22 years ago. Michel would go to his dad's for the weekend and, in the initial stages, I would cry because I was so sad. I'd walk by his bedroom door and he wouldn't be in there. My baby wasn't at home. It didn't seem right.

I had to recondition my thinking about that. I had to recognize that Michel's dad is his parent as well. His dad loves him with every ounce of his being. Michel's being taken care of. He's being loved and it's good. When Charles and I were together, it wasn't a good environment for Michel. There was hostility. It wasn't healthy. This was better for him. Although it was a very challenging time for me, it was a wonderful growth experience because it was through that experience that I recognized that I had to love myself and let go. I had to trust that I was deserving of love and that this relationship may have fulfilled a certain role in my life, but it was no longer serving me. If I wanted to experience fulfillment in love – a feeling of a soul connection and being in a healthy, loving relationship – I had to experience it in my life. I had to be very clear about what that was, define it, feel it, and attract it into my life.

That took a while, because I had created a belief system that relationships cause massive pain. Many people are afraid of relationships because they've been hurt before. I had that belief system. Relationships cause pain. I wasn't going to attract another relationship into my life. I dated casually, and I wouldn't allow anyone in, because if I fell in love, it would hurt and I didn't want that. I had to work on myself and create some new conditions. I opened myself up and then I attracted my husband, Denny, into my life. I thank God for him every single day. I love him so much. We've been together 12 years and I love him more today than I've ever loved him. We are soul-connected. He's a blessing in my life.

My best and worst experience was the divorce, because it was painful. Yet, it caused me to dive deep and to understand more about myself. It allowed me to turn up the volume of love within myself and grow and learn. It stretched me. I had to take care of myself. I had a responsibility. It was at that point that I ended up buying a home. I didn't have any money, but I bought a home. Many benefits came out of that experience. It was my worst experience and my best experience at the same time.

When you hear the words "Universal Laws", what do they mean to you?

Peggy: The Universal Laws are set. They're set in motion and they are for everyone. There's not a different set of laws for you than there are for me. We're all operating under these same Laws. There are many different Laws – the Law of Gestation, the Law of Vibration, the Law of Attraction, the Law of Compensation – and when I hear the Laws of the Universe, I get excited because I know that if I just understand these Laws and apply these Laws, I can have and create anything that I desire, within limitations. If I go to the top of this building and I jump off, I'm not going to fly. There's an element of common sense. I also know that if I decided that I was going to be a gold medal winner in some sport, that's not going to happen at this stage in my life either; it's within reason.

The Universal Laws work. If I decide that I would love to experience something, I know that working with the Law – and Raymond Holliwell wrote an entire book on it called *Working with the Law* – I can create anything that I desire in my life.

You don't even have to understand it for it to work. For example, when Bob first started his business, the first year he made $175,000; within five years, he was making over a million dollars. He wondered what had happened. He didn't understand the Laws at that time. You don't have to understand the Laws. They're working whether we understand them or not.

Can you tell me about one specific goal you managed to accomplish?

Peggy: When I was getting divorced from Charles and our matrimonial house was on the market, we couldn't sell it. We kept dropping the price, but no buyers would come. It was a weak market. It was a very weak market and specialty homes, like ours, just weren't selling. However, I was very clear that I was going to buy a home for my son and me. I had a goal card written out that said: "I, Peggy McColl, am grateful that I own my beautiful four-bedroom home." I had no means to buy this home, but I still saw myself in the home. One thing that I learned from Bob, which is probably one of the most valuable lessons that I've ever learned, is that you don't have to know how. You don't have to know how you're going to do it, but set the intention, see yourself in possession of it and get on with the work. Start doing things to take you in the direction of your goal.

I visited show homes. I went to open houses. Charles used to say to me, "When you have your apartment...." I'd say, "I'm not getting an apartment." And he'd respond, "You don't have any money to buy a house." I'd say, "I don't know how, but I'm getting a house." He'd roll his eyes; he didn't believe in this stuff. He thought it was a bunch of garbage.

One day, I heard about a fundraiser lottery in our city for the Children's Hospital of Eastern Ontario: the CHEO Dream of a Lifetime Home. You could buy a ticket for the lottery for $100, and the prize was a beautiful home. It was decorated. It was furnished and it came with everything. It was a beautiful home.

I drove to the home to check it out. It was open. People could go in and buy tickets. They could view the home and they did this during the month before the draw. I went to the home and I discovered that the home was exactly what I had written on my goal card. I took it to the next step and I visualized living in the home. I'd go to the family room and I'd sit on the couch. I would feel the furniture and close my eyes. I would imagine being there with my son, maybe watching a Disney movie and cuddling up by the fire. There was a little fireplace in there. I'd sit at the kitchen table and I'd look out the window. I'd go and sit in the formal dining room. I'd sit at the head of the table and I would imagine my family there for Thanksgiving dinner or Christmas dinner. Then, I'd sit in the formal living room and imagine having guests over and entertaining. Upstairs, there were four bedrooms and three bathrooms, just as I had described in my goal card. They were all beautifully decorated. I chose which room would be my son's. I imagined Michel being in there – he was two at the time. Then, I went into the master bedroom. There was this beautiful sleigh bed; it was gorgeous. I lay on the bed and I looked up at the ceiling. I imagined waking up in the morning and seeing that ceiling. There was an ensuite bathroom with a big, Roman tub. I jumped in the tub and I lay back and closed my eyes. I could almost smell the bath salts. I just saw us living in this home.

Down the street from the home was a park and, in the other direction, there were trails in the woods. My son and I love being outdoors. We love going to the park. I love going for walks on trails. I saw us living in that home and, because the home was open, I could go and visit it over and over again. That's what I did. On my goal card, I changed my goal to say, "I, Peggy McColl, am so happy and grateful now that we own our home at number 71...." I added the address to the goal card and I saw it every day.

Having this home would allow Charles to keep the matrimonial home, which we couldn't sell anyway. Then, I could buy this home. On December 7th, the CHEO draw took place and Dr. John Goodman won the home. I didn't win. One of the things that I've also learned is that we have to detach ourselves from the outcome. We don't have to know how it's going to happen. Don't throw your goal away when it doesn't show up at the time that you wanted it to show up. I thought, *Maybe it's not that home.* Maybe the timing is out. I changed my goal card and I took off the address. "I, Peggy McColl, am so happy and grateful to own my beautiful four-bedroom home." A few months went by. I was at my brother's cottage for the weekend with my son. I woke up in the middle of the night and sat bolt upright. I received a message that said, "Go to the house." I knew exactly what it meant. It was a weird experience for me. I didn't know where it came from, but I knew it meant that I should go to that CHEO dream home.

The next day, my son and I were driving back from my brother's cottage. I exited off the highway, and I went to the neighborhood where the dream home was. I pulled onto the street and I could see from a distance a "For Sale" sign on the lawn. I guess Dr. John Goodman didn't want to live in it. He already had a beautiful home and he didn't want to have this home. I immediately called the realtor and asked to see the home.

The real-estate agent didn't know that I didn't have money or that my house hadn't sold. I asked him to show me the house the next day. He met me at the house. When he put the key in the door, unlocked and opened it, and allowed me to go inside, I stepped into my visualization mode. I thought, This is my home. I imagined that my friend – who had come to the viewing with me – and the real-estate agent were visiting me. I walked through the home. All the furniture was there. All the decorations were there. All the window coverings were there. Dr. John Goodman didn't want any of it and he left it as it was.

I went back again and I brought my son with me, because I wanted to see my son in the home. I asked for a second visit and I came with Michel. Michel ran around the house. I thought, *I'm going to do this.* I was listening to an audio tape one day in my car and it was talking about the philosophy of stretching. Stretching means that if you think you can't, you must – not for what you get, but for who you become.

Bob says that all the time. Goals are not for what we get; it's about who we become in the process. I called the real-estate agent because an idea popped into my mind. I said, "Meet me at the house. I want to make an offer." He met me at the house; we sat at the dining room table. I said, "I'm going to move in in two months. I'm going to give Dr. Goodman 10% of the purchase price the day I move in. I'm going to pay him an occupancy fee for six months and we're going to close eight months down the road." He'd never heard anything like that before, but he took it to Dr. John Goodman and the offer was accepted.

I didn't have the money to buy this house. I had to come up with the money and I made a firm offer. I even wrote a check with the offer of a small deposit. I had to run to the bank and take out a cash advance on my Visa to cover that check. I'm not advocating buying a house on your credit card, but that's what I did in order to get it.

This is the belief that I have within myself. When I am committed, I will find a way. Not everybody believes that about themselves. But, it's easy to create that belief system in your way. If I sign my name to something, I commit to it completely. That's why getting a divorce was a really difficult decision for me; I had signed my name on a marriage agreement. I made a commitment to buy this house, so I had to find a way. Two months later, I moved in and I paid the 10%. Six months later, I closed the deal on the home. In the six months that I occupied that home, I had to figure out how I was going to come up with the rest of the money. I had no idea how I was going to do it.

The company I worked for at the time went public. I learned what that meant for employees; we could buy shares and sell them on the day the company went public. The house deal was closing on December 1st and the company was scheduled to go public in October; however, they ended up changing the date to November 26th. That was really tight, because I took all the money that I had saved for a deposit and I put it into this stock. I didn't know whether it was going to go up, down, or sideways. I went to the broker and I said, "If the company goes public on the 26th of November, when will I get my money?" He told me, four days later, which was the 30th of November. My house deal was closing December 1st. Fortunately, the company went public on the 26th of November and the stock skyrocketed. I got my money on the 30th, I closed the deal on December 1st, and I lived in that home for eight years and sold it for almost twice what I paid for it. That was a stretch experience.

It's true that it's not what you get, it's who you become. The home I'm sitting in right now is a CHEO Dream of a Lifetime Home. I bought this home five years ago and this home is worth about a million dollars more than the one that I was in because these homes keep increasing in value. This is a spectacular home. It's gorgeous. It's beautiful. I bought it for well above seven figures. It's not what you get; it's who you become. It causes you to grow.

Sometimes, goals can bring out the worst of who you are, but you have to manage that. Through that experience, I created what I call switching techniques, which allow me to switch from what I don't want over to what I do want. Sometimes I think, "What have I done? I'm a fool." But then I stop myself and say, "Wait a minute. That's not going to serve you. What is it that you would love? I would love to experience owning this home. What's that going to feel like? It's going to feel great. I'll feel grateful. I'll feel relaxed." That's what you need to feel and that's what I do. I have these little dialogues with myself, I create these techniques, and I switch. I look at my goal card. Looking at your goal card, affirming things, reading, and studying; these things don't do anything unless you internalize them. You must feel it in order to experience the results in your life.

What were you prepared to give up to arrive at your goal?

Peggy: Sometimes, people think that they have to sacrifice their health or their family. You don't have to sacrifice any of that stuff. I was prepared to give up doing things that were a waste of time, like watching television. I stopped wasting time and started using time, getting up a little earlier in the day.

I also choose to take care of myself physically. I consider myself a professional and I don't drink alcohol very often. I might have a glass of wine, but I don't go to bars or parties. I choose to take care of my physical body and to get enough sleep. As much as possible, I try to live and maintain a healthy lifestyle. My physical body is my vehicle. It takes me where I want to go. Even if I feel like having a glass of wine or staying out late, I don't do it because I choose to stay in my professional space and serve people.

I heard Bob say one time, "You wouldn't want a surgeon to have a couple of drinks before he opens up your physical body and does surgery on you." Some people say alcohol takes the edge off. Do you want your surgeon to have taken the edge off while he's conducting brain surgery or some other kind of surgery on your body? No!

It's the same idea. I don't take the edge off in order to feel more relaxed, because I know there's an impact. There's a chemical reaction that will happen in my physical body if I drink. It's not the same for everybody. I've seen people perform and they're drinking. I've seen comedians do their act and they're drinking. Beethoven was known to be drunk when he composed most of his creations. It's not always a bad thing, but for me, that's what I chose to give up. I choose to give up things that I don't believe are going to fuel me or serve me because I'm here to serve the greater good.

What is the one key lesson you can give to everyone who wants to reach their goal?

Peggy: I don't think it's necessarily one key emotion or one key thing because there are a number of things. One is to set your mind upon your goal, set your heart upon it, grab hold of it, and don't let go. Don't let anyone else take your dream away from you. Decide you're going to do it and get on with the work.

Be a dog with a bone. I became an author and I realized I have to be absolutely focused on having that experience in my life and not let anyone take it away from me. Maybe that's the key lesson as well. You've got to work on yourself every single day. Get a mentor, because somebody else can save you a whole lot of time and prevent you from doing things that aren't going to get you the results. I love working with authors, I love working with experts, and I love working with entrepreneurs. I'm not saying I have it all figured out, but I've been at this a long time. I've created phenomenal success. Ask those people who blazed the trail for you to help you and give you guidance. Follow that guidance.

What is your next goal?

Peggy: My next goal is a financial goal that I'm looking to create in my life. Giving thanks for something in advance, but feeling as if it's already here, is so incredibly powerful.

I also recognize the value of continually giving thanks for goals that I have reached. I'm happily married to my husband, Denny, and he is happily married to me. I have a wonderful relationship with my son, Michel, and my grandson, James. I include my family in my goals. One of the greatest statements we can give is that we are grateful.

What would you like to accomplish in your life before you leave it?

Peggy: I want to reach millions of people. I'd like to be recognized in the world as Bob is: as one of the leading experts in this space that I'm in and positively impacting millions of people all over the world. That's what I live for and that's what I would love to do before I die.

If you had to choose one sentence that has a lot of meaning for you, what would it be?

Peggy: You are the source. You are the source of everything that you experience in your life. In other words, the power is within you now to create anything that you want in your life.

My upbringing and my divorce fueled the paradigm that I was not worthy. Through study, I realized I could change that and that I deserve success, prosperity, abundance, and love. Now, I work at being the source of happiness in my life and I live to give love to my family.

About Peggy

Peggy McColl is known as the Bestseller Maker. A faithful student of Bob Proctor's work, she became the author of many international and *New York Times* bestseller books that have been translated into more than 12 languages.

Now, she is a mentor, key speaker, and the coach of many bestselling authors. She has developed successful online courses that are helping hundreds of authors.

Contact Peggy at:
http://peggymccoll.com/
peggy@peggymccoll.com

9

I Can Is More Important than IQ

Inbal Hillel

Israeli entrepreneur Inbal Hillel lives in the south of Spain with her family. Inbal is a distributor of an innovative early education software. She is a passionate photographer, designer, and traveler. Inspired by Bob Proctor and driven to grow her awareness, she decided to write this book and share this information with the world.

Can you please introduce yourself?

Inbal: My name is Inbal Hillel. I'm originally from Israel. I have two beautiful boys, Tom and Gil, who are seven and nine years old, and I share my life with my amazing partner, Alberto. For the past six years, we have been living in the south of Spain on the Costa del Sol. I'm passionate about traveling, taking pictures, design, and vintage stuff. I love to dance. I laugh and smile all the time. I love to surround myself with good friends and to enjoy myself with them. My life is wonderful.

Three years ago, I started a company called Multinational Kid, which helps children all over the world to achieve their potential and learn languages, math, and music easily and quickly from the age of four months old. I founded this company because I was passionate to raise my children as multilingual. One of my goals in life was to give my children the opportunity to speak many languages; I wanted them to have every opportunity to communicate with people from all over the world. I am happy to say that I have achieved my goal. My children speak three languages perfectly and they're currently practicing a fourth.

What inspired you to create this amazing book?

Inbal: In the past, I was a wedding photographer, but I stopped working in photography when I became pregnant with my first child, as it was very physical work; I thought that it was not something that I could possibly continue doing as I aged. Through studying Bob Proctor's material, a few years later, I discovered my roots again. Bob continuously asks, "What do you want? What do you really want?" That question got me to thinking. After a lot of reflection, I came up with the answer – my passion is a combination of traveling, taking photos, and surrounding myself with high awareness people. Continuing with photography had been on my mind for a long time, but I didn't take any steps toward it. I just continued working in my own company. One day, my friend and coach, Berenice Basavilbaso, sent me a video showing a penguin walking on the edge of a swimming pool. The penguin in the video went backward and forward, wanting badly to jump, but he didn't jump. He hesitated. Talking to Berenice afterward, she explained, "This penguin is you." And I wondered, *What is she referring to?* She said, "You love photography, that's what you really want, but you keep doing something else, things that you may like, but that aren't actually your real passion. These things don't really drive you. In other words, you're not jumping. You're not taking action toward your real life's purpose, exactly like the penguin." Something hit me at that moment and I realized she was right! I needed to go back to the things that I loved. Right there, I made the decision and jumped.

What is the connection between this decision and this book that you're reading now? My vision was to make a book with wonderful stories and to combine my love for photography by including a portrait of each of the interviewees. However, things turned out differently from my plan and, finally, I created this book without including any photos. But, I did go back to practice photography and revitalize my skills.

When did you come upon Bob Proctor's material? What was your situation in life then?

Inbal: All my life, I was shy. At parent-teacher meetings, the teachers always said that I never spoke. I would never speak in class. I'd hate it if they asked me a question and I'd blush deeply. I had no self-confidence. At 17 years of age, I became a guide with the youth movement in Israel. At this point, things started to change inside me and my self-confidence started to grow.

Later on, after I finished high school, I spent a year as a volunteer with the 'Moshavim Movement'. We performed different activities with young children in different villages in Israel. We taught them, by example, how to respect, love, enjoy, and take care of nature; how to keep natural spaces clean; how to work as a team; how to experience sleeping outside their home and travel, etc. I guided small children and gave them everything that I learned from my parents, who passed on so many important values to me. I had an opportunity to share and help them think differently. This position provided me with a lot of confidence and was the second step forward on my internal journey.

After that year, I started going to courses and listening to self-growth material. I learned from many coaches in Israel. I would listen to their messages while doing laundry, walking outside, driving in the car, cooking, doing sports, and so on. Everywhere I went, I listened and always looked for more; I was thirsty for knowledge. One day, I heard that Bob Proctor was visiting Israel. I was in Spain at the time, so I couldn't go to that event, but I found out that they made a package of books and CDs of his event, translated into Hebrew. My English wasn't that good at that time, so I was keen to buy these materials in Hebrew. I listened to these CDs over and over, and once I had exhausted their potential, I continued looking for more material.

Looking at Bob's website, I found a one-year coaching program, which cost $5,000. I had never spent that amount of money on any course before. This sounded like a lot of money for me at the time, but as I was convinced that this was what I wanted, I signed up. A year later, when I consulted with my friend Amanda about attending another event that was even more expensive, she said, "If you're asking me, I'm going to all those events!" Hearing that, I thought to myself, *This lady is a little bit crazy.* But after a while, I thought, *If she can go, why can't I? I will go also! Why not?* I made my decision and went to the 3% event in Arizona. At that event, I had the opportunity to meet Bob Proctor and Sandy Gallagher in private and I even recorded an interview with Bob. He explained about the baby's subconscious mind, the importance of early education, and my educational software's benefits. At the time, I thought of things as being expensive or cheap, but those concepts are explained by Bob Proctor through the Law of Relativity: nothing is good or bad, big or small, until you RELATE it to something. You say that things are cheap or expensive according to what you relate it to. "Everything expensive is cheap for us," Amanda said, and she explained to me how she used these words in her life. It's only the way we look at things; it's our mindset. Amanda, for example, chooses to say, "It's very cheap," about everything. What a nice way to look at the world. This idea sounded so good to me that I began using it also, and my feelings and vibrations became very positive. Everything is easy and possible.

Sometimes at events, Bob takes out a wad of dollar bills. He wants to demonstrate that people who carry a lot of cash can always see, feel, and touch it. It's all about developing money consciousness and a different attitude toward expense and abundance.

It's about your state of mind, how you see things. Money is just paper, numbers. You need to think about money as if it is just like any other thing. Expand more awareness for money because the money is there. Even if you don't see much around you, it doesn't mean it doesn't exist.

Recently, Amanda put a lot of money on a bench in her room and we just threw it in the air, had fun, and took pictures. This is the abundance mindset that Bob talks about. You need to feel it before it will become real. It's like you're part of a show in the theater. You're an actor who needs to fake it till you make it, till you really become the character that you're playing.

I started studying Bob Proctor's material two and a half years ago and my life totally changed. Then, I met Amanda and started observing her way of thinking and conducting herself in life, based on Bob's material. That caused my thinking to shift once more. Thanks to her, I took another big step forward in my life.

What did you do differently at the moment you connected with Bob's material? What did you change in your life to have better results?

Inbal: I started to bring order to my mind and my life. I started to clean out the negativity and the people that were around me who were not acting as allies to me, who couldn't match my level of vibration and awareness. For example, I had local partner who spent work time arguing instead of lifting the business up together with me. Getting support from my coach and my mastermind group, I understood that, as difficult as it would be, I had to make the hard decision and end this business relationship.

I also became more focused on what I want. Another thing that I learned from Bob's material was beginning to understand the concept of giving and receiving. When you give, you don't always receive from the same person. I always expected to receive from the person I'd given to. I was frustrated that I was giving to some friends and I never got the same amount back from them. I learned from Bob that it's not important. If you give, you give. You don't expect to get it back from a specific person at a specific time. You'll just receive it one day from the universe or even from another person, in a different way. For me, that was a big 'aha' moment. Realizing that you don't have to control who you receive from, that this energy will be returned to you in unexpected ways, is so powerful. Understanding this released a lot of frustration from me. I found that I no longer had this expectation from anybody. You give and the universe gives back to you. It's so easy and so incredible. *When you have no expectations, you live in a very relaxed way. You act and you forget about it; then, you get it back one day.*

Inbal: I had been focused on money and how to earn it, and I was not relaxed. If you believe that you live in abundance, then you already have everything you need. You don't need to be stressed or afraid anymore. Bob Proctor talks about the calmness of the mind. I learned that I needed to be very calm and when I was calm, things would come naturally to me. Being stressed and busy, not having time for anything, doesn't help you reach your economic goal.

There is the Non-resistance Law which teaches not to resist things, but to let things flow. If you start to resist things, this Law will not work for you. You try harder and harder, but you get nowhere. There's no flow. However, let go of your stress and desire to control, and you'll see that things will turn out fine.

When you're more relaxed, more things come in a natural way – like rain. When it rains, it doesn't try to rain; it rains. And when a bird flies, it just flies naturally. No effort is needed. When you relax absolutely, you get much, much better results. Your desires will be fulfilled when your feeling is as natural as possible.

What was the paradigm you realized you needed to change in the process?

Inbal: A big paradigm for me that I needed to change was the paradigm of "I can't." I can't do this; I can't do that. I was always telling myself that I can't speak English. I would also tell myself, I can't speak Spanish. Here is an example: I had a road accident when I was younger. I broke a vertebra in my spine but, luckily, it didn't affect my nervous system, so I left hospital walking, without a weelchair. That event affected my father a lot and he became very protective of me. He'd start saying things like, "No, you can't ski. It's dangerous for your back. You could break something. You can't be a photographer. The equipment is too heavy and it's not good for your back." Even though he meant well, he was always telling me more of the same, reinforcing this paradigm. A big change for me was to realize that I can; I can do everything. There is nothing that can stop me from doing anything except myself and there is nothing that I can't do.

My other big paradigm that I needed to challenge was learning to be focused and finishing each task to the end. I would jump from idea to idea and not see anything through to the end. I couldn't focus on one task.

It's our nature; many people have so many goals and ideas that they don't know where to start. But you need to choose and focus.

Inbal: To reach something, you need to focus on it, and only on it.

I also had to change my paradigm about abundance and money, as I mentioned before. I came from a family that had no concept of abundance; therefore, they didn't think in an abundant way, and neither did I.

Changing this approach to money was a long process from me; it included learning, listening, and repeating the material over and over. I know now that learning this is a lifelong process that never ends.

What were the most difficult moment and the best moment during this journey?

Inbal: A very difficult moment was when I was writing my goal on a goal card and putting a date next to it the way Bob suggests. The day came and I hadn't reached my goal; I was still very far away from it. However, Bob says that it doesn't matter if your goal hasn't manifested itself yet. Maybe you wrote down the wrong date – the truth is, it was just a guess from the beginning. In that case, what we need to change is the date, but not the goal. The best moment was writing the goal and expanding my awareness.

What do the words "Universal Laws" mean to you?

Inbal: When I first heard about 'Universal Laws' I didn't know what they were. I had seen *The Secret* and that had been a spiritual experience for me. When I started to understand deeply how this world works, I knew that if you work with these laws, you'll get whatever you want. In that case, I needed to know them well and start applying them in my life. From that moment on, things start to change immediately.

I want to mention another law; there is a Law that states that whatever you give to the world, you get back. *Have you noticed that when you are aware of the Universal Laws, you are kinder, nicer, and more thoughtful? You have more empathy.*

Can you tell me how one of these Laws has affected your life? For example, consider the Law of Vibration and Attraction which says that everything vibrates. Nothing rests. You are always moving toward something and it is always moving toward you.

Inbal: When I was very young, I told two of my friends that I was going to travel all my life. They started laughing at me and asked, "Where will you get the money from?" I didn't know. I had never thought about this. That was not important. The important thing was that I was sure I was going to travel all my life. Many years after, one friend reminded me of my statement and added, "We're all stuck here in Israel and you're traveling all over the world. You're traveling every year. You were right. What you said came true." That's how the Law of Vibration and Attraction work. I said it, I believed in it, I attracted it, and it became my reality.

Can you tell me about another goal you accomplished in your life?

Inbal: I had a dream home in my mind. I visualized it, from the inside out, and I built my vision out of the many pictures that I took and clipped from magazines. I took all of this to an architect, and I described my dream home to him. When I viewed the plans, I found they were not close to my vision at all, so I decided to change architects and start from the beginning. With the second and third architect, I had the same issue. I described what I wanted again and again, but I was unhappy because they planned their dream home, not mine. I threw out the plans again, sacrificed a lot of money, and went to the fourth architect. This time I chose a nice lady from Jaffa. She managed to understand what I wanted and created the plans for my dream home. Thanks to her, I finally got the home that I desired, not the home that others wanted to build for me. I didn't compromise by accepting a home that I didn't want. I manifested my dream home because I was very clear on my goal and didn't let anybody or anything coax me away from my dream.

Now I have a big financial goal. I would like to make a quantum leap and arrive at my goal quicker and easier.

What difficulties did you face? Did you have to give up something you liked?

Inbal: For me, it was difficult to read Bob's material in English. Reading and translating took hours and hours. I missed out on a lot of events. I gave up going out with friends and playing volleyball all day on the beach. Even though I was living on the beach at the Costa del Sol, I gave up lying in the sun. I can say that I gave up relaxation.

I also gave up reading all the fun Hebrew novels that are still waiting for me on the shelf, as I focused on reading Bob's material in English, a language that was challenging for me. I wanted to be focused and pay attention full time; as they say, "When you pay, you pay attention." I paid a nice amount of money, so I paid careful attention.

People always want to get free things, but sometimes when you get them for free you don't value them and you might not even use them.

Can you give one piece of advice to people about how to make it easier to achieve their goal?

Inbal: As Bob says, you first need to decide what you want. When I arrived in Spain the first time, without a word of Spanish, without friends, family or connections, I thought, *What am I going to do here? How am I going to earn money?* I loved early education software and concepts like that, and it was also aligned with my goal to have my children speaking several languages, so I became a distributor and opened my business, Multinational Kid. It's important to define what you love to do and write it down. Then, you've got to dedicate your life to that goal. Be persistent. Be the dog with the bone, as Peggy McColl writes in her book.

You need to do this with your dream, your goal, and your life. Hold it tight and don't let go. It doesn't matter if you invest a lot of money in it. It doesn't matter how long it takes. It doesn't matter what people say. Don't let it go. If this is your dream, go for it, and be persistent till you achieve it.

What do you want to accomplish in life before you leave this planet?

Inbal: I have a dream of living in many countries – one year here, one year there. I'd like to live out in the world, not in one specific place. I want to change countries, not as a tourist, but as a resident in different places.

We all need this. I always say, we don't need permanent residences. You can earn money by managing online multiple sources of income and also teach others how to do it as well. Have you noticed that when you give, it is much better than when you get?

Inbal: Yes! Bob says that the biggest problem in the world is ignorance. People who don't know this material walk in the world with ignorance. They cannot change anything if they don't know how to and they don't make the effort to learn. The key to success in any area is to start learning the material, for at least a half an hour to an hour a day, and expanding your awareness.

Investing in yourself is very important. Most of the time, we invest in our houses, furniture, or cars. However, I think the real investment is in ourselves.

Inbal: I choose to invest in myself and I sacrifice material things for that, as I know that investing in myself is the most important investment in my life. When you invest in yourself, you can have anything you want. In the end, you will have all the money you want, because when you apply the Laws, material things come so easily.

If you had to choose one sentence that has a lot of meaning for you, what would it be?

Inbal: I have three sentences that I'd like to share. The first is: failure cannot cope with persistence. The second is: it's not what you have, it's what you are. The third is: "I can" is more important than IQ. People can have a very high IQ, but if they don't believe in themselves, they will not succeed or progress.

Growing my awareness by studying this material changed everything in me: my life, my relationships, and my "I can" perception. Doing new things in my life that were challenging for me has made me stronger; this book, for example, took me out of my comfort zone and made me grow new levels of awareness and manifest new opportunities.

About Inbal Hillel

Inbal Hillel is a professional photographer and the owner of Multinational Kid, a company that developed and distributes award-winning, revolutionary software aimed to teach language to children as young as four months old. She is also the author of this book.

Contact Inbal at:
inbal@inbalhillel.com
www.inbalhillel.com
www.multinationalkid.com

10

Who I Am In The World

Ryan Pack

Ryan Pack lives in North Carolina with her husband, Rick, and their puppy, Molly. As a woman of a color, Ryan has had to deal with her belief that she needs to work harder than everyone else. Today, she is an adept businesswoman, blogger, coach, and advocate. Ryan quit her corporate sales job to commit to starting her own business.

Can you please start by introducing yourself?

Ryan: I am originally from the California Bay Area. I grew up in a small town 30 miles east of San Francisco. I lived there until I went to university and then I moved to the east coast. I'm an African-American woman. San Francisco is extremely diverse, culturally rich, and full of life. However, Benicia, the town I grew up in, was teeny-tiny – about 18,000 people, one middle school, and one high school. More often than not in social settings, I was often the only African-American person represented in a sea of Caucasian faces.

Growing up, I tried to figure out who I was in the world. The fact that others did not look like me provided its own set of challenges. I was well-loved by a lot of different people who did not look like me and did not come from the same background. Race was an issue back then and I grew up with the belief that as a woman of color, I was going to have to work twice as hard, and I would need to be twice as good to get half of what any of my white male counterparts would have gotten.

I was very driven; I was very motivated. I played a lot of sports, including soccer. I did leadership activities in the Girl Scouts, including selling cookies. That's when I first fell in love with sales. All throughout school, I was involved with various student council activities because I wanted to do more. I wanted to be of greater service.

It took a lot of courage. I was driven by the importance of representing my race and embracing my individuality, but even then, as a child, you don't want to be different. You want to be like everyone else. My hair was kinky, my skin didn't look the same, and all I wanted to do was fit in. Everyone's searching for meaning and you just want to belong.

I think that's something I struggled with as a child. I also had a proper, suburban accent, so when I would interact with urban minorities and other black kids, they would say I didn't sound black enough for the prevalent hip hop culture that dominated the scene. What does that mean? Some of my white friends would say, "You're not really black, because you don't sound black." But I was and I am.

Once, I ran for student government treasurer in high school and I lost. I was devastated. That took the wind out of my sails, because it took a lot of energy for me even to want to put myself out there. I felt like I wasn't good enough; even when I tried my hardest, I failed. But, I became resourceful. There was a role called club commissioner that was wide open. I ran for it and I won by default.

I'm a big proponent of diversity and embracing all the differences that make us unique and special. While celebrating our diversity, we can still figure out what connects us and unifies us. We're not as different as we may seem on the outside. If we can appreciate what those unique things are, we can be better connected.

The club commissioner role launched my public commitment to diversity. I created a multicultural week at my school, and I worked with the principal and the superintendents to create a festival of celebration and participation. We had Hawaiian-Polynesian dancers, we had Persian dancing, and we had African drummers. It brought the entire student body of about 3,000 students together. We planned a whole week of activities and every morning we would share a unique fact. In that week, everyone's awareness shifted. People were excited and they wanted to participate. It was an incredible feeling to know that I had something to do with bringing us together on a much deeper level. It transformed my life. That was my first foray into doing diversity and minority work. I included the event in the school's bylaws; that festival still happens at the high school, almost 20 years later.

Initially, when I went to university, I struggled with trying to find myself. I went to a very large institution, the University of Arizona, with around 40,000 students. Growing up, I knew everyone, but there I just felt like a number. I studied chemistry and I wanted to go on to be a pharmacist. In my class, I had the only brown face out of 450 students. My self-confidence was shaken because I didn't have a firm sense of myself.

That first semester was very tough. I nearly flunked out and it wasn't for lack of trying. There was a lot of pressure. I wanted to do well and I held myself to an impossible standard. I hardly went out with my friends; I was always in the library, studying like crazy.

It was the first time I lived away from my family. I had to try to figure out who I was as a new adult, who I was as a person, how to survive in this new environment, and, without the foundation of my family to rally around, how to build a new community to help me power through. I'm grateful for that experience, because it struck me that maybe that institution wasn't the right one for me. I felt I needed to do something radically different.

I got my grades up and I transferred to a small, historically black college, Kentucky State University. They have a different university system. In the past in the United States, blacks weren't allowed to go to the same institutions, colleges, and universities as whites because of slavery and later due to segregation, so there was a strong need for all-black educational institutions. This university holds a special place in my heart, because it's where my grandparents met during World War II; even more than that, my father attended this college as well. A lot of my insecurities during my formative years came from feeling that every time I spoke, I was speaking for all black people, not just Ryan. When I went to this smaller school, I met smart people who looked like me. I could speak up. I embraced my individuality and I began speaking for me, not for every black person in America.

I am not the authority on everything. That situation changed my life in the best way possible. I had an Indian chemistry professor from Mumbai, Dr. Javid; he believed in me so much, he told me that I could do anything. He made me feel like I could do anything. I believed in myself and that's how I was able to get through chemistry, which was not my natural gift. I had to work hard, but because Dr. Javid believed in me, I felt I could do anything. The classes were much smaller and I thrived. My self-confidence was much stronger because I had a better sense of who I was as a young woman and as a person of color. I felt unstoppable. That is a powerful feeling.

I have a boy's name and I'm black. Kids would say, "Aren't you a boy?" But I really came to love my name. I am grateful that my mother named me with a more masculine name because when I applied for jobs, the interviewers didn't know what to expect.

My first job after college was working for a Fortune 500 technology firm. When I walked into the room, I could see them looking at the resumé and then looking at me. They saw "chemistry, student government, 3.0* GPA, Ryan Pack." They said, "You're Ryan?" I said, "Yeah, I'm Ryan. Nice to meet you."

Long afterward, they said that when they first saw my resumé, they were expecting a white guy to walk in the door. When I got into the corporate arena, I already had experience working with executives from working in the marketing sales training department for a global company. That gave me great exposure and mentoring; I could see that I knew things that my counterparts had not been exposed to.

I always had a passion for business and an understanding of what it meant to be successful. Having those kinds of experiences transformed me and I did really well; I was promoted and I ended up having my own territory in the mid-West. The mid-West has historically been a challenging territory. I was scared to move to the mid-West because I had grown up in California, and now I was going to be covering states like Iowa, Nebraska, and Kansas. I had never been to any of these states, nor had I ever imagined that I would ever go to them. These were agricultural, blue collar, hard-working states. I wondered how they were going to treat me. Was I going to be good enough? I didn't realize that I had to confront my own prejudices. The people in my new territories loved me. They were so good and kind to me. That shifted my awareness, and I had to remove all of the perceptions and limiting beliefs that I had about them.

I met my husband in college, like my grandmother before me. After graduate school, we moved to Kansas City. That was a great experience, but I had come to a point in my career where I wanted to do more. I am a chemist by training. I knew that I no longer wanted to stay in the technology sector and I wanted to use my degree. I wanted to work with purpose.

I read a recent research study which says that purpose is probably more important than salary when identifying a new job for women. I wanted to be of greater service and I wanted to be in healthcare, but I wasn't going to be a pharmacist; that's not why I went to graduate school. I worked in a pharmacy and I hated it. I also knew I wasn't going to be a doctor. I knew I wasn't going to be a nurse. I lucked out and landed in the pharmaceutical industry.

When I moved from technology to pharma, I took a 50% reduction in salary. My husband said, "Go for it." He was very supportive and so I made the leap. Initially, I got a job, but I became depressed. I knew that I had jumped industries to create a better life for myself. I could see that pharma was the way to go, but the role that I started out in was the most junior entry level role you could start out at. I had taken a massive pay cut. I had a graduate degree, but I was stuffing binders and fetching coffees. I was over-qualified and underused; it was depressing. It was the height of the recession, so finances were tight and we had to provide for other family members. My husband's father passed away from cancer during that time. It was a very traumatic time and we struggled.

One day, my boss pulled me into the office and she said, "We need to talk." I almost got fired that day. I had always been a high achiever and I heard, "You're not up to par. What the hell are you wearing?" In the workplace, I was wearing these hideous yoga pants, ugly sweaters, and horrible shoes that my grandmother wouldn't even wear. I looked a mess. I looked crazy. She said, "What the hell are you wearing?" I said, "Oh my gosh, what am I wearing?" I had been in a fog. I was very depressed, I had lost myself in the process, and I didn't realize it.

When traumatic things happen, you don't have your oxygen mask on. There are a few things that can happen in your life that shift your paradigm; one of them is a traumatic emotional event. For me, that was the traumatic emotional event that rocked my world. That was my moment of brutal radical honesty. I had to confront my integrity. I had not been honest with myself. I hadn't been showing up and bringing my full self to the table. I was below par and I needed to do better. When I drove home that evening, I looked at myself in the rearview mirror. I had tears in my eyes and I decided that the woman who had just left the office wearing yoga pants and an ugly sweater was never walking back in like that again. I knew I could do better.

I picked myself up. I changed my clothes. I committed to being my very best. No matter how far below me I felt a task was, I was going to be awesome and put my whole heart and soul into doing it. I did it to show the universe and God that I was grateful; I appreciated the gifts that I was blessed with and I would use them to my fullest capacity. That changed my life.

One night, I decided to stay a little late and I received an instant message about a new job opportunity within the company. One of the women working there said, "I've been watching your performance and you're amazing. You're really good at what you do. I want to put you forward for this promotion. I'm going to pass along your resumé to the hiring manager." The job hadn't even been posted. She said, "You should go for it."

My self-confidence was still a little shaky; I didn't think I could do that role. But this woman insisted, "Yes, you can." That made all the difference. I subsequently earned five promotions in five years. The biggest promotion was when I transitioned from an operations role back into sales. From the moment I decided to be great, I charted a course – I didn't know how it was going to happen – to sales at the company. I wanted to get closer to the source of wealth. I loved sales when I worked in it previously and I knew that's where I wanted to go. That was my stretch goal because I didn't know how I was going to get there. But I was drawn to it; I was pulled into it.

In 2010, my husband and I watched *The Secret* for the first time. We became aware of attraction and manifestation. Things started to slowly come together for me, and I thought, Maybe I do have some control in this. When I went for that second promotion, they wanted me to relocate to Raleigh, North Carolina, from the mid-West. We had just had horrible snow where we were living, so we agreed because North Carolina is much warmer.

We made that big leap of faith and I found myself located at the company's headquarters, which is where the sales department and sales roles are. One day, I was working in my operations role, I saw a listing – I would check the listings every month to see when a sales role would come up – and I became very excited. I called my mom on my cell phone out in the back parking lot. I huddled in a corner and I said, "This job says you need all these qualifications and experience. This is exactly me." She said, "What are you doing talking to me? Go apply for it."

There was a restriction that you had to stay in your current role for at least one year before you could apply for another role. I had only been promoted to my last role six or seven months previously. I thought I could either play by the rules or go for it. I went for it and it turned out to be a very long process. I had fourteen interviews. At one point, my confidence was shaken and I started to lose hope. My husband said, "Hang in there. I can see you in that role." That helped me to build up my confidence and get emotionally involved again with the dream and the hope. After the fourteenth interview, they finally said, "You have the job."

The job was in business development; it was a sales role for the inside sales team. The sales roles are highly coveted and it is a very tight team. There was another candidate that I was up against, and they were having a tough time deciding between him and me. I ended up getting the first role and they later brought him on too. I will never forget the day I came home and told my husband. We started jumping up and down in the middle of the floor in our teeny-tiny apartment. He pulled out a piece of paper that he had written on; it said that on that day, we would jump together celebrating my getting the job as the new inside sales person. He wrote the date and the month. He didn't share that with me, but that was his belief and conviction. He had written the note after we watched *The Secret*.

I worked hard. I won several sales awards. The first award I won was to be part of the $100 million RFP* (new business proposals) club.

That was a huge honor. The next year, I was promoted to associate account director, and I ended up securing the $100 million RFP club again and being recognized as the Global Inside Sales Manager of the Year. It was very exciting. However, I was confronted again with the idea of not being good enough, feeling as though I had to be Polly Perfect and very positive all the time. I didn't feel fully myself in the role. I was holding back. I was confronted again with the fact of being the only black person. I was the only black person on the entire team and it was a global team. It was a company of 12,000 people and I was the only one.

That idea was holding me back. Finally, I ended up working with an executive coach called Kelly. I wanted to go to the next level and where I was going, no one in my family had gone; none of my friends had been there. I decided to take a leap. I was terrified, because I had never worked with a coach before. She told me how much it was going to cost and I choked. She said, "That lump in your throat is the insecure woman who knows that she's made for more. You need to make a change."

Kelly changed my life. She helped me increase my awareness. She helped identify my limiting belief that because I am black, I have to work twice as hard and be twice as good. She helped me shift that paradigm and call it what it was, which is a lie. I can't create more hours in a week to work twice as hard as you.

The hard work had paid off, but then I hit a ceiling because I wanted to earn more. I wanted to earn well over $100,000, but I was stuck. It was because I did not have the confidence. It was because my self-image had shifted. It was because I kept bringing the idea of not being enough to the table. I kept trying to cover it up with, "I'm happy. I've got it all together." That held me back, because people could not connect with me. I was not being genuine.

As a coach myself today, I like to train women that a genuine attitude is far more important than a positive attitude, because a positive attitude alone is not enough for you to go the distance. If you constantly feel you have to work twice as hard as everyone else, your mental energy is not focused in the right way. You're focused on pushing through something hard, not figuring out more creative ways to succeed.

Once I accepted this, my career exploded. I went on to earn over $200,000. I took a poorly performing territory that was doing $1 or $2 million a year; I grew it to over $50 million a year. I was on fire and I put my whole heart, my whole soul, my passion, my full self into it. I worked with global team members from Germany, Spain, Italy, and all over the world. I worked with some of the biggest names in pharma. I loved it. But I didn't get that love until I let go of all the pain, all the resentment that I had been carrying. What had fueled me for the longest time were hate and the idea that I had to prove myself. I resented people who said that I couldn't do it; I wanted to prove them wrong. I should have been loving myself and loving everything that was wonderful about the world and the role, engendering a true passion for making a difference, focusing on the patients, and making people's lives better. When I put in more love, my whole world just exploded.

When did you first come across Bob Proctor's material and what was your situation in life at the time?

Ryan: I first watched *The Secret* in 2010. In 2015, I found myself searching for more meaning; I was searching for something different. I listened to one of my favorite podcasts – *The Model Health Show* with Shawn Stevenson. Bob was on that podcast, talking about shifting your paradigm. I was making plans for 2016 and that podcast made so much sense. I replayed that one podcast over and over again. That's how I entered 2016 with a new mindset, a new paradigm, and a new idea.

The year 2016 was when I first started getting serious about my morning routine. Being more conscious and aware of doing all those little practices of gratitude and meditation made a massive difference in how I interacted with others and the world.

What happened from that moment and what did you start doing differently to change your results?

Ryan: 2016 was a huge year of revelation and transformation. My husband and I became really serious about examining our results. We made a commitment that we wanted to be millionaires. To do that, we had to confront all our insecurities about money and look at those limiting beliefs that were holding us back and keeping us at the same level that we had always been at. In 2016, I made a commitment that I wanted to be one of the top performers on the sales team; I wanted to do more than had ever been done in the region. Instead of looking at things as a dollar amount, I shifted to thinking about how many people I could help.

I thought, *This year, I'm going to make it my mission to provide enough revenue to support 400 families. If I can do that, that will make my world a lot better.* When I was on the road, it was lonely; but when I thought about the families, that transformed things for me. Shifting my perspective and awareness helped. It allowed me to close $75 million in business in 2016. In October, we did the Shift Your Paradigm live stream. It made me confront that I'm here for a higher purpose and that, as much as I love sales, I need to serve in a much bigger capacity.

I had been mentoring a lot of women. They started coming to me and asking questions. "How did you earn five promotions in five years? What are you doing differently? How can you help me with my career?" Around that time, the US elections were happening and a lot of women complained about earning less than men and wage gap issues. Around October, I had begun to shift my paradigm and I decided to start a little blog with my sisters, Danielle and Shannon. It's called *Ms. Rising* and it provides helpful content to support women discovering their power in college, career, health, and mindset. That's really when the idea was born.

My husband said, "I think you should go to *The Matrixx* event. I see this thing having a bigger impact on the world around you and you need to be around like-minded people." He told me, "I think you can help more people." I met people who were launching businesses and contributing to the world. I met Peggy McColl and my life changed. On Monday, I called him and said, "You need to come to Toronto." My husband flew up that night and joined me at the event.

I quit my job. It was hard to say goodbye. I had been there seven years; these people had become like my family. They were sad to see me go and I had adopted the beliefs and paradigms of that culture. But, it was time for me to do more. It took Bob Proctor and Sandra Gallagher to point that out to me. I got reconnected with my purpose. Now we have our company called Impackt Squared Solutions, where we facilitate *Thinking Into Results*. I have my six-week course, which supports women and teaches them how to earn six figures in corporate America.

What paradigm did you discover that you needed to change?

Ryan: The biggest paradigm I had to put to bed was the idea that as a black woman I would always need to be twice as good and work twice as hard as my white counterparts. That one idea held me back. I think that idea and that mindset no longer serves people of color well, especially today when there are many opportunities for people of any color and people of any gender; there's no better time than now. That idea needs to go.

How long did it take you to start seeing results?

Ryan: If someone had told me that I would leave my corporate job, I would have told them they were lying. I loved what I was doing. I would have said, "I'm going to be here forever or at least for another five to ten years." My shift has given other people courage. Some of my friends, who were afraid to start their own businesses, are now starting their own businesses. Women who were afraid to go for promotion are going for promotion – one woman whom I shared tips with earned $20,000 in less than eight months. She got a new role in the corporate world.

I have people signing up for my course now. I secured a corporate client the other day. In the darker moments, I persist and I reread the chapter entitled "Persistence" from *Think and Grow Rich*. I do exercises for calmness of mind and serenity. I do my daily gratitude *** and I send love; all these little things make an exponential impact.

This has been the first full week that we've had our webinar automated. We now have over 400 people on our list and we're recruiting 60 to 70 people every day. We started a Facebook group just two months ago. At first, we had 100 people, of which maybe 40 were close friends and family who felt sorry for me; now we have almost 1,200 women in the group. My mind is blown. I'm really excited.

I have all these new ideas. I've got a new zest for life. I lost twenty pounds. I'm healthier. I sleep better. My marriage has improved. Our communication is so much better because we have a unified goal, and we did not have that goal initially. I think couples need a good goal or something that excites them both. Now we're connected and working on this shared vision.

What was the most difficult moment and what was the best moment in the process?

Ryan: The most difficult moment was being honest with myself about what it was that I really wanted out of life. I was used to staying in my little safe box. I was very judgmental. It's scary to decide what you truly want. I have a vision to fulfill and I need to not be afraid of it, even if it feels huge. I need to open my arms and run toward it; that's very scary.

The best moment in the process has been becoming better connected with spirit. I can interpret different things as signs for me. I did not have this strong connection with God before. I think that's been the best part, because I know that if I have that connection with God, no matter what happens in the outside world, it's okay. I trust that everything happens at the appointed time for a reason and if I can keep my thoughts in alignment with God's plan for me, the sky's the limit.

When you hear the words "Universal Laws," what do they mean to you?

Ryan: The Universal Laws enhance my faith and give me strength and courage, because they let me know that things will happen. The Universal Laws reduce a lot of the anxiety that I used to feel. The Universal Law of Gratitude gave me a better understanding as to how things circulate; before, I didn't have this awareness. I didn't know why things were happening. I didn't know why I was being promoted. I didn't know what it was that I was doing that was triggering these things. Looking back, I can see I was using certain principles and Laws, and that's why these things happened.

It's comforting to know that if I abide by these Laws, my life is going to get better and better. The impact I'll be able to have on other people's lives is going to increase and expand. I'll meet more amazing people and life will be richer.

Can you talk about the effect of a specific Law on your life?

Ryan: I believe the Law of Gratitude has been the one consistent Law that has shown up time and time again throughout my life. I did not have a deep understanding of it until now. I can see how it has transformed my life. In *The Science of Getting Rich*, Wallace Wattles says that the nearer we draw to the source and the more open our hearts are to the source, the nearer the source draws back to us. By speaking and by being grateful, it keeps the lines of communication open with the source. The more grateful we are, the more abundance we shall receive. We shouldn't only be grateful for the good things, but we should be grateful for all things and really understand that everything just is.

Once, I went for a job promotion and I did not get it right away; but, because I didn't, I was able to create a role for myself and the people I worked with. Everything worked out so much better than if things had gone the way I initially wanted them to.

I am also grateful because I feel that the universe loves us, and that until I am ready for something, I cannot receive it, because the universe loves me and does not want to see me fail or hurt me. When things aren't going my way, I'm reminded to be grateful.

If I don't receive an opportunity or if a client says no, I need to figure out what I don't know or how to change my plan. I am thankful if I have been protected from a situation that could have been bad. The Law of Gratitude changed the game for me.

When we get overwhelmed or anxiety strikes, gratitude helps you to snap out of the spiral. It's easy and seductive to get caught up in negativity when you're already feeling bad. It's important to be grateful for the little things. I'm grateful that I can write; I'm grateful that I can breathe; I'm grateful to be right here, right now, in this moment. I'm grateful that I was born in this country, that I have fresh air and clean water, that I have an education.

Can you talk about one specific goal that you managed to accomplish?

Ryan: One of the things that I'm working on is to refine my goals so that I can focus on one goal at a time. I have a lot of ideas, and I can have too many goals and want to do them all at once. I had a goal of writing an article that I wanted to have published on LinkedIn. I couldn't find the inspiration, but I finally completed it last night. The article I originally had planned for LinkedIn ended up being published in the *Huffington Post*. That made me feel really good and it helped me feel that I'm on track with all the things that I set forth to do.

What were you prepared to give up or to sacrifice to arrive at your goals?

Ryan: I walked away from everything that I knew because I'm so committed to the goal of developing and growing my program, *Six Figure Spirit*, to having a successful company, and to serving the world. I want to connect the best people in the world, the best talent in the world, and the best companies in the world with each other. I'm willing to stake my existence on it, and I let go of my former way of life to try something new and different. I'm also more open to and grateful for divine inspiration, and I take action immediately when I'm inspired.

What is the one key lesson that you can give to everyone who wants to reach their goal?

Ryan: Be radically honest. Get a crystal-clear vision and then bury it deep in your heart. You've got to feel it. The goals that I've set that I did not bury deeply have not manifested. The ones that I really felt and believed in – I studied them, I meditated on them – showed up.

What is your next goal?

Ryan: You'll hold me to it, so it has to be good! I've made hundreds of millions of dollars for other companies. My goal is to scale my company to be a multimillion dollar company. I want to do it for myself and my family.

What would you like to accomplish in your life before you leave it?

Ryan: I want to use every single gift and talent that I have. I want to know that when I leave this world, I left it all on the line and I gave everything that I had; that I did not let it go to waste.

If you had to choose one sentence that has a lot of meaning for you, what would it be?

Ryan: A quitter never wins and a winner never quits.

I'll never quit trying to impact others in a positive way. By being radically honest with myself and grateful for what I have, I became better attuned to inspiration; I intend to act on it to scale my company and grow my program.

About Ryan Pack

Ryan Pack is the president of Impackt Squared Solutions, a businesswoman and coach, and a facilitator of *Thinking Into Results* materials. Ryan is an active member of the Junior League of Raleigh and sits on the Board of FemCity Raleigh. She holds a Masters of Public Administration with an emphasis on finance and health care administration from the University of Kentucky and a Bachelor of Science in Chemistry from Kentucky State University.

Contact Ryan at:
ryan@impackt2solutions.com
www.impackt2solutions.com

*A 3.0 Grade Point Average (GPA) from a possible 4.0 total GPA is equal to a 'B' letter grade. GPAs are determined by a combination of course credits, individual grades, and semester hours spent in the class.

**A Request For Proposal (RFP) is a document issued by an agency or company interested in the procurement of a commodity, service, or valuable asset, which solicits a proposal inviting potential suppliers to submit business proposals, which are often considered in a bidding process. It is submitted early in the procurement cycle, either at the preliminary study or procurement stage.

***The Three Steps Powerful Exercise (a Bob Proctor tool to enable people to be in the attitude of gratitude):

1. Gratitude: Write 10 things you are grateful for. Write in the present tense, as if it is already so. For example, "I am so happy and grateful now that...."

Gratitude is an attitude that hooks us up to our source of supply. The more grateful you are, the closer you become to your maker, to the architect of the universe, to the spiritual core of your being.

2. Guidance: Sit quietly for five minutes and ask for guidance for your day.

3. Send love: Send love to three people who are bothering you. Send love not for the other person's sake, but for yours. Sending love puts you in a wonderful vibration that will attract good things to you.

11

Think and Grow Sober

Austin Thomas

Austin Thomas grew up in the methamphetamine capital of the world and became addicted to drugs and alcohol at a young age. After his life fell apart, he got sober and discovered spirituality and Bob Proctor. Today, he works as a solutions architect and is president and co-founder of the Power Within Institute.

Can you please introduce yourself?

Austin: My name is Austin Thomas. I'm the author of *Success by Design: Blueprint for a Prosperous Life*; I wrote the book with my brother, Josh Thomas. I'm also the co-founder of the Power Within Institute and co-creator of a revolutionary new addiction recovery program called *Think and Grow Sober, Visualization Course* and the *Ultimate Life Course*. I have four daughters and a beautiful wife of five years, Shyann Thomas.

I am completely ecstatic and passionate about personal development. It's helped me change every aspect of my life. I grew up in a very poor town that was completely overrun with drugs and alcohol, in an environment where partying was a nightly occurrence. I became addicted to drugs and alcohol at the age of nine years old. Exposed to that lifestyle from a young age, it became a part of my culture. It became my lifeblood and who I was. All the way through grade school, high school, college, and my adult life, I used and abused alcohol and other substances. For the majority of my life I was in denial, but the truth was that I was a hardcore alcoholic.

In spite of being addicted to drugs and alcohol from a young age, I was still really successful at pretty much everything I turned my hand to. I was a high-functioning alcoholic. I graduated high school with honors and a 4.4 GPA. I got a scholarship to college and I graduated college with honors. I was also successful in the IT industry and my success made me blind to my substance abuse problems. I didn't know anybody else who could drink as much as I could or do as many drugs as I could, and still get really good grades, be a star athlete, win state competitions, and excel in life.

Drinking was a daily occurrence for me. It was part of who I was. I drank to celebrate. I drank to grieve. I drank to cope. I drank on every single occasion. I figured that since I was a highly functional drinker, I didn't really identify as being an alcoholic. I just thought that I drank.

What is a high-functioning alcoholic?

Austin: That means that you can drink copious amounts of alcohol and still function in your daily life. I wasn't necessarily dependent on it. I did it because I liked it. I could stay up all night and drink, party, and still get up in the morning, go to school or to work. I could still remember things, function, pay my bills, and get on in life. My life wasn't falling apart as a result of my alcohol abuse.

I started in the IT industry during college and, in my sophomore year, I landed my first corporate job. Two years later, I lost that job due to alcohol abuse at a Christmas party. I blacked out, I did some things that I regret, and I was fired. That ended up being a blessing in disguise for my IT career because, the next day, my college professor told me that there was a job opportunity at a bank. I applied for that job and 24 hours after I had been laid off, I found myself running a bank's IT department at the age of 21. I was in way over my head. I had no idea how to run a bank. I didn't belong there. I didn't have the skills, the knowledge, the academic experience, banking experience, or the IT experience to be successful in that role. That was my first experience of putting myself in a corner; I realized then that I really excel when I put myself in a position where it's sink or swim.

I swam and I excelled. That led to another job and to yet another. I thought that life was great. However, I was earning a mediocre salary – about $75,000 a year – when I first discovered personal growth and personal development. I have the type of personality where, when I take on something and I learn something new, I get really invested. I consume every bit of information and soak it up.

I started learning, experimenting, and looking into different things. I discovered the Law of Attraction and from that I discovered the movie *The Secret* in 2010. This was after my life had fallen apart due to my drug and alcohol problems. My life was in a shambles at that point. My seven-and-a-half-year marriage had just ended in divorce. I still denied that alcohol and drugs were the cause of my life falling apart. I was always blaming my spouse, my circumstances, or anything else in the external world and the environment for the results that I was getting. I was divorced. I lost my house. I was broke. I was alone. I was depressed and that fed the alcohol and the drug abuse.

What happened in your childhood that led to your abuse of alcohol and drugs?

Austin: I grew up in a household that was steeped in that way of life. I lived in a city called Oildale, California. It's about two hours north of Los Angeles and it's considered to be the methamphetamine capital of the world. In the beginning, I didn't do hardcore drugs. I mostly used pot, alcohol, and minor drugs. In my late twenties, I started consuming harder drugs like cocaine, ecstasy, and meth. It was a part of our environment. There was a party every single night in our house and every weekend was a gigantic party. Our dad used to take the food out of the fridge, put it in the sink, and put ice on it to make room for beer. That was just the lifestyle. It wasn't my parents' fault; they grew up in that environment. It was just how life was at that time.

It became a way of life. It was a part of the culture, so it was ingrained in me. A lot of people say that it's genetics, but it's really more about learned behavior and epigenetics. Our environment has great control over who we are and what genes are turned on and off in our bodies, which ultimately determines the lives that we live.

I didn't discover this until many years later, but, essentially, I had observed and learned behaviors from my parents, friends, and family, and I was programmed from a young age that this is the life you live, this is how you cope with life, and this is how you deal with stress and emotions. It forced me to bury my emotions and never really get in touch with my feelings. My father always told me that emotions are a sign of weakness. I rarely saw him cry.

Anytime I had a feeling that I didn't know how to cope with, I would drink. My only feelings were complete happiness, complete anger, frustration, and outbursts. I was never afraid of anything and I'm still not that afraid of anything, especially now given what I know about life and how things really work. However, back then, I didn't know that.

How did your parents have the money to buy alcohol and drugs?

Austin: My parents worked to live and party. My dad always said, "I don't live to work, I work to live." He'd go to work and earn a living so that he could come home and live the lifestyle he wanted, which was to have fun with his friends. I don't want to give the impression that my childhood was horrible. I had a fun time as a kid. It was a wild lifestyle; we went swimming in the river, we partied, we went camping – we had a blast.

Looking back on it, it's not an environment I want my kids to grow up in. But I don't have any in ill-will or ill-feelings toward my parents at all. It was learned and observed behavior for them as well. They were also functioning alcoholics. They were able to go to work, earn a living, put food on the table, take care of us, and provide medical insurance.

We were loved. If anything got us through those hard times in life, it was pure love from our parents. But that was their life, that's what they were taught. They didn't realize the consequences and impact it would have on their kids.

In fact, I wouldn't be who I am today if it wasn't for that experience and I am eternally grateful for that. It's not a lifestyle that I would condone or want other people to live, but it was a way of life that shaped who I am.

When my life fell apart, I started taking a close look at who I was. I started getting into spirituality – not so much religion, but I started to dive into what really makes people tick, what makes people happy. How can I find happiness? Divorce is just something that happened. It led toward a slippery slope. I had the majority custody of my kids and within a year I saw the impact of my alcohol use on them. They would ask me not to drink; they didn't want me to pass out and get drunk. Their desire for me to get better set me on a path of self-discovery.

At the time, Bob was not a part of my life. I saw him in *The Secret* and he stood out as a very prominent, positive, influential person. But I didn't seek him out to learn from him. Several years later, when I told my brother about *The Secret* and the Law of Attraction, Bob stood out to him. He wanted me to join him in learning more from Bob and his material. I thought, that's stuff I already know. I used to be very arrogant and very egotistical, because I learned things very quickly and I was always successful at everything I did. I always believed that I knew better than everybody else. As I got older, I realized the more that I know, the more I don't know. That really opened up my perspective and my view of the world. I started to take a hard look at the life I was living, because it was no longer getting me the results I wanted.

I saw my brother completely change. He went from a hardcore alcoholic to completely quitting overnight. He turned his life around. That inspired me. I saw his business take off like a rocket. I thought, he's doing something that I'm not doing. I was always the success-ful one in the family and now he's outgrown me. He didn't have the education that I have. He'd always struggled. That caught my attention.

One day, he said, you need to come to a live event with me. That first night changed my life completely. It opened up a whole new level of awareness within me. I started to dig into the material and my life started to turn around.

Did all your brothers grow up with alcohol and drugs?

Austin: I have two brothers and two sisters. My oldest brother, Shawn, didn't really live with us and my dad growing up. He lived with his mom in another city. He wasn't exposed to that kind of lifestyle as much as we were. My half-brother Josh decided to live with us when he was a teenager. When he lived with us, he was exposed to that lifestyle on a nightly basis. I had been exposed to it my whole life.

My oldest brother and sister weren't around that much and they didn't adopt that lifestyle.

After the first Bob Proctor event you attended, what happened and what did you start doing differently to change your results?

Austin: At the first event, everything changed because I met Barbara Daoust. That first night, she convinced me that I needed to hire her as my personal coach and mentor. At the same time, I was trying to start several businesses in the network marketing space; that's why I'd gone. I wanted to learn how to grow my business like my brother had done for his plumbing business.

I started working with Barbara on the *Thinking Into Results* program and everything started to turn around for me. I started several businesses; I had tripled my income within a year. I ended up buying a 3,500 square foot house – my dream home. I used the material to attract my perfect soul mate: my wife and my best friend. I also used it to break my addiction to drugs and alcohol. I ended up discovering my passion through all of that, which is helping other people to achieve success, break their habits, and create new, empowering beliefs.

I ultimately changed my belief system. I started understanding how my thoughts, my feelings, and my habits created my paradigms and how my paradigms were controlling everything about my life and the results that I was getting. I discovered who I really am and what I'm capable of.

I owe my entire life and the success that I had in the last three to four years to Barbara and to Bob's material. Once I started, I wanted to consume more and more. I'd go to every one of Bob's live events that I could. I continued to study *TIR*. I watched all his videos. I read every single one of his books. I read like crazy. I studied, studied, and studied. To this day, I get up early every morning – around 4:30 to 5 a.m. – and I read, meditate, visualize, and write down my goals and my gratitude list.

How did you get rid of your physical and mental addiction to alcohol and drugs?

Austin: Your body is affected, but your mind controls everything: your anatomy, biology, physiology, and everything that happens from a chemical and electrical perspective. To overcome it, I started installing empowering beliefs to replace my limiting beliefs. I started changing my self-image. Once I understood the power of the mindset, the power of the Law of Vibration and Attraction, the power and the control self-image has over who we are and what we're capable of achieving, that ultimately led me to breaking that addiction. I started seeing myself and believing that I was somebody different.

Even though there is a biological reaction and a physical addiction, our mind controls everything within our bodies. When you change your mind, shift your beliefs, and start seeing yourself as the person you want to be, everything else falls in line.

Since then, I've discovered that our diet and nutrition have a huge impact on our ability to get sober and break addiction to drugs and alcohol. I'm now studying the nutritional and diet aspects. I'm still not living the healthiest lifestyle that I possibly could; there's always room for improvement. I'm starting to understand how the foods that I eat and the sugars and carbs that I consume impact my ability to cope with life and to be healthy. It all starts with the power of the mind. You are the only problem you're ever going to have and you're also the only solution.

What is your diet like now?

Austin: I understand that my diet controls my mood and my energy levels. I understand that sugar is probably the root cause of almost every ailment and illness out there and sugar is in every processed food. In American culture, we eat horribly: hamburgers, cheeseburgers, pizza, and processed food from the grocery store which is infused with nothing but sugar. Sugar is eight times more addictive than cocaine; that's been scientifically proven. Once I understood that and became aware of what I ate and how I ate, I shifted my diet to start eating more organic fruits and vegetables and grass-fed meat. I started getting away from things like antibiotics and hormones. I took on a holistic approach to living and feeding my body the proper food with the nutrients that it needs. I also started consuming a lot of water.

Water and lemon water are the two best things that you can drink. They hydrate your body. They flush all the toxins out. This changed my life for the better. Now that I understand the power of nutrition on every aspect of my life, I make it a priority.

What paradigms did you discover that you needed to change when you started this process?

Austin: Every single paradigm I had was wrong. One big paradigm for me was understanding that emotions are not weakness. I realized that our thoughts, emotions, and feelings determine what we attract into our lives. Emotions are the key to getting everything that you want. When I understood that, a light switched on.

The second paradigm I had to overcome was my need to be a perfectionist. Now, I'm not a perfectionist. I would rather get something done and put it out there and be wrong, than sit back and try to make it perfect. Nobody's perfect.

Another paradigm that I overcame was the need to prove that I was a success or accomplished to others. The reason I was an overachiever at a young age was because I wanted to be loved and accepted. I wanted to be looked up to. I felt that I had something to prove to the world. The moment I started believing that I was already enough and I didn't need anybody else's acceptance or approval, that changed a lot for me.

I also used to believe that I was better than others. That paradigm put me on a pedestal and pushed a lot of people away. Nobody likes somebody who's arrogant, cocky, and egotistical – I was definitely that person. I'm a lot humbler now than I used to be. Once I changed that, a lot of people, circumstances, places, and opportunities started coming into my life, because I was open to that paradigm shift.

The biggest paradigm change for me was realizing that I didn't have to drink to enjoy life. I broke the addiction by rewiring my programming, by changing my self-image, and understanding how my mindset, my beliefs, and my emotions control everything. Now, I'm at the point where I don't drink daily. I don't drink as often as I used to. I enjoy a glass of wine every now and then, in moderation, whereas before I depended on it to cope. I had to have beer or liquor every single day. Now I just enjoy it. Wine pairs really well with food and I've become a wine connoisseur, but I never get drunk anymore. I don't drink to the point of oblivion. As soon as I get a buzz, I cut myself off. I enjoy it for the sake of enjoying it and it also has some health benefits. Everything is good in moderation. When you start using it too much, that's when it impacts your life.

How long did it take you to start seeing results?

Austin: At first, it was rough. Paradigms are very difficult to change. Bob always says, "It's easy. It's just not simple." For me, it was an 'aha moment' when I understood the stick figure* and the power of the mind. I immediately connected the dots and it made perfect sense to me. The first night that I saw Bob live, I couldn't sleep. Everything started to click and make sense. I started to understand why I was the way I was. I was programmed that way. The subconscious mind controls everything.

I was working against some paradigms and had to go through a lot of pain and challenges. A lot of things cropped up in my life while I was making paradigm shifts and changing my beliefs which prevented me from making progress. Learning how my emotions control my vibration and that my vibration attracts and dictates what I bring into my life was a discovery for me. As soon as you start expecting change, you will get change. You have to be and act as the person you want to be before you can really become that person. You have to believe that you are and that you can. Shifting one limiting belief to its polar opposite – to an empowering belief – can change everything in your life instantly.

What were the most difficult moment and the best moment in the process?

Austin: The most difficult part was being addicted to drugs and alcohol and changing my paradigms. During that process, I suffered a lot of injuries, illnesses, and obstacles which would come up every time I tried to change a paradigm. Paradigms work at the subconscious level and because of that our subconscious mind wants to protect us. They don't want us to change and they create circumstances in your life to prevent you from accomplishing your goals, from changing and growing as a person. Every time I tried to change a paradigm, I would get sick, my wife would get sick, or I would break a bone.

The best moment was when I helped to change someone else's life in a positive way. That helped me realize my real purpose and passion: to serve and to contribute. That breakthrough moment helped me understand that I have to push through these challenges. I have to continue to work to make changes and to better my life and help others improve their lives. That's my life mission now.

Barbara helped me realize that my subconscious mind was working against me to keep me trapped in my current life. Our minds want to go into survival mode and keep us in our comfort zones. The mind doesn't want a lot of changes.

When you hear the words "Universal Laws", what do they mean to you?

Austin: I'm a man of science and I like things to be proven to me. When I made the connection between the spiritual side, the material, and the physical side through Bob's work and through science, it really helped me understand how everything worked in life. The Universal Laws really underpin everything that we experience. We literally create our own world. Every single day, we wake up and make a conscious choice to live a positive, happy, healthy life or live the opposite of that. Once I really understood how the Universal Laws worked, – that they're fixed and that we can't change them – I decided to start using them to my advantage.

I started understanding and believing in the fact that I am a co-creator with and through God, Spirit, or Universe – whatever you want to call it. I have the ability to co-create my own life by utilizing the Universal Laws. That really turned me onto this material because I love science and technology so much. When I started to understand how I could combine those to change my life, I felt like the Universe was on my side. The Universe is on your side too. You just have to understand how those Universal Laws work, how to become in harmonious vibration with them, and, when you do, a new world of opportunity will open up for you.

Can you talk about the effect of a specific law on your life?

Austin: The biggest one is the Law of Vibration and Attraction which states that everything vibrates. We live in an ocean of motion. Nothing is what we think it is and everything is constantly vibrating. Quantum physics and quantum mechanics have proven this. That's really the key to getting what you want in life. I wasn't in tune with my emotions in my previous life. I was constantly living in a state of fear, doubt, neglect, regret, and I was a pessimist. I was never known as an optimist.

The Law helped me understand that if I continue to think negatively and believe that bad things will happen, they're going to happen. I got in touch with my emotions. I understood that my emotions change my vibration and my vibration attracts into my life whatever it is that I want or that I don't want. It works 24/7, just like the law of gravity. You drop something from a building and it will fall down. It's not going to float. The Universal Laws are as precise as that.

It's a very empowering and freeing idea to know that you can change your destiny by changing your thoughts and your emotions. Most people live life thinking that they're controlled by their circumstances, their environment, and that they're victims. Quantum mechanics and quantum physics have shown and proven that the moment you observe something, you bring it into existence. So, why not observe and create the life that you want?

Can you tell me a story about one specific goal that you managed to accomplish?

Austin: When I first started studying this material, I wanted to find my dream wife. I used the Law of Attraction. I used the goal card, visualization, and meditation to do just that. Six months later, I had found her. The night of our first date, I went home and told my roommate, this is the woman I was meant to marry. This is my soul mate. She didn't know it yet, but I did.

How did you meet her?

Austin: I was visualizing and I wrote down the qualities that I wanted. I meditated on this and visualized this every day. I kept that picture constantly in my mind and I kept that goal card in my pocket.

I was part of several online dating sites, but none of them were successful for me. One day, I decided to close my dating accounts because I was continuously getting spam or matches that didn't work out. I had never really been on a date with someone from online dating. I didn't believe in it very much at the time.

As I was closing my accounts, a window popped up in one of the websites with a bunch of women; it said, "You could be a match". In the very center was the most beautiful woman that I'd ever seen. She matched the description of what I had been visualizing. I clicked on her profile, I messaged her, and I told her she had beautiful eyes. I'd commented positively on women's looks before, trying to get their attention, but it didn't work. She responded and we started talking. We met up within a couple of days. We've been best friends and soul mates ever since.

Another big goal that I accomplished was buying my dream home which I live in now. I knew I wanted to start my company, *Power Within Institute*, with my brother and we're going to be creating videos and training courses. I set out to find my dream home that would allow me to work from it and have a studio. I found my perfect dream home, but it was way outside of my price range. I didn't have the down payment and I couldn't afford the mortgage. I started writing down my goal, declaring my goal as what I have now. I started visualizing it and meditating on it. I started 'being' in that place.

My dream home was actually a model home. I visited it every single week. I would go into that home with my wife and kids and we would walk around. I would act as if I lived there. I existed in that space as if it was mine and I felt the emotions of living there. That sped up the process.

One day, I got a piece of junk mail. It was a loan offer, which I didn't take, but it sparked an idea. I had money in my 401k pension plan. You're allowed to pull up to 50% of your 401k pension value to purchase a home. My down payment was the exact amount I was allowed to pull from my pension.

That is not a coincidence. That is the Universe telling you, "I'm here and I support you." That was something that was really awesome for me. We closed escrow on Christmas Eve and that night we told the kids, the family, and everybody that this was our new home. Thirty days prior to that, I didn't even know I was going to be living in that house. It all happened so quickly.

Can you talk a little bit about the process of visualization? How do you do that exactly?

Austin: Barbara Daoust and I created a program that teaches people how to do this. Essentially, you have to go to a quiet place and control your breathing. I learned some processes that helped me get myself, my body, and my mind into a relaxed state very quickly. Just breathe in slowly and deeply for five seconds and then breathe out for five seconds and imagine your breath coming in and out of your chest. I hold my hand right on my chest, over my heart, and it activates the connection between your brain and your heart.

If you look up the Heart Map Institute, they scientifically prove that there's a connection that opens the doorway to your subconscious. It makes your body very calm and it upgrades your intuition faculty, lowering your brainwaves to the alpha state so that you can get into a relaxed state of being. Breathe for a couple of minutes and express and feel the thoughts, feelings, and emotions of love, gratitude, and care. That's very powerful.

Within two or three minutes, you will have activated this connection between your heart and your brain and you go into visualization. The process of visualization is simply imagining yourself living a life that you want in the future. You just picture yourself accomplishing a goal, living a lifestyle, taking that dream vacation, or meeting your spouse. Whatever your goal is, whatever you want to manifest, you just go in your mind's eye and you imagine it being real. You actually create a movie on the screen of your mind and you start using all five of your senses.

When I visualized my house, I went into the house and I felt the energy. I closed my eyes and I would imagine enjoying family vacations or family time in that house. I imagined Christmas, spending time eating dinner, inviting friends over. I started to feel the emotions of what that felt like. I would hear the sounds of the people in the house. I would smell my wife cooking food. I would literally imagine myself touching the counter, lying on my bed, or walking in my front door. I created a movie that was so real that my subconscious mind believed it to be true. You enhance it with emotions. You have to involve all five of your physical senses when you visualize. You have to see it, hear it, smell it, touch it, and taste it. You have to wrap it in the senses, because it creates the feeling of something that is real and your mind cannot determine the difference between what's real and imagined. In order to visualize properly and manifest, you have to create and convince your mind that it's real. Then you express gratitude for having achieved it.

Emotions are the key. They enhance and bump up your level of vibration. Positive emotions change our vibration faster than anything else that we can possibly imagine and we attract into our lives whatever we're vibrating at.

You have to create a future environment that doesn't exist yet and you have to bring it into your now moment by expressing gratitude for having already achieved it or experienced it, as if it's already real. You can practice visualization and meditation in just five minutes a day. It doesn't take very long, but it's the constant repetition that is important. You have to do it consistently. You create a crystal-clear picture in your mind of what it is that you want and then you empower that and bring it to life with your senses. You've already created it in the quantum space, where every possibility exists. It's all infinite potential. You just have to reach out, grab it, and bring it into your life.

One of the primary reasons why people say the Laws of Attraction or Visualization don't work is because they don't create that realistic environment using their senses and they don't involve positive emotions. If you don't make it real for your mind, your mind will reject it. When you involve your physical senses, your brain cannot tell the difference between the real and imagined. Science has proven that and studies show that visualization works if you involve your senses and express positive emotions, because it creates new neural pathways in your brain. The more you activate that in your brain and light it up, you convince your mind that it's real. Once you convince your mind that it's real, your ego is diminished and your mind accepts it to be true. Expectation is the key; expect it to come. The moment you do that, you'll start witnessing magic.

What were you prepared to give up or to sacrifice to arrive at your goal?

Austin: I was prepared to give up everything. When you pursue a goal, it should scare you and excite you at the same time, and you should be willing to do anything and everything it takes. I'm not condoning anything illegal, immoral, or unethical, but you need to be willing to burn bridges. Give yourself no other option.

I'm a firm believer that I will do anything it takes to accomplish my goals and my dreams. You cannot expect to live the life that you want without making changes. You have to clear the way and make room to allow new people to come in and have an impact. I've lost a lot of friends, family, and network connections, because I now have a radically different view of life. Those people aren't on the same level of vibration and frequency as I am, so they've been removed out of my life, clearing the way for new people to come in. It is a painful process, but at the end of the day it's well worth it.

What is the one key lesson you can give to anyone who wants to reach their goal?

Austin: Focus on what you want, not on what you don't want. That's what I teach and believe in. This is how to start seeing results immediately in your life.

What is your next goal?

Austin: My next goal is to help a million people overcome their addictions and get sober, stay sober, and live healthy. I'm doing that through my program Think and Grow Sober. It's a revolutionary new approach that's based on science, personal development, neuroplasticity, epigenetics, health, and nutrition. By understanding the power of the mind, people can overcome their limiting beliefs, their addictions to drugs and alcohol, and create a new life.

What would you like to accomplish in your life before you leave it?

Austin: I want to create a legacy. I've always wanted to be a billionaire. I believe I'm going to build a billion-dollar empire. I want to leave a legacy that displaces the idea that Alcoholics Anonymous or Narcotics Anonymous are the only ways to get sober. These programs leave out science, cutting-edge technology, and the power of the mind. They make people feel powerless and that they're going to be an addict, surviving one day at a time. I want to displace those ideas and bring in a new model that people can rely on – one that's proven to work and that helps people change their lives.

Austin, is there anything that you want to add?

Austin: Figure out your life's passion and how you can contribute to the world. Go out there and live your mission for the rest of your life, because there's no other form of happiness or fulfillment than improving the lives of others. The moment that you learn how to contribute back to the world, that's when you'll feel more peace, joy, serenity, and fulfillment than any other form of life that you can have.

The knowledge that you can change your destiny by changing your thoughts and your emotions is empowering. Expectation is the key; expect it to come. The moment you do that, you'll start witnessing magic.

About Austin Thomas

Austin is President and Co-Founder of the Power Within Institute, a sobriety and life coach at Think And Grow Sober, and a solutions architect in the IT industry.

Contact Austin at
austin@powerwithininstitute.com
https://powerwithininstitute.com

* Stick Figure: The idea behind the stick figure concept is that in our minds, we think in images. Val Van De Wall said that since no one has ever seen the mind, he would create a picture of it. He explained that the mind functions on many levels, but it is simpler to deal with two levels: the conscious mind and the subconscious mind. He drew a circle with a horizontal line right through the center. Everything above the line is the conscious mind; everything below is the subconscious mind. Below the circle, he drew a much smaller circle to represent the body. (Source: TIR material).

12

Believe to Your Core and Live It

Lorrie A. MacGilvray and James La Trobe-Bateman

Married couple Lorrie A. MacGilvray and James La Trobe-Bateman live on Fuerteventura, one of the Canary Islands. They are in business together and are both now Thinking Into Results consultants.

Can you please introduce yourself?

James: We started our business 20 years ago, in 1997. At that time, I worked for a medical device company. I'm an engineer by profession and we still have those types of companies as our main business clients. It was our search for better ways to help those clients that brought us to the *Thinking Into Results* system. We have both completed the certification program to formally become consultants of the Proctor Gallagher Institute.

I'm English. I was born in London, but my childhood was spent on the small island of Sark in the English Channel. It has no cars and no streetlights. It's a very beautiful, unique place; Enya made an album about it called *Dark Sky Island*. I had a wonderful childhood there because it was a small community of only about 600 people. At that time, Sark was not a place you could live if you intended to work in the professional world. It was inevitable that if you grew up there, and if you were going to do anything with your life, you'd have to do it somewhere else. That set me loose in the world, if you like. Still, because of where I grew up, I love islands, beaches, or anything to do with the sea and water. I swam in the sea today… in the rain! We now live in the Canary Islands. To go swimming in the rain here is a special thing.

I grew up loving the beach, but because Sark is in the English Channel, it's not always warm. It has a British climate. Here on Fuerteventura, I'm outdoors all the time, walking or mountain biking. That is how I relax to better think about our customers' needs.

Lorrie: I'm the co-founder and chairman of Remodel International. I'm originally from Detroit, Michigan. I moved away from Detroit during times of economic difficulty in the late 1970s. I moved to Colorado, found work within a couple of days, and made my life there. Many years later, I met James and lived in Wales.

While James loves the beach, I love the mountains; I love the dry climate. When we moved to Fuerteventura, we combined our dreams. When we started our island search, it was about number five on our list out of twenty options. As soon as we arrived, we knew this was it. It was a matter of seeing if we could continue our lives from here – if we could build our business from home in a sustainable way, given that most of our clients are in America and the UK.

We met online. At the time, Internet dating was brand new. My girlfriends would talk about doing it, but I was always like a mother hen, telling them, "You don't know what might happen." I was checking my email one day and I absentmindedly clicked on an advertisement with a heart that said: "Click if you're looking for love." At the time, I wasn't consciously looking for love. I scrolled through the dating site to see what my girlfriends had been talking about and this man popped up on my screen. He was so unique and the words he used grabbed my attention.

I had just been out to California and it was beautiful – sunshine and magnolia trees. I came back home to Colorado; the snow was blowing sideways and it was several feet deep. I thought, *That's it. I'm done with Colorado; I'm done with snow.* I made my decision right then. This was a couple of months before James and I connected, but I had already made the decision that I was going to move somewhere else. However, Colorado had become my piece of heaven, so the new place had to be spectacular to get me to leave. Then, the magic of the universe turned up this amazing man. I thought, *I'd like to get to know him as a friend.*

We wrote back and forth and it was like magic every time. There was an instant connection, but both of us had been married before. We each had our paradigms, though we didn't know what those were at the time. It was like old-fashioned dating, except you're not sitting face-to-face.

James: I hadn't even seen your picture.

Lorrie: I was not very technical at the time. I had to go to the print shop and ask the people there to show me how to put a picture onto Match.com. In the meantime, I asked if he was coming to America anytime soon, because he was doing business on the east and west coasts; I was in the middle of the country in Colorado. The chances of us ever meeting were a bazillion to one. He dared me to come to the UK from America. I had been to Mexico, Puerto Rico, and Canada. I had traveled around America, but I had never been farther than that. I had a huge project coming up. I was very busy, but I had about one week that was clear; otherwise, it wouldn't have happened for another six or eight months. I found a flight for that week and I booked it. I didn't check the dates with him first. I just sent him the itinerary and I went to bed. He got up the next morning and realized I was coming.

I thought, *There's nothing to lose. I've never been to the UK. I would love to go there and see the place. If he's not there, or if it doesn't work out, I have nothing to lose. It's an adventure; it's an experience. I have everything to gain.*

James: At that point, we hadn't even spoken to each other.

Lorrie: I hadn't even heard his voice yet. We were in different time zones with a seven hour difference. My mobile phone rang the next day. I didn't recognize the number. I answered and I heard this British voice. His first question was: Do you have your passport in order?

I said, "Don't I just need my driving license? That's all I need to go to Mexico or Canada or Puerto Rico." I had a week to get a brand new passport. I was in Colorado and the passport offices were in Chicago or Washington, DC. The universe moved in the most amazing ways.

We kept saying that my grandfather and James' father were up there in heaven, conspiring with each other and helping us get together.

You made a quick decision and followed your heart. Most people can't do this.

Lorrie: I was there for six days. During that time, we put together our entire business plan and we knew we were going to go forward together. He was living in the UK; I was living in Colorado. We thought, *what next?* In that very short time together, we put together our business plan. We had a vision of where we wanted to go. We worked out how I could leave my job. I had a substantial position and I needed to find someone to fill it. He came over to Colorado for a while, I went over to the UK for a while, and it went on from there. The original plan – which we set out all those years ago – is pretty much the way it's gone. There have been twists and turns, and much better things have evolved from it. But setting our goals and setting out what we wanted to do is what started everything.

James: It's amazing that it doesn't at all occur to people that they should want to do something specific. I often wonder why it took us so long to get where we are. That's because it was only really when I started doing the Thinking Into Results program that I understood the significance of a goal. If I was to think of one thing that acts as the blockage for most people, it's the mindset that goals are for other people. They're not for me.

We hand-wrote the plan. We still have it and Lorrie shows it to me sometimes to remind me what the plan was. At the time, I didn't want it in the way you have to want something. When I look back, there were things I definitely wanted, but I didn't make the connection between the business plan and wanting something.

Lorrie: I was always setting goals. We knew that this was the goal, to come to Fuerteventura. We didn't know how it would happen or the long-term sustainability of this plan. We didn't know any of those things. We only knew that between us, this was the scope. We created a picture of what we wanted. I wanted the mountains and the dry climate and the warmth; James wanted the sea. We got it all. He says he doesn't set goals, but that was his goal when I met him.

James: I had that goal. It's true and it's why I had my profile on Match.com. It was spontaneous. I couldn't tell you what drove me to do it; it just happened. In the same way, Lorrie responded spontaneously. It wasn't as if I was thinking about it for months. It was spur-of-the-moment.

Lorrie: He kept saying, "I'm a numbers man; I'm not a man of words," but his emails kept getting longer and longer. If you think about the amount of time it took to write and post the ad, visible for just a few days, it was just a few days of our whole lives, a tiny window of time. I responded and I immediately decided that I wanted to get to know this person. I thought, *I'm going to meet him.* I told no one because I knew I would get negative reactions. I wrote my brother an email and I said, "I'm going on holiday to the UK. Here are the address and phone number of where I'll be staying."

If I had said to people, "I'm going to meet this man that I met on the Internet," the whole world would have tried to talk me out of it. I'd already thought that through. It's like Bob Proctor says, "Don't ask everyone around you what you should do. You know what you should do. You know what the answer is and you know it when it's right." Sandy Gallagher says the difference between your big goal and your small goals is the difference between catching a tiny fish and a big, fat salmon. You know the difference. I thought, *If nothing more, he is going to be a lifelong, great friend. I just know that this man is somebody I want to meet.*

Bob says to make decisions fast and change them slowly.

Lorrie: In my business life, I had a very short window for when I could actually travel; otherwise, it was going to be another six or eight months before there was another opportunity. I thought I had to do it right then. That was the time.

We look for security, we need to be sure that our decisions are okay. We need to know that it doesn't matter if we are correct or not. It's better to make the decision.

Lorrie: Absolutely. You have to decide. You don't have to know how. You don't have to have all the answers before you do it. You just have to know that this is what you want to do and then do it. Don't decide this is what you want to do and then think of all the obstacles to it. You have to be open to seeing the next door opening and then go through it. Don't start with the tenth thing down the road. Don't overthink it. By the time you get 10 steps down the road, things will have changed. If you let it evolve, it will be greater than you could ever possibly have imagined.

Equally, you can't just say, "I'm ready now. Let's go." You must make the next step. You must move toward it. You must bring it to you – Sandy calls this "visioneering."

James: On the way, sometimes things will go backward as well. This is where faith comes in. For example, we were in the UK for quite a few years and the US part of our business looked a bit dodgy because of the economy.

Lorrie: Our clients in the US were outsourcing consultancy and there was a pull back. They said, "Where is your US base?" I kept saying to James, "We have to go."

James: The other driver was Lorrie's family. Her mum and dad were ageing. We'd already set our hearts on coming here, but we found ourselves going 4,000 miles west instead of 2,000 miles south. It felt like the wrong direction.

Lorrie: In fact, it was the right direction, because we needed to stabilize our business. We needed to get our US base in order and I was also able to look after my parents. There were lots of things that went on during that six- or seven-year period.

James: We've lived in Fuerteventura for three years now. We started visiting in 2002 and we realized straight away that this was the place we'd like to be. It took another 11 years from that moment to get here.

Lorrie: Communications were not great when we first started coming, so it made long distance work very difficult. We would take longer and longer holidays here. We would keep trying to see if it worked any better. Then, we stayed for 10 weeks and that time we knew that communications had gotten better. It was also easier to book flights to where we needed if we had to visit a client quickly. Our clients felt that we needed to be somewhere near them. We worked with clients on-site and when they needed us.

James: Our clients said they wanted us to be near them, so we sold our house in Michigan, and we bought a motorhome. We thought, *We'll park outside their front door!*

Lorrie: Our mobile office will come to you. They loved the idea.

How long did you travel in this motorhome?

James: We had it for about three years. One time, we got an email from a client we hadn't heard from or seen in seven years, now at a new job on the West Coast. He wrote to us and asked, "When are you going to be in Los Angeles?" At the time, we were driving west on Interstate 10 past El Paso, Texas. So we answered, "In a couple of days!" While we were there, we had a call from someone who needed us in Puerto Rico, so we drove back to Florida and then flew out from Orlando to see them. Then, the first company needed us back in Los Angeles, so we drove back to Los Angeles and parked at Dockweiler Beach there. It was great fun, as you can imagine.

One time, we found ourselves parked in New Jersey. New Jersey's the worst place to be in a motorhome, by the way. There's nowhere nice to park. It's too crowded. We spent a couple of weeks in New Jersey, but no one wanted to see us, even though most of our clients were there.

Lorrie: Clients would arrange meetings with us, but the day before, they'd cancel or ask to do a conference call. We thought, *What are we doing? It's time to sell the motorhome.* Our mindsets had shifted, but so had our clients'. A lot of our long-term clients became our friends, then they all started retiring. We now work with the younger generation; they're very used to Internet communication. Many work from home. They want to do conference calls instead. Once that shift started happening, it released us from being stuck in their paradigm of having to be right there.

James: In the end, we bought a house and we went to Fuerteventura for the winter. My next goal is to have the clients come to us.

We never know when our goal is going to manifest. Finally, your goal has manifested – you're in your dream location.

Lorrie: It may not happen exactly in the timeframe you planned because there are other things that you must do first, in order to be better prepared. That's the way we saw all of it. You feel it when you're supposed to be doing something else first. There were a lot of times we'd think, What is this about? But then it would reveal itself, and we'd be really happy that we experienced and took care of that thing first, so that everything that followed was in order and fell in line with our objectives.

I was able to spend the last six years of my mother's life being close to her. It was lovely. From the time I was in my early twenties, I had lived away from her. We had the greatest friendship, and I spent time with both my mother and father in their last years. I'm so grateful to have this fantastic business that allows us to do these things. Our coming together all those years ago put us in a position to do this.

When did you first come across Bob Proctor? What was your situation in life?

Lorrie: Once we fulfilled our big dream of moving here, we thought, Now what? We were searching for something bigger and greater. I had taken a step back in our business. I dealt with clients behind the scenes, but I had six years to focus solidly on taking care of my parents. I was no longer confident about getting in front of the big corporate clients. I wondered if my purpose was something bigger and better. I researched and read everything from the Tao to *The Secret*. I was devouring all this personal development material.

James: Lorrie has always been a natural at this stuff. She's an unconscious, competent Bob Proctor. The issue she had was simply that nobody compensated her for all this work she'd been doing. In her family, she is always the one who picks them up, brushes them off, and gets their heads straight enough for them to get going again. She was doing this stuff naturally, without really knowing. They thought she was great, but nobody paid her or acknowledged her for it. Something was missing.

Lorrie: I love helping people turn themselves back around or get themselves to a better place.

How did you learn about Bob Proctor? What kind of course did you take?

Lorrie: It was through *The Secret*. I researched each person who was in it to learn a little bit more about them. I looked at Bob and Sandy's website. I started the *Six Minutes to Success* program, and I did that every single morning. That's an email that you get every day with a short video of either Bob Proctor or Sandy Gallagher. It's more than motivational; it's more than inspirational. Each video deep-dives in just a few minutes into one of the Laws of the Universe. It takes about six minutes to watch and think about it. That was how we got started.

What did you start doing differently from the moment you came across Bob Proctor?

James: I didn't really respond to *Six Minutes to Success*. It all made sense, but it didn't go in. I began to take Bob Proctor seriously when there was something I wanted to do and his material was the solution. Without going into the details, when I first started a business on my own in 1997, I wrote down my mission and vision statement. My mission was to make corporations fit for human habitation. I had left corporate life because it had not been very good. I wasn't very productive. I could see all this waste of human effort. I wrote that down as my mission statement and I must have put it away in a file. I dug it out again last year and, when I read it, I got quite emotional. I thought that this must be what I want to do. Nothing that we were doing in our current business was fixing that problem. All our clients were downsizing, which happens in corporations when business isn't too good. I didn't feel as though we were able to help people.

Lorrie: We were able to help stop several factories from closing; if we hadn't done that, people would have lost their jobs and it would have made a massive hole in the local economy. Those were the kinds of things we were doing. We were helping turn people's thinking around; for example, they didn't need to outsource things that they could take better care of themselves. They could introduce new products. We were doing major work like that, but we weren't getting to the fundamental core of these problems.

James: We weren't addressing the issues of how people worked together and why they were so unproductive – why people in general don't want to be at work.

Lorrie: We were working with people who couldn't get other people to shift. We could show them the way and help them start moving toward it, but there were all these roadblocks that were bigger than what they could push through.

James: There was no one who could tell you how to shift the paradigm. We knew about the problems of paradigms, but we had no idea how to fix those problems. Next thing we knew, along comes Bob Proctor, and he was saying, "I know how to fix that."

Lorrie: We went to three live streaming events. One time, they mentioned something about *Thinking Into Results* and it planted that seed in our minds about becoming *Thinking Into Results* consultants. In the third event, Arash Vossoughi came on stage and he gave a more in-depth description of the program. During the breaks, I did some research and I saw that you could buy the program online. I bought it right then. I told James, "This is it. This is what we've been looking for. This is how we can better help our clients." When you know, you know.

I tried to sign up for the consultant training in Toronto, but you had to be a consultant in order to sign up for the training. We decided to do the consultant training in June. We regularly go back to America to do a nine-week tour, visiting all our clients. We knew we'd be there then.

James: I probably wouldn't have bought the program, but we also needed to understand online marketing, which is a whole different field. We had bought quite an expensive program a couple of years ago. We'd worked through it and there was going to be another live event in Phoenix a couple of weeks after the live stream event. We said, "Let's do that too and let's just go for everything."

Lorrie: For me, that was a game changer; it gave me self-confidence. As soon as I started getting into this material, that was it. It just cleared the way.

Which paradigms did you discover you needed to change in this long process?

Lorrie: Regaining my self-confidence was a big one for me. I am an expert in my field, but I felt like I had lost that part of me. I needed self-assurance to realize that I do know how to help people in great ways. The journey has been amazing. I've always wanted to help people make quantum leaps in their lives. My greatest joy is watching the transformation in my students.

James: This morning, a student who lives on the island, one of our neighbors, drove over and said, "Lorrie, I've got a little present for you." He gave her a book he had written. It was like a snowball effect. She signed this guy up as a client last week. Within two days, he had signed someone else up for his own program for a similar sum of money. He couldn't believe it.

Lorrie: He had his return on investment within two days. It was something that he had inside him, but he didn't have the confidence to do it. This allowed him to believe. I'd been talking with him for a while about doing it and he couldn't see how he could raise the money. He finally just did it. He was our gardener.

James: Here's the irony of it: he would come around purportedly to do some gardening but, in fact, he would sit down with Lorrie for a couple of hours and he'd get her wisdom.

Lorrie: I'm happy for him, but now I have to find a new gardener! He went from something like 15 euros an hour to 30 euros an hour. From there, he took on project work and he was able to make 100 euros an hour. He just believed in himself more. He took on bigger projects and bigger gardens in big hotels. He'd been working on this quietly and privately. He started talking to other people about it after he bought the program. He immediately went home and watched everything. It gave him the confidence. Two days later, he went out and spoke to somebody about his mind, body, and spirit program.

James: You could see that he had some childhood paradigms. I found myself going back to my own early childhood. In many ways, I was very lucky. I came from a very functional family. When you have a really good childhood, you accept everything. You don't challenge it. But I realized that there were things that I had accepted in my early childhood that weren't appropriate to me. These were paradigms that stopped me from doing things. I found that I needed to go back and address these. It was difficult, because I thought, *How dare I challenge what my mother said when she was so good to me?* We see this in a lot of our clients. They have enormous respect for the people that they received these paradigms from and they don't want to challenge them because of that.

James: I studied engineering at Cambridge University. Having a university education and a profession turns you into a ballistic missile.

It catapults you into life with such a force that you don't have to think. By the time you come down again, it's time for retirement, you have a nice pension, and you don't need to think any further. You're not really challenged to think in this way, in the way that you need to: the way that Bob Proctor teaches you.

I can understand why Bob Proctor says some of the things he says about people who have a lot of education. Those are the people I'd like to work with more because I understand their problems. I'm a lot like them. A lot of people working in corporations and professions have deep-rooted paradigm problems. These people have adopted the education paradigm hook, line, and sinker because they've done all right out of it. Why should they think differently?

How long did it take you to start seeing results using the new material?

James: It was immediate for both of us. We're still working on how to be truly effective in corporations. The *Thinking Into Results* program was designed for corporations. That was the motivation Sandy had when she put it together. We're trying to further develop those ideas.

Lorrie: When we work with our clients, we interweave the program into whatever the conversations are. Our personal business has just exploded. It's gone crazy.

James: At the moment, I have to contract work back to our established clients because I can't cope with the volume. It's as if clients sense that you've reached a greater depth or a greater ability to help them; they want you to be involved with them.

Every corporation has one place that's causing a blockage. It could be marketing or sales doing something that's not quite right, or some other internal issue. For one of our clients, it's a finance issue. You can pinpoint the blockage and apply the *Thinking Into Results* techniques to that point; it doesn't mean that you have to fix all five thousand employees at your company. You just need to address the people who are central to that issue.

What was the most difficult moment and what was the best moment in the process?

Lorrie: The most difficult thing is continuing to believe when it looks like something is not going to happen. We all have moments of doubt when you think, "Is this really the right thing to do?" It's difficult, but in the face of that difficulty, don't change the goal. Change the plan. You need to hang on and believe. Keep that burning desire. Don't let external circumstances change that. Change the direction slightly. Don't change your goal.

James: We had a client who was difficult to deal with in a number of ways. I thought, *This is a classic case of trying to turn a negative into a positive.* They weren't paying us; they kept demanding things. They told us we'd made mistakes, but they were someone else's mistakes. How can you make this positive? I wrote down the opposite of every complaint they had. We made a point of going to see these people when we were in the States, because I thought seeing them face-to-face would allow us to work out their paradigm and turn the situation around. In the end, we could see what their paradigm was, but the truth was that they didn't want to fix it. We had to let them go as a client. For the first time in 20 years, we fired a client – and we felt good about it.

Lorrie: All our client testimonials are so positive. They say we're amazing, that we give 1000%. When you keep giving at that level of intensity, and a client doesn't want to respond or do the things that need to be done, and they keep blaming you, something's not right. We consistently over-delivered, but in the end, we just had to say, "Thank you," and terminate the project. There comes a time when you have to acknowledge that they don't want help.

James: That was probably also the best moment: letting it go. We told them to call if they needed us, but the deal would be different the next time.

When you hear the words "Universal Laws," what do they mean to you?

Lorrie: That brings to mind the story of how I met James. The chances of us ever meeting were so small, but the opportunity manifested itself.

James: I have a more scientific outlook; I think that there are Laws that science hasn't pinned down yet. Gravity existed before Newton discovered it. That law's always been here, but we've only been able to say exactly what it is in the last 300 years. A lot of the things that we refer to as the Laws of the Universe are of a similar nature. They exist, we can't deny them, but we can't pin them down. We can't prove them. This is one of the big issues. They are real nonetheless. That's my understanding of them.

Can you talk about a specific Law that affects your life?

James: The Law of Vibration, which Bob talks about, is really interesting to me. We know from quantum physics and astrophysics about energy that exists in the universe, but we don't know what it is. We know about action. We know that one end of the universe can communicate with the other end of the universe instantly. That's what quantum theory tells us. We know we have pieces of that story that science tries to understand. Timeless, instant communication really intrigues me because, in fact, there is no time. Time is an invention of our minds. I try to think of it as science that hasn't yet become science.

What were you willing to give up or to sacrifice to arrive at your goal?

Lorrie: When I hear that question, it strikes me as negative. I don't ever look at it from a negative perspective. I don't consider that I'm giving anything up. I don't ever feel anything is a sacrifice.

My grandfather was a businessman, and he lived with us until he died when I was five. I would sit on his bed and he would tell me about business. At the age of seven, I had Kool-Aid stands out front of our house. I knew what kind of Kool-Aid the postman and the newspaper man wanted. I've never felt anything is a sacrifice. If it's something that I really want to do, I do whatever it takes. It's a matter of eliminating non-productive things and attracting productive things.

James: For example, I don't see cutting out time on Facebook as a sacrifice.

Lorrie: Both of our daughters, mine and James', are great business people. Every minute I have with them is quality, not quantity. We make every moment meaningful together, and they have done the same thing with their families. They're highly productive people, and they're very people-oriented.

James: However, they also need to challenge our paradigms because we must have put stuff into their heads that was inappropriate too. I say to my daughter, "You need to stop listening to what I say. There's no universal right or wrong; what's right for me may not be right for you."

Lorrie: Both our children are independent business people and have beautiful families. We wanted to show them a better way of living and being independent: a way of not having to rely on other people.

What is the one piece of advice you would give to someone who wants to reach their goal?

Lorrie: Believe to your core. Live your dream. Believe it and live it. Don't let anybody tell you you can't do something.

James: Lorrie takes belief for granted. I think it's part of her nature. It has to be a strong feeling, and it has to be internalized. I have to say that one of the revelations of the whole *Thinking Into Results* process for me was the nature of belief. We have conscious beliefs, but believing emotionally is a whole different thing, and that's where it has to be. How do you create that? That's where the strength has to come from. The strength of the goal has to be at that place. The key lesson is how to make that. I know having goal cards is all part of the process of internalizing it. At first, you think it's a strange ritual. It makes you think it's some kind of religion. But you have to have that goal implanted strongly. The significance of the emotional connection was a big surprise to me. I opened my mind to this material when I realized there was an emotional connection with something I wanted. I was brought up not to have emotions; I'm culturally British in that sense.

Lorrie: You have to be prepared to put the work in; it doesn't just drop in your lap. I think James and I make things look easy to most people; when we do what we do, we just do it. Nobody sees what goes on in the background. It's like an iceberg. The success that people see is that little bit that sticks out at the top; everything that goes into it is invisible to the outside world. That's what you have to be prepared to do. You also need to be prepared and have your goal crystallized so that when a door opens, you know if it's the right one to go through. You need to see the next step and do it without hesitation; it's a small window and it passes by quickly.

What is your next goal?

Lorrie: I have a workshop in February and probably another one in Detroit in May. That will take all this work we're doing to a much bigger scale. I will be working in collaboration with people who all complement each other in the areas of mind, body, and spirit. Four of us will be presenting.

I would also like to bring people to Fuerteventura for a holiday. Well, to tell you the truth, it won't just be a holiday; we'll be doing something constructive with that time as well. I've had a lot of interest from several Americans who are very excited about this. We're starting small at first, but we have other clients who want us to make the next event larger. We've wanted our corporate clients to come here for a long time and we're working toward that.

James: My most immediate goal is to get one or more of our corporate clients to come here to do something similar to what Lorrie's talking about. They all go on retreats and off-sites. Our event will have a different twist to it.

Lorrie: James works with people in the area of data insight and he will use *Thinking Into Results* for that field, which also requires a different kind of goal-setting.

What would you like to accomplish in your life before you leave it?

Lorrie: I would like to put my work which helps others into a format that continues long after I'm gone. For example, Napoleon Hill is still helping thousands of people every year, even long after his death. We're working on writing down our material – like you, Inbal!

James: I would like to help create a corporation that is fit for human habitation. How do you make Johnson & Johnson like Google? Actually, I'm not even certain that Google is fit for human habitation. What I mean is, how do you create a feeling of humanity at work? Humans don't want just to be part of some machine that's been invented to make money for somebody else. It's important that work is a contribution to life and not just something you go to every day.

I saw a TED talk yesterday. It was by a Brazilian businessman named Ricardo Semler. He has a completely revolutionary view of organizations, schools, and life. He spent a lot of time walking around cemeteries, looking at headstones, and thinking, *What do I want to be remembered for?* A thought occurred to him: *Why do I want to be remembered at all?* He says this is a better question. It made me think, *Why are we here? What's the meaning of life?* When my daughter was three years old, she would always ask, "Why?" Ricardo Semlar talks about three levels of why. You have a sort of answer to the first "why". Then you think, *Why is that?* You come up with an answer. But when you get to the third "why", usually you're stuck. This is when you end up with an answer like, "That's the way the universe is made." You're more or less saying this is the Universal Law.

Lorrie: One of the most exciting things I'm working on at the moment is with a teacher in Detroit, Michigan. It's a difficult area; I grew up there and I know how challenging it can be. He teaches at the school I went to. He's one of my *Thinking Into Results* students. He teaches psychology to 10th and 11th graders. He interweaves what he's learned from *Thinking Into Results* into his psychology class, and he's seeing results with them. They use a flipped classroom, which is where the students are the focus of the learning experience instead of the teacher and non-traditional types of resources are employed; it's a better way to learn. They're very innovative. Teaching the teacher is another area that I'm starting to work in. That has a ripple effect, reaching beyond what I had ever imagined possible. I'm teaching a teacher, and he is sharing some of what he's learning with all these students. Their lives are being affected in positive ways. These children are thinking about what they really want to do. My student is very pleased with the results he's already seeing.

Hopefully, we can start introducing this sort of teaching in more schools. Some of the other teachers are seeing the positive changes in his students. They ask my student what he's doing because they want to learn how to implement it in their own classes.

James: I did well in traditional learning in terms of it setting me off on a career. But, what traditional learning couldn't do was to teach me to fly. You need to think to be able to learn to fly. University education teaches you to go with the flow. You just jump from one thing to another.

Lorrie: James' parents paid attention to what naturally came to the surface for each of their eight children and they nurtured that part of them. They sought out the best schools for each individual child to go to, schools that would nurture that part of them. I love that they took that deeper, more focused approach with each child.

If you had to choose one sentence that has a lot of meaning for you, what would it be?

Lorrie: A childhood friend once said to me, "Every time I see a Nike commercial, I think of you. All you ever said from the time you were a young kid was, 'Just do it.'" I didn't even realize I did that. I thought, *I've got to change that. I don't want to sound like Nike.*

James: You don't say that anymore. Now, you say, "It's done."

Lorrie: That's true, that is what I say now. "It's done" means, focus on the ends rather than the means. You don't have to know how. You just have to know where you want to go. Have that crystallized picture of what you want. I always ask my students, if they had two million euros in the bank, and all their dreams were fulfilled, what would they do? That takes them to the next level. You've got to remove thoughts about making money from any decisions because you'll make the wrong decision for the wrong reason.

James: My sentence is from a poem called *Little Gidding* by T. S. Eliot, which I remember from my childhood:

> We shall not cease from exploration;
> And the end of all our exploring;
> Will be to arrive where we started;
> And know the place for the first time.

It's like the theme of *The Alchemist* by Paulo Coelho. We're all sitting on our acres of diamonds, but we don't realize it.

We made a plan and combined our dreams. Now we're working on writing down our material and attracting clients to Fuerteventura so they can be inspired by our story and the manifestation of our goal.

About Lorrie A. MacGilvray & James La Trobe-Bateman

Lorrie A. MacGilvray

For more than two decades, Global Innovation Award Winning Mentor, consultant, and author Lorrie A. MacGilvray has shown results again and again, helping multi-million and billion-dollar global corporations.

Prior to joining reMODEL, she worked in the USA for Wells Fargo, the original stagecoach company of the Western Frontier, specializing in multi-site operations and people.

She has 20 years' experience of understanding manufacturing improvements, market data, and the global medical device industry. She can identify WHAT to improve, WHY to do it, and HOW to make change happen. This is where she has invested thousands of hours of research, training, and in-the-trenches development.

James La Trobe-Bateman

Thirty-five years ago, James started predicting the effects of one change on all parts of an organization while working in the oil and petrochemical industry. Now, after 25 years in the healthcare manufacturing industry, James very passionately continues to drive highly successful, ongoing operations improvements, as well as resolve new product development and market issues internationally.

Over the years, James has also successfully shown several international manufacturing facilities very specific, pinpointed steps to keep their facilities open when faced with near-certain closure, saving jobs and creating economic security.

James is also co-author of *Design for Manufacturability* and *Bridge of Faith for Operations*.

Contact Lorrie & James at:
http://www.remodelinternational.com/
info@remodelinternational.com

13

Think Beyond What You Know

Oddmund Berger

Oddmund Berger grew up in Moss, Norway. He runs a successful network marketing business and is the author of Your Life's Echo. *He and his wife, Angelika, live on the Costa del Sol.*

Can you please introduce yourself?

Oddmund: My name is Oddmund Berger and I'm from a small town in Norway called Moss, where I grew up with my parents and my sister. I went to business school in Oslo. I was given a chance to work in New York for a year with all kinds of people from different countries, with the IBM Corporation. When I came back from that experience, I had it in my blood; I wanted to work abroad again.

I worked in sales and management consulting for IBM, first in Oslo, then in Stockholm. In Stockholm, a travel company approached me and offered me an executive position. I was made executive vice president of international sales and was responsible for about one billion dollars of sales per year. I learned a lot, but I also traveled 150 or 160 days out of the year, whenever other people wanted me to travel. I worked on average between 60 to 80 hours a week.

After five years in that job, I thought to myself that there must be more to life than just work. I wanted to start my own business. I didn't know what I was going to do, but I met a friend who suggested network marketing or multilevel marketing. I created a company that I ran for 16 years. I built a strong global business. I was named European Consultant of the Year and I was one of the top earners in the world. Everything was going well. I made many mistakes because I was new to the business, but I also did many things right. I had a great career there.

I left the company that I had been working with about two and a half years ago. For a number of different reasons, I didn't feel like working there anymore. I wanted to concentrate on my coaching, consulting seminars, and a couple of investments that I have. I had more than enough to do. Then, another network marketing company offered me to join them and their opportunity. I met the founders and the owners. I joined them a month after leaving the other company and now we're building that business around the world. Network marketing or multilevel marketing is a profession that most people do not know very much about, and I made it part of my purpose to help people understand how good that opportunity can be.

Network marketing can initiate many things. That's how I met my wonderful wife, Angelika. She's from Germany. We both traveled with our former business partner to Australia via Hong Kong. On our way to Australia, we got to know each other; soon, I started commuting between Hamburg, Germany, and Stockholm, Sweden, and two years later we were married in Oslo. Today, we live in Spain. We have our base here in the beautiful Costa del Sol, a little south of Malaga. That's where we travel from; this is where we work from. We have an incredible life.

A big contributor to my success throughout the years was Bob Proctor. Bob and I have known each other for many years. I was introduced to him through a friend fifteen years ago. At the time, I asked Bob if he wanted to coach and mentor my wife and me. We had had some good successes before, but we wanted to be even more successful. We wanted to break through to the top of the company we were working with. I was surprised to learn that Bob doesn't coach just anybody. When I asked him if he would like to coach us, he said, "Maybe." I thought everybody would be happy to get a client or somebody to coach. He said, "I want to make sure that you really have the right intentions and that you want to make something out of this."

He interviewed us over the phone for about an hour and a half, and then he agreed to work with us. He was an incredible inspiration, mentor, and coach to us. We worked very closely together over the first five years. After that, it was a little more sporadic. I have attended every single training session he runs. I've done every program he has. I've studied his book, his programs, everything. I would recommend that any person who wants to have more out of life study Bob Proctor's products and attend his training sessions. As a matter of fact, I learned about a lot of the things I teach and train people from him and a few others – among them, Jack Canfield, who is a friend of Bob's and is also from *The Secret*.

Bob teaches things that you don't learn at business school. You don't learn them in any sales school or sales training. That kind of training usually focuses on teaching people how to do things on an intellectual level, but a lot of the things we do are caused by what's going on at the subconscious level, and we communicate with people from subconscious to subconscious. The frequency we're on – the vibrations we send out – has a lot to do with the results we get.

I took Bob's teachings and materials from some other people, and I drew on my own experiences as a management consultant, a top executive, and a sportsperson. I've been a sportsperson my whole life, playing soccer and tennis. A lot of the things we learn in sports can be applied to business and other areas of life.

Bringing all these things together, packaging them, and making a business out of them, all this was very much inspired by Bob. Bob came to me one day and told me to write a book. I didn't realize I needed a book. He said, "Of course you need a book. A book can be there when you're not. You have a lot of experience. If you put that in a book, it can provide valuable information to people, so they can learn even if you're not there." It's true. It's about leverage.

He said, "For your business, a book is like a brochure on steroids." It's a kind of commercial, because when people see that you have a book, they think that you know more than they do. I usually say that it took me 25 years to build up the book and just three or four months to write it. I wrote for four to six hours every morning for three months and I finished my book. It's called *Your Life's Echo*.

The title was inspired by one of the Universal Laws: The Law of Cause and Effect. What you put out comes back to you. A friend of mine said, "You should call it your echo." I thought about it, and I decided to call it *Your Life's Echo* because it's like screaming something out in a valley and it comes back to you like an echo.

Bob was right. As soon as I had written a book and people heard about it, they asked me to talk about the book. It became a seminar. The seminar became several seminars. The seminars became a three-month program, a six-month program, and now a twelve-month program. I have a twelve-month program that I have been running for eight years. It's called *Become a Master Communicator*.

It is my belief and my experience that whatever you want to be successful in, communication is the key. Your ability to communicate effectively will help you become a better parent, a better spouse, a better neighbor – but also a better salesperson, a better executive, a better coach, or a better trainer. Communication is important. This is a program about how to master all aspects of communication. It's a twelve-month program consisting of live seminars, webinars, and a retreat here in the beautiful Costa del Sol at the end of April every year. That's when the group travels to come and see me, as opposed to me travelling to them. This is a beautiful experience and people come back year after year. We have a good time studying because you can never get enough of this. You can never get too much of this material.

As Bob says, it's a lifetime commitment to daily studies. That's why I'm here. My purpose is to inspire and encourage people all over the world to understand that it is in your hands to create your own future. That's what I'm here on this planet to do – to inspire as many people as possible. Network marketing is also part of the portfolio.

Tell me about the history of the business. How did you start it?

Oddmund: I was very lucky to have loving parents. They had all the love in the world for me, but they couldn't teach me things they didn't know. They could only teach me what they knew and what they had experienced. They told me to get a good education, work hard, get a good job in a big company, get a secure job, and then retire after 50 years or so. I reached the top of a company when I was 33. I was a top executive in a large company and I saw that I still had maybe 30, 35, 40 years to go before retirement. I started asking myself, "Is this the only answer?"

I was lucky enough to be in an environment where people around me were entrepreneurs. A good friend of mine ran three restaurants. He was working, but he didn't work too many hours. I remember one day seeing him sitting in his restaurant – he had just come from the golf course and he just collected the money in the evening. He had people working for him at the restaurant and he was working at the golf course, taking clients out to play golf. He had a nice tan! It was the middle of the summer. I came from work, pale in my dark suit, white shirt, and tie. He looked at me and said, "Oddmund, you look terrible." I said, "Thank you very much. That's exactly what I needed to hear." But he meant it in a friendly way, because he said, "When are you going to learn that the thing in life is not to make everybody else happy? You have to make sure you are happy." Then he said, "Stop building everybody else's dream and start working on your own." His words infected me like a virus; I started thinking about them night and day. That's how I ended up wanting to start my own business and be independent.

What paradigms did you discover that you needed to change when you met Bob?

Oddmund: Paradigm is an interesting word. A paradigm is actually a multitude of habits and it starts with the fact that we get information from the outside. We collect information through our five senses. We see, hear, smell, taste, and touch. We hear what people say. That starts when you're a young child. You're impacted by what all the grown-ups, what your parents and the authorities around you suggest and repeat over and over. Before you know it, these things are programmed into your subconscious, because as a young kid, you haven't really developed your mental muscles. You can't reason or have your own perceptions about things. You don't really fantasize or think. You take for granted that everything that has been said to you is true. It goes straight in. As these thoughts are repeated, they become ideas. Ideas repeated over time become fixed ideas and fixed ideas are what we usually refer to as habits.

Habits are things that are stored in your subconscious mind and they express themselves without any conscious thought. That means that you suddenly find yourself thinking in a certain way about certain things, and you act in a certain way when you're in certain situations out of habit. You don't even have to think about it. Some paradigms, some habits, are good to have. For example, I don't particularly like shaving. I shave every second day when I'm in Costa Del Sol and I don't really think about it. It's an automatic skill. I get up in the morning, I do what I need to do, and I think about everything else. Driving a car is not something I get a lot of pleasure out of; it just takes me from one place to another. It is an automatic skill. It's a paradigm.

You could say that the biggest paradigm that I was stuck in was the paradigm that says: study, work hard, get a job in a good company, and become an employee. There's nothing wrong with being an employee. It's perfectly okay as long as you are comfortable with it and it provides the happiness that you're looking for. You earn the money you want to earn to provide the things you want, the things you choose. If you're totally happy with that, then that's what you should probably be doing.

However, I was not happy with that situation. I had a discussion every year with my boss, the chief executive and the president of the company. I was a top executive. He wanted me to be happy, but not too happy. We were good friends. We had a joke about it every year, when we discussed how much I was worth. I always thought I was worth more than he thought I was. In the end, I suggested that he pay me nothing and give me a piece of the cake instead, but he said, "That's not doable. We have a union; it would be unfair to other people, etc."

It struck me that the only way I can prove what I'm worth is to start my own business. I didn't know exactly how to do that. I ended up starting with network marketing and I became a professional network marketer. A passion of mine was to be a trainer and teacher, helping other people to grow and see how they can achieve results. I built this network marketing business in order to create residual leveraged income and have the income and the freedom to build other businesses that I'm passionate about. I like many elements of both things. That was probably the biggest paradigm to get over: the habitual way of thinking when it comes to work life.

I thought it was all about having a job, but my good friend there in Stockholm put those viruses in my head, saying, "When are you going to build your own thing instead of only building other people's dreams?" That's what made me change, what made me start studying entrepreneurial life.

How long did it take you to start seeing results from the moment you started reading this material?

Oddmund: To tell the truth, Bob and I agree about most things, but we also have discussions and we have different opinions sometimes. He says that if you don't have a purpose or if you're not aware of your purpose, everything else goes wrong. I don't necessarily agree with that. I think it is a sign of strength if you have your purpose clear. It certainly has been for me and Bob has been a great contributor to helping me define and discover my purpose. It's not something you decide, it's usually something that you discover through a process and it takes time. That doesn't mean that you can't be successful. I had a lot of successes in different areas because I was always very goal-oriented. I think having a goal is extremely important.

My wife and I were at the second highest level in the network marketing company that we could reach. We had all my parents' markers of success. The reason why I wanted to go to Bob is that I realized that no matter how much success you have, or what level you are at, you can always improve. And we saw that we could become even better. I always look for people that can help me improve. I always try to learn from people who are good at what they're doing, and Bob is one of the best in the world. So, I started learning from him, and being coached by him and mentored by him, and started looking at what he was doing, how he was doing things.

It went very quickly, but that's also because I started at the pretty high awareness level. It was not a huge shift. It was more an extension, an improvement of where we already were. I took off like a rocket once we started with Bob; it took only four or five months and we made a huge jump. I tripled my volume in the organization and tripled my income; I tripled the organization's size in just a few months. We couldn't even explain exactly how it happened. We didn't really care how, either, as long as it did happen. That, I guess, is the long answer to the question, but I would say it went very fast.

For my wife, it took a little longer, which is very natural because we are very different. She came from a background as a secretary. She was working in a kindergarten with children. She worked in restaurants and was not used to sales. She was not used to leadership. She had to learn all these things through network marketing, which is a beautiful school for sales communication and leadership. But she had to go through some major personal growth and it took a little longer time, but she also managed to do that.

She's with you in the business right now?

Oddmund: Yes. Now she's joined, and she's doing very well. The beauty of it was that we met through business, we were both independent and working by ourselves, so we didn't have to ask for permission. We both already had the lifestyle that we could afford and we had the time and freedom to live it, so we started travelling between Hamburg and Stockholm to see each other. Two years later we got married in Oslo. Today, we live in Spain.

How did you arrive in Spain?

Oddmund: We asked ourselves, "Where do we want to live?" We had certain criteria. It had to have easy access to the destinations that I travel to; for example, the flight connections are good from Malaga to the rest of Europe. I guess the major thing was the weather. The climate here is unbelievable. It's the best possible climate to live in and, on top of that, it's very near to both snow and colder climates if you want that. That was the number one factor.

What were the most difficult moment and the best moment in the process?

Oddmund: I guess, as with most things, the most difficult moments are before you make a decision. As soon as you have made the committed decision, things usually fall into place. Most people make that mistake. I did too. It took me a long time to really understand that how things are going to happen has nothing to do with the fact that they are going to happen. The decision comes first. You go back and forth, especially when it's a major shift in a career; I went from being a top executive of a company with a high salary and all the perks and benefits, prestige, respect, and credibility that comes with that. All these things come in a package and then I jumped ship and started my own business, not really knowing how it was going to happen.

I think the hardest time was all the discussions I had with myself before I made a decision, because you have a tendency, like I did, to start thinking about how it's going to happen before you have even made a committed decision that it's going to happen. You say to yourself, *How am I going to make this work?* How am I going to find the people I need to find? How am I going to find the money to finance these things?

I've been a student of personal growth and development for 30 years and, by studying Bob's material, I started thinking about what I learned and I found out that, actually, 'how' has nothing to do with it. You have to make a decision first and then the 'how' will appear. You will always find a way to do it, you will find the teachers. There's some truth in what they say, that when the student is ready, the teachers appear, and the 'how-to' appears as well. I guess that was the major hurdle for me, but once it was done, I've never looked back. I love this life and it will probably be a part of my life for the rest of my life.

What is the best moment in the process?

Oddmund: There are many, but probably the best moment is when you start to get that feeling where you actually know that it is working. For me, it was when I saw that I could make a living by myself. I didn't have to work for others and have a job. I felt that I had value. I knew intellectually, before this, that I had value; otherwise I wouldn't have started my own business. But most of us do have a certain value and if we put it into our work and do it with passion, if it's something we love doing, we can always find a way to earn money that way.

For example, if a person loves golf, they may not be good enough at golf to be one of the top players in the world and earn a lot of money.

But, there's a lot of ways to earn money doing what you love doing in golf. You could be a golf trainer, a pro. You could be working in a golf shop. You could arrange golf trips and tours to beautiful Costa del Sol. There's all kinds of ways to do what you love doing. And that's what I found out, too. I love teaching and training people. I discovered my purpose is to inspire people to understand that they can create their own destiny, their own lives; it is in your own hands to create your own future – that's what I believe. That's what I found to be the most beautiful thing, that I have the ability to teach and coach and mentor people so that they can achieve what they want. When I saw that, or got that confirmed, I think that was one of the best moments.

When you hear the words "Universal Laws," what do they mean to you?

Oddmund: I'm not a very religious person and that was a challenge for me in the beginning because Bob, among others, referred to God. We had a conversation over coffee once, down in Florida, after one of his seminars. He asked me to speak at his seminar. We sat down and I asked him, "What about this God thing and how do I explain these Universal Laws?" He smiled at me and asked if I had a problem with God. I said, "I don't think so, but I don't know." He started laughing. "Would you be more comfortable talking about universal science or universal power? If so, that's what you should call it."

To me, that's up to every person, whether you call it God or science. I truly believe that people are spiritual beings. We live in a body and we have an intellect. You can choose whatever you want to call it. I call it "universe." I address it from the scientific perspective rather than the religious perspective. You can choose what you want to do. The Universal Laws to me mean that there are some powers that are stronger or bigger than us. We normally call these the seven great Universal Laws and then there are a number of sub-laws or side laws. There are Laws for many things. If you choose to live your life in harmony with these Laws, I truly believe that you can accomplish a lot more. They will work in harmony with you and help you achieve what you want to achieve. If you choose to violate the Laws and work in disharmony with the Laws, they will probably not benefit you.

Can you talk about the effect of a specific Law on your life? For example, the Law of Perpetual Transmutation says that energy moves into physical form. How did knowing or using this Law affect you?

Oddmund: This Law affects me every day. It is a Law based on the fact that there's all kinds of thought energy out there in the world, and we can tap into that by using our mental muscles – the ability to reason, to choose our perception, our imagination. We can fantasize. We have our will, intuition, and our memory. We use these mental muscles to think. When we get all this energy in, all this information is channeled to us and through us, and it ends up in physically manifested results. We take that energy and we do what we want with it, with our intellects. The way we handle that information, the way we choose to think about it, will affect how we feel about it.

Our thoughts cause our feelings, our feelings have to be expressed, and they're usually expressed through the vibrations we send out and the actions we perform. The actions also cause a reaction from the universe. The actions we produce will actually dictate what we attract. Therefore, action causes this reaction and enhances our circumstances, our condition, our environment and, hence, our results. If we don't like our results, or if we just want to improve our results, I suggest that we be grateful. We should be grateful for the results we have, but also dissatisfied. Healthy dissatisfaction will always cause us to stretch ourselves to become better. That explains that whole Law to me. To put it very simply, our thoughts produce our feelings, which cause our actions, which produce our results. If we want to change our results or improve them, we need to go all the way back to our thoughts and start thinking differently because the thoughts cause the results.

The Law of Vibration and Attraction says that everything vibrates; nothing rests. You're always moving toward something and it's always moving toward you. How has knowing or using this Law affected you?

Oddmund: That is the Law on which Rhonda Byrne based the story of *The Secret*. She wanted to help people understand that what you focus on is what you will get. You can test this in simple things and you can experience it in more serious things. Every time I set a goal, I use my reasoning, capability, and my imagination, and I fantasize. This is a time of year for revision. What did we do? What worked, what didn't? What do you want to accomplish next year? You break it down and you set goals. You start moving. As you repeat the goals and you get more and more emotionally involved with the goals, they grow on you. It becomes a burning desire to achieve them. When you do that, your thoughts become focused on the goal.

I use visualization, affirmation, and goal cards to program that goal into my subconscious. I look at it, I read it, I think about it several times a day. When I meet a person, for example, I don't focus on me. I always focus on the person I meet in order to see how I can contribute to that person's life in some way or another. That is a kind of an explanation for this Law because when you know where you're going, you're in harmony and you're on a certain frequency of thought. You move forward, and you tend to attract what you want, because you vibrate in a certain way that attracts people on the same frequency as you. You start attracting people to you. It's a wonderful thing because you are going toward the goal, and you feel as if the goal is coming toward you. It moves both ways and it happens all the time.

In order to attract, you have to act. When *The Secret* came out, I liked that DVD so much that I bought a bunch of them and I gave them out as presents to different friends. Some people came back and said, "That was interesting." Some people came back and said, "This doesn't work for me." I said, "What do you mean it doesn't work for you?" A friend of mine said, "I did everything they said to do on the DVD. I walked in the woods and I screamed my goal out loud," she said, "and nothing happened." I said, "What do you mean nothing happened?" "The results didn't arrive," she said. I asked her what she did then. She said that the DVD didn't say anything about doing anything. She thought it was just about focusing on and thinking about things.

That was something that, for some people, was missing from that DVD; in order to attract, you have to act. Actions cause reactions. It's no good just thinking about things. Those thoughts have to go down into your subconscious. You have to be emotionally involved with your goal. You have to get into the vibrations that are expressed through your actions, which cause the reaction and then produce the circumstances, the environment, the conditions, and the results that you need.

The Law of Relativity says that nothing is good or bad until you relate it to something. How does this Law affect you?

Oddmund: Nothing is good or bad, warm or cold; everything just is, until you relate it or compare it to something. For example, when I'm selling something or asking people to invest their time and money, some people say it's expensive. That Law comes in handy because I know that nothing is expensive in this world. I also know that nothing is cheap. It just is. For example, if I suggest that people buy some products that will enhance their health, they may look at it as a cost. Perhaps it's an investment for your health, but it's still money out of your pocket. Some people will say, "I don't have €500 to buy that." People tell me that it's impossible to find the money – they can't borrow it, they can't find it.

I say, "Imagine that I have a BMW outside. Let's assume that you like BMWs. They're nice cars. This car is worth €100,000 brand new. If I told you that you could have it for €10,000 as long as you give me the money within 48 hours, would you buy it?" Every person that I ask this of immediately says yes. Suddenly, there's no problem finding the money. Then I say, "A few minutes ago, you said you couldn't find €500. How can you now find €10,000?" One person replied that he could find 20 friends who could lend him €500 each and he could even repay them double because he would make 10 times what he paid.

Everything just is. When we relate things to other things, that's when they take on meaning. We can use this Law to our benefit. Instead of thinking of everything as a cost, we can think of things as an investment. Instead of thinking about squandering, we can think about how this is an investment that will improve our lives. It's a great Law to use in sales, communications, and leadership.

The Law of Polarity says everything has an opposite and we need to find the good in people and situations.

Oddmund: We're all human beings. We can all have bad moods or be annoyed. But there's always a chance to think the opposite. Take, for instance, a situation in which you have to decide whether you should do something or not – you're not sure if you have the competence. You can always ask yourself if you can find a thousand reasons why you can't do it, you must also, by this law – because there is an opposite of everything – be able to find a few reasons why you could do it. Then you can decide to focus on why you can and how you can do it, rather than wasting energy on the reasons why you can't do it.

This is very helpful in many situations. If you do not have the self-confidence to do a certain thing, you would probably be able to write down all the reasons why you could not do this thing. You can then look at all the reasons and, then, on the right-hand side of the page, you can write their opposites. You will suddenly find out that there are just as many reasons why you could do this as there are reasons that you can't do it. Then you strike through what you can't do, and focus on what you can. This Law will help you every day.

The Law of Rhythm says that night follows day; there is a season and a cycle to everything. How does this Law affect you?

Oddmund: We don't start at the bottom and go straight to heaven. Life has rhythms. Relationships and marriages have rhythms. You have highs and you have lows. You have businesses that go up and down. Countries go up and down. Spain has been through a few tough years and now it's starting to improve a little bit; there is more optimism in the country. I worked for three years as a management consultant. I looked into a couple of hundred companies during that period of time. I have never seen one single company that just started and then went straight to heaven. Every company has problems. Every company has challenges. Every person has problems and challenges.

The Law of Rhythm works like that. It goes up and down. The only thing that you can be sure of is that if things are down, they will go up. If you're up, you'd better plan for a crisis, because one will happen every now and then. That's why people are so well paid to be top performers, managers, and chief executives, because they face these problems every single day. If you run your own business, welcome the problems. In my network marketing program, I say, "Welcome the problems. We may not have problems right now, but I'm sure we're going to meet them." We are well-paid to lead companies because we're trained at solving problems and facing challenges. You will not find a successful person in any area who has not solved many problems to get there.

The Law of Cause and Effect says that whatever you send into the universe comes back.

Oddmund: Ralph Waldo Emerson once said that this was the greatest Law of all Laws. It was the Law that inspired me to write the book and call it *Your Life's Echo* because if you put something out, it comes back. Put out good things and they come back. Put out bad things and they will come back too. It's a beautiful Law because it also shows that if you give good things to people, you shouldn't think about it as a trade, but think of it as something you put out, not necessarily expecting to get anything back from that person or that situation. It will come around and it will come back to you, in one way or another. That's what I really like about that Law. If you can live in harmony with that Law, you can benefit from it in that way.

Sometimes, we think wrongly about what actually causes results. For example, most people who don't like their results go back and look at their actions and they try desperately to change actions and end up doing more of the same. If we don't like our results, we need to go back to the main cause of all the results, which is our thinking, and start questioning how we've been thinking because the results we have today are nothing but a manifestation of the ways we were thinking up until now.

The last law is the Law of Gender, which says that every seed has a gestation and an incubation period.

Oddmund: When we set a goal, for example, that's a mental seed. Many people go wrong here because they're afraid to set goals. It is a fact that most people who have success in life are usually people who have set goals. They go after something. The interesting thing is, only around 3% of the world's population actually sets goals the way we are talking about here – writing these goals down, envisioning them. The question is, if we know they are important, why don't more people set goals? I think, most of the time, my experience is that people don't set goals because they're afraid not to reach them. They set a goal, they set a date to achieve that goal, and then they are afraid not to accomplish it. They feel sad about it.

That's a mistake because the goal and the date you set are two different things. The goal is the goal. The date is part of the plan. You can set a goal and give yourself a short amount of time, because nature abhors a vacuum. You don't want to give yourself too much time because you're going to fill the time anyway. You work toward the goal, then you miss your deadline, and you feel miserable. You don't have to feel miserable. There's nothing wrong with the goal. You didn't fail to reach the goal; you just estimated your plan incorrectly. All you have to do is come up with a new plan, a new date. If people could understand that, I think many problems would be solved.

It's worth mentioning that when you plant a mental seed, it's different from a physical seed. When a woman gets pregnant, it takes approximately nine months and then the baby comes out. If a gardener plants a physical seed in the ground, the plant will grow after a certain time. However, when you set a goal, you're guessing. You guess the date. Ask yourself, when did you ever reach a goal at the exact minute or second that you predicted you would? You reach it either a little bit earlier or a little bit later. We're just guessing at the plan for mental seeds. There's nothing wrong with the goal itself. Keep the goal, change the plan if it doesn't work, and feel good about it.

Can you tell me about one specific goal that you managed to accomplish?

Oddmund: When I started in network marketing, I remember setting a goal that I wanted to reach a certain level in the organization. My goal was to achieve a volume of $120,000 in sales within a certain time period, in order to achieve that rank. I remember that I set a very specific date – June 28th at 8 o'clock in the evening. By the beginning of May, I had no idea how that was going to come together because I could not see on the horizon how I could pull this off. However, I kept working, believing that if I did the right things, things usually fall into place.

We started recruiting. I needed to attract a couple of leaders who wanted to work with me in the business. Unexpectedly, a person came up to me in an open training session that I ran and asked me to be her mentor; she asked me to recruit her and to teach her. Out of nowhere, she came in and produced an incredible result in the first month, helping me reach my goal.

A friend of mine, whom I had asked to join my business 15 months earlier but was not interested then, suddenly came to me and said, "Life has changed. Are you still looking for partners for your business?" I said, "Sure." He got on board and started with a bang. I still don't really know how it happened, but we created an incredible amount of volume in the last month. On the 28th of June, I came home to my apartment in Stockholm. I logged into the back-office system to check the results. Remember, I had set a goal of $120,000 in sales volume six months previously. I logged on at 9 o'clock in the evening, one hour after the 8 o'clock deadline that I had set, and the results showed $120,402. I remember it very well. More than anything, it convinced me that if you set a goal and you burn it into your mind, you can achieve your goal. You need to visualize it as if it has already happened: write an affirmation describing it as if you're already there, and read it aloud to yourself several times a day. Put the essence of it on a goal card that you have in your pocket or purse. Place it near where you put your hand all the time and every time you touch it, you'll think about it. By doing those simple exercises – it doesn't take more than a few minutes every day – you burn it into your mind; it becomes a burning desire. You get emotionally involved with the goal and things like this can happen.

I very seldom miss a goal that I set. I set high goals that inspire and excite me at the same time. Most of the time, I don't know how I'm going to accomplish the goal when I set it. I usually reach those goals. However, quite often, I don't reach them by the deadline I set. So, I set a new time. Sometimes I reach it at the third or fourth deadline. That doesn't mean that you're a failure. It only means that you guessed the wrong date.

What were you prepared to give up or to sacrifice to arrive at your goal?

Oddmund: For this particular goal, I had left my job, but I was still a consultant – management for hire – as a temporary Managing Director for a company. I worked a full-time job to finance my start-up. I had to find time. I'd say, "I don't have time to do what I want to do." But, in reality, we all have time; it's what we choose to do with the time that matters. I chose to, for example, stop reading newspapers for a while. I saved 45 minutes every day by doing that and I didn't miss anything, because if something really important happened, someone would call me by the time I had finished breakfast to tell me about it.

I chose to stay fit and exercise, but I also chose to cut out a couple of other hobbies that I liked to do for a while. I cut out certain TV programs. I did not see some people for a while, because I chose to be around people who encouraged me and supported my adventure. I chose not to spend so much time with people whom I really liked and loved, but who were negative about what I was doing or not supportive. I didn't need that kind of energy around me as I was building up my business. I made sacrifices but, looking back, they were nothing compared to what I got back.

What is the one key lesson that you can give everyone who wants to reach their goal?

Oddmund: The most important thing is to decide what you want. Most people set their goals from a perspective of what they know they can do. Maybe they dream a little bit about what they think they could do, but then they go back to what they know they can do. Most people don't get to the place where they use fantasy to really imagine and dream big about what they really want out of life. That would be my number one encouragement. Think about what you want, not about what you don't want. Think beyond what you know.

As Bob says, a goal should be inspiring and scary at the same time. It should be scary because you shouldn't know how to reach it when you conceive it. If you know how to reach it, you've probably done it before or it's just a small stretch for you. There's no inspiration in that. It should be inspiring so that when you reach it, it should feel really good. This will force you to become a different person on the way, because it's not about reaching the goal. The most important thing is the person you grow into on the way to the goal. If you set a goal of something you've done before, you're not going to learn anything new. You're just going to repeat what you've done before.

If you set a goal that stretches you – that forces you to learn new skills, to meet new people, or get into uncomfortable situations – that's when you really grow as a person. When you set that goal, find a mentor, because there's always a person that has achieved similar things before you. Find a person that has proven with results that they know what they're talking about, that they've done it. Ask them what you should do. Accept what they say and do what they tell you to do. Many people receive this information or this advice, and they say, "I think I can do it better." I would try the mentor's way first. If that doesn't work, talk with them about a different way of doing it. But do what they tell you to do. That would be my key lesson. As Bob taught me many years ago, you're the only problem you'll ever have and you're the only solution.

Try to understand that you are capable of doing so much more than you think you can. Once, someone wanted me to give a talk about a certain topic. I was a little uncertain if this was within my competence. I doubted myself. I asked Bob, "What do you think I should do? Should I do this?" Bob looked at me, and he started laughing. "Oddmund," he said, "you care way too much about what other people think of you. You don't have to worry about that, because they don't think."

I was confused and he explained, "Most people don't think at all most of the time and if they are thinking, what makes you think that they would think about you? They have more than enough to think about themselves. Don't worry too much." He asked when I was going to do the speech and I told him in about two and a half months. Then he started to laugh loudly. He said, "Say yes and then you have two and a half months to learn whatever you need to talk about."

That's the way he teaches and that's the way I suggest you think about it. Find out the reason why you should be doing it rather than focusing on why you can't do it.

What is your next goal?

Oddmund: I have several goals. I have financial goals within the business, for example, and personal goals that come from that. I have relationship goals. I have happiness goals. I have physical goals. You never have any guarantees in life, but we can certainly try to stay as healthy as we can.

I have goals for friendships; there are things I want to accomplish over the year with friends and family. I have goals for making a difference in people's lives. I have goals for how I want to impact this world while I'm here. I don't want to get into the details, but I think about them in November and December, and I typically set goals for the whole year, breaking them down into quarters – ninety-day rhythms and goals – so that I have something to keep me on track.

I also have goals for personal growth. I want to make sure that I can sit on New Year's Eve, look back at the year, and make sure that I can say to myself that I had several uncomfortable moments. The worst thing I could tell myself on New Year's Eve is that I've been totally comfortable all year. If you're totally comfortable, it means that you have not developed at all. There's no personal growth. That would be sad because there should always be personal growth. You can always become a better and bigger person. Many people are scared of this and they choose not to be uncomfortable. I usually encourage people to seek discomfort and learn to live with being uncomfortable until that thing becomes comfortable, because then they will have learned it. Then you can seek new challenges.

What would you like to accomplish in your life before you leave it?

Oddmund: I tell my wife that I intend to have great health when I'm 110 years old. I don't have a bucket list, but I have a lot of things that I want to accomplish. These can be trivial things; for example, I like soccer, and I enjoy traveling to different places in Europe to see and feel the atmosphere of different stadiums. I walk around those streets for a couple of days and think. That's the way I think and how I live.

My wife and I have a good rule in our relationship. It's not up to us to make the other person happy; that's their own responsibility. I take full and complete responsibility for my happiness and she does as well. We can always do good things for each other to help each other become happy. But it's not just our responsibility. That's each and every person's. That allows me to do these kinds of things. I can fly to Bilbao or Sevilla or Valencia or Barcelona, go to a football game, and stay for a couple of days just to soak up the atmosphere, sitting in an outdoor restaurant.

One of my favorite cities in Europe is Berlin. It has a lot of history. I like to walk around the city, sit down in a café, and eat a typical

German meal; it gives me good energy. I like simple things like that; they make my life worth living.

I'm also a big family man. I appreciate family and family traditions. I love my parents and sister. My wife and I do things together every year that are focused solely on family. These are simple things, which I think most people want to do anyway.

If you had to choose one sentence that has a lot of meaning for you, what would it be?

Oddmund: You're the only problem you will ever have and you're the only solution.

Having caught the travel bug early on in life, I realize now that the most important form of travel is the journey you take toward achieving a goal. I seek out discomfort so that I can constantly achieve personal growth and I enjoy the simple things in life.

About Oddmund Berger

Oddmund Berger is an international trainer and public speaker. He runs a successful network marketing business, ASEA, and he is the author of *Your Life's Echo*. He and his wife, Angelika, live on the Costa del Sol, Spain.

Contact Oddmund at:
oddmund@oddmundberger.com
mailto:info@oddmundberger.com
www.oddmundberger.com/

14

Follow Your Heart

Peter Hurley

Peter Hurley is a portrait photographer in New York City. A former Olympic sailor, today Peter travels the world teaching people about photography. He founded the Headshot Crew – the world's largest team of headshot and portrait photographers.

Can you, please, start by introducing yourself?

Peter: I've been a photographer for almost 17 years. I picked up a camera in the late '90s and officially started a business around 2000. I was training to sail in the Olympics while this was happening. I raced sailboats all over the world; that got me into modeling, which inspired me to pick up a camera.

When did you first come across Bob Proctor's material and what was your situation in life then?

Peter: I was modeling in New York City and I met another model who was working with a network marketing company. That company brought Bob in to speak and my friend asked me along. I couldn't believe what I heard. When I was training for the Olympics, the US team sports psychologist had us do a lot of visualization and things of that nature; I had been doing the things that Bob spoke about without knowing it. As Bob would say, I was an unconscious competent. I didn't know what I was doing, but it was working.

At the time, I was trying to start a new network marketing business, because I was not making enough money modeling. I was also a bartender. I lived in a fifth-floor walk-up, and I could barely make ends meet in New York City. I was in my late twenties and I was looking for a better life. I knew I couldn't be a model forever, so I tried to get into acting. But I wasn't a good actor; that wasn't going to work. Bob's material gave me a new direction.

What happened from that moment on? What did you start doing differently to change your results?

Peter: Bob's teaching was all about repetition, creating goals and figuring out where you want to go. I wasn't aware that photography was going to be my thing, but once I started photography, I used all these principles to build my business. I started shooting actors, because I was one and actors need headshots. Now I've written a book called *The Headshot*. I look back at the goals I had in the beginning – some were monetary, some were about getting enough people to my studio to provide for my family – and I'm amazed to see how far I've come.

What paradigms did you discover that you needed to change on the way?

Peter: If you don't check or break the paradigms that you're immersed in, you're never going to get the results that you want. That can mean making big and scary moves. I was in a workshop, and Bob was talking about decision-making. He asked me to stand up, and he said, "Why aren't you going for the gold medal?" I had trained for one Olympic Games before that. I had no plans to train for a second; it seemed too lofty a goal. He told me to come back the next day and tell everyone if I was going to do it. That night, I couldn't sleep. I thought, *I'm bartending until 4 a.m. every day. I'm living in a fifth-floor walk-up. I can barely make ends meet. I'm in my twenties. I could train for the Olympics and this is my last chance to do it.* I decided to do it. I dropped everything in New York, and I went to the west coast.

Decisions like that force you to break your paradigm. Everything in my life was in turmoil at that moment because of that one decision.

All sorts of incredible things happened. It's really interesting when you turn your life on its head to see what happens. I had the ability to do it at that time. I was young; I didn't have any responsibilities. I had a little bit of money saved. Along the way, things just fell into place. I met my wife. I picked up a camera. It was an amazing time, but I had to take that initial leap to break the paradigm.

Was one of your paradigms that you didn't make decisions?

Peter: No. I made decisions all the time. I just didn't know what the right decision was. Bob helped foster that decision in me. Bob says that successful people make decisions quickly and rarely change their minds. People who aren't that successful are wishy-washy. They take a long time to make a decision, and then they flounder around and go back and forth. I've always been an excellent decision-maker. I wasn't a complete loser, but I was young. I wasn't sure what my next step would be. I flew by the seat of my pants. I'd take whatever was in front of me. When Bob asked why I wasn't going for the Olympics, I decided. Boom, done, let's go! Living like that becomes very interesting and that's the way I still do it now, to this day.

How long did it take you to start seeing results?

Peter: It took a while. I had no monetary results until I started my business, but when I started sailing, I saw results right away. It was a year out from the Olympic trials when I started sailing again. I finished sixth on the first day of my first regatta and I was in contention to win by the end of the regatta. I used these principles when I was sailing. I was winning the Olympic trials after the first day and then I had a couple of rough days. Bob talks about psycho-cybernetics, where you get off track, but you have this mechanism that always brings you back.

I was winning, but I felt off track because I wasn't comfortable winning. I hadn't really seen myself winning the Olympic trials and representing the United States. At first, I was winning; then I started doing poorly. I became upset and then I came back. At the end of the Olympic trials, I made the United States sailing team, which is something that would have never have happened if Bob hadn't helped me make the decision. That meant a lot to me. It means a lot to me to this day.

What was the most difficult moment and what was the best moment in the change process?

Peter: When I got back to New York after the Olympic trials, I was trying to get my modeling and acting going again. I decided I wasn't going back into bar work. I wanted to figure out this camera thing. I didn't have any income. I remember working out and really wanting a new pair of sneakers. I looked everywhere online for these sneakers to find the best deal; I remember how much those sneakers cost and how it was a big deal for me to purchase them at the time. I remember how I felt at that moment.

Now, I feel so blessed to be able to buy whatever I want and to have a successful business. I look back at those moments when a pair of sneakers was a big deal to me. I was near the bottom then and I didn't see how I was going to get out of it.

The best moments for me have been about supporting my family. I have twin daughters who are 14 years old. I'm able to support them in New York City. I have a studio, an apartment, a loving wife, and a wonderful family. When my business took off and I could support my family with it, I was very proud of myself. In that moment I thought, *Wow, I did all right.* There's been constant growth since then. It's always challenging, but when I look back, I'm proud of what I've done.

When you hear the words "Universal Laws," what do they mean to you?

Peter: I know they're out there and I know if we abide by them, they work. But I think it's hard to wrap your brain around them, think about them every day and be strict about the way that you work with these Laws. Studying is critical. Taking time out to know where you're at, what you're thinking, and how your brain is reacting to the world is important.

Bob always says, "I'll show you exactly what to do. You can do it. I'm going to tell you exactly how, and if you do this, this will work." I don't know if it's disbelief or just human nature, but we get off track, and then we get back on track. If you know that the Laws are there and you abide by them, things will happen.

It blows me away when things fall into place, when you're behaving in a way that allows for it, the Laws will help you. It amazes me when that happens. I always know I'm on the right track when things start popping out of the woodwork. How did that happen? Where did that person come from? Wait a minute, I needed that, and there it is. It's always about getting back on track for me. Sometimes you fall off, but you get back on the bike. It's no big deal.

Can you talk about the effect of one specific Law on your life?

Peter: My goal was to be the best headshot photographer in New York. I knew I had to work at it. I also had to believe that it was possible for me and I had to see myself in that role. For years, I called myself the best headshot photographer in New York and people would laugh. But my belief created this momentum and it opened up doors for me; now I am considered the best headshot photographer in the world.

Did you tell this to other people or just to yourself?

Peter: I did tell it to other people and they laughed. I was always aware that that was the goal. I don't have an off switch. I love what I do and I wanted to be successful at it. I worked as hard as I could, and I enjoyed every minute of it because it's amazing to be able to take pictures of people and produce something for them that helps their dream of becoming famous or getting to Broadway or being in a movie. These pictures opened doors for them to be able to do that; for me, that was very fulfilling.

Did you have one specific goal that you accomplished?

Peter: To be the best headshot photographer in New York was my specific goal. I don't know how many photographers are taking headshots in New York. At the time, there was a pecking order. When I was sailing, you were ranked. When you're taking pictures, I don't think you're ranked, but the industry becomes aware of you. After a couple of years, the industry became aware of me and embraced what I was doing. It was also monetary. People would think, "He's not that expensive. He must not be that good." So, I raised my rates. In fact, a casting director told me to raise my rates, because I was as good as any $1,000 headshot photographer, but I had been charging $500 or $600.

Every month I was busy, I raised my rates by $50 until I was charging $1,000 and was considered at the top of the game. Then I went a little higher, to $1,050. Then I thought, *If they're going to pay $1,050, they'll pay $1,100.* Achieving those monetary goals was always something that I had in mind, because my vision of success was also being able to provide for my family or being able to live the way I choose. I envisioned having a photography studio. I'm sitting in a photo studio that I could never have imagined having when I first started this. It's a beautiful space, right?

It's amazing.

Peter: It costs $8,000 a month to have this space. When I started, my first studio cost $1,000 a month, and I had difficulty deciding if I should do it. But I did and I eventually expanded to having this type of space. These things happened along the way.

What were you prepared to give up or to sacrifice to arrive at your goal?

Peter: I never looked at it as a sacrifice. I didn't give up anything, because I didn't feel like I had anything. I was a nomad. I didn't know how I was going to make a living. All I knew was that I didn't want to do a nine-to-five job. I didn't want to be behind a desk. I don't think I'm good with authority. I didn't want a boss. I wanted to do my own thing and I knew that I enjoyed the craft and the art of photography. It made me feel like I was creating something special. My sailing meant a lot to me, so maybe I gave up a little bit of sailing. Maybe I gave up a little bit of time with my family. If you speak to my family, they'll tell you I'm a workaholic. My girls say, "You're always traveling, Dad." That's a price to pay. But I enjoy everything I'm doing and they're so supportive of me doing it that it works out okay.

What is the one key lesson you can give to everyone who wants to reach their goal?

Peter: A goal has to be something that you're passionate about. There was no way I wasn't going to figure out how to make money with a camera. I was determined to shoot anything I could and figure it out. I worked so hard at it and it was non-stop because I loved it.

Finding the right goal can be difficult, but it has to be the right one.

It has to be big enough that it's worth it. If it's not big enough and it's easy to obtain, then what are you doing? It has to be lofty. It has to scare you and it has to thrill you at the same time.

What is your next goal?

Peter: I do a lot of teaching and I speak all over the world to photographers. I've created a website with over 12,000 photographers, who I coach. It's exciting to see their success. I want to figure out how to get them jobs, how to arrange a system of referral fees for placing them in jobs. If I can help them have the life that I've had, that would be pretty great. So far, I've coached them on how to do it and now I have to figure out how to orchestrate the process of connecting them with the clients. That's the plan.

What would you like to accomplish in your life before you leave it?

Peter: I would have liked to win a gold medal. I don't know if that's possible anymore. I am going to the World Masters Games; maybe I'll win a gold medal there, even if it's not an Olympic medal.

I'd like to photograph some people that I idolized when I was growing up – some actors or rock stars. I always wanted to photograph Bono or Sting. I photograph celebrities; I don't think it would be that much of a stretch to get one of them in front of my camera.

I want to start mobilizing this team of photographers into something and creating a legacy for myself that nobody else has ever done. I want these photographers to be able to make a living for their families. That would be cool.

I was standing on the street today on a call, and this guy walked by me. He said, "Peter Hurley?" I turned and he looked at me in shock. He saw that I was on the phone and he waved at me and started to walk off. I called after him and said, "Hold on." He came back and he said, "My name is Kevin. I just moved here from San Antonio and you've been my inspiration to become a photographer. I just moved here two weeks ago and I can't believe I'm seeing you on the street." I gave him my cell phone number, and I told him I'd send him my tutorials and to come by the studio and say hi. That happened this afternoon. I think it went both ways. I got as much out of it as he did.

When things like that happen to me, I know I'm on the right track. Those are the moments when I think the universe is speaking. When I go to different countries, and people stop me in the street, it's a remarkable feeling.

When I meet celebrities that I've looked up to, I don't want to talk to them. I'm nervous as hell. Being in that situation made me feel what these other people feel now that I've gotten some of that status in the photography realm. I understand what they're going through and I want them to know that I want to talk to them and say hi to everybody. It's important.

If you had to choose one sentence that has a lot of meaning for you, what would it be?

Peter: What is my purpose? My purpose is to touch anyone in front of my camera in a way that captures a human expression that's authentic, reactive, and based on trust. The phrase "human expression that's authentic, reactive, and based on trust" is an acronym that spells heart. That's what my purpose is. I needed a purpose because my purpose before that was getting this studio or becoming the best headshot photographer in New York. But I was shooting so much, I burned out. I did this over and over again. I thought, what am I going to do? I turned my attention to the people and I realized that it's more fun to give them an experience in front of my camera than it is for me to be shooting them and collecting a paycheck. I started doing that and it meant a lot to me. I think it means a lot to the people that I've photographed. That's what it's about for me.

Making a big leap forced me to change my paradigm and create big, scary goals. I followed my heart to my purpose, which is to capture human expression that's authentic, reactive, and based on trust.

About Peter Hurley

Peter Hurley is a portrait and headshot photographer with studios in New York City and Los Angeles. He is known for the genuine expressions he captures in his actors' headshots and executive portraits. He has spoken on the subject for TED, Google, Apple, Microsoft, Adobe, and GoDaddy. Peter teaches his signature photography workshops all over the world and is the author of the book *The Headshot*.

Contact Peter at:
https://peterhurley.com/
peter@peterhurley.com

15

Do it Anyway

Rodney Flowers

Rodney Flowers suffered a paralyzing injury in his youth that lead to a long road to recovery and reinvention. He is now a motivational speaker and best-selling author; he lives in Maryland, USA.

Can you please introduce yourself?

Rodney: My name is Rodney Flowers and I am originally from North Carolina, USA, but now reside in Maryland. I am a transformational speaker and a three-time international best-selling author. I help people deal with the paralysis of life. You don't have to suffer an accident or injury to experience paralysis in life. A lot of people look at paralysis and they think it's purely physical, such as using a wheel-chair or having a physical disability. Some of that is true; however, people can be paralyzed mentally, emotionally, intellectually, and sometimes even socially. People get stuck in a rut in those areas and they don't know how to get out of that.

I sit down with these people and help them identify what's keeping them blocked. I ask them, "What's keeping you stuck?" I help them develop comprehensive plans on how to get out of that situation and understand where it is that they want to go, where they want to be, what's stopping them, and how they go from where they are to where they want to be in life; I help them live life joyfully, purposefully, fulfilled in every area of life. That's what I help people do. That's who I am.

223

Can you tell me a little bit about your life, your story?

Rodney: The story of how I got into this field of training is very unique. I'm very thankful and grateful for where I am in life, but I also have a little bit of pride about being able to help people get over their challenges and get unstuck, because I know what that's like. I myself was paralyzed at one point in time in my life and I still deal with a level of physical paralysis. At age 15, I loved football. I wanted to make football my life. I wanted to be in the NFL*. My life revolved around football; how I ate, how I took care of myself, all of it was for the sake of the game. I was a star player, devoting myself to my dream.

One day, while playing the first game of my sophomore year, I made a tackle, went down, and realized I couldn't get back up. My mom and the doctors ran out onto the field. They discovered that I had suffered a spinal cord injury. They rushed me to the hospital and they flew me out to Duke Medical Center, where they ran more tests. They found out that I had a C5/C6 spinal cord injury, which is very similar to what Christopher Reeves** suffered. They diagnosed me as paralyzed from the neck down, with no movement or sensation. I had a 91% chance of remaining paralyzed and a vegetable for the rest of my life. That's what they told my family. I was 15 years old and I was devastated.

Several times during this process, I wanted to kill myself. I wanted to give up on life. I had this dream of doing big things and being this person, and all of that was destroyed in an instant. I had dedicated my life to this and it was over. I had to figure out how to move on with life, how to get over this challenge, how to still be productive, how to be someone that could contribute and take care of myself and be an effective member of my community. I had to figure out how I was going to do this because I couldn't do anything; I couldn't get a job, buy a house, or do any of the things that a normal person would want to do. Someone had to wait on me hand and foot, 24 hours a day.

Even with all that against me, there was still something about me that just wouldn't quit, that just wouldn't give up, that wouldn't accept what the doctors said. It didn't come out immediately; it took about a year, because I was mad at the world. I felt that God was doing me wrong, that I was dealt a bad hand, and that it was unfair. But, I found that having that negative attitude and blaming God, or blaming my circumstances, wasn't getting me anywhere. I would go through the motions every day of being mad at the world and thinking it was unfair, and at the end of the day, I was in the same place with the same feelings. I felt that if I continued with this cycle, 10 years down the road I was going to be the same, feeling the same way, and that was just going to be miserable.

I thought about suicide, but I felt that suicide would cause me to lose the game of life. Giving up on life because of this situation would be quitting. At times, it felt like it was worth giving up; I felt like I didn't have a reason to live. But I didn't kill myself. In my book, I talk about that moment where I wanted to roll myself out in my wheelchair in front of a tractor trailer and just get it over with. I sat by the road several times, thinking about doing that, but something kept me from doing it and that something was all about opportunity. It was about the 'what if' in life. Everyone has challenges, everyone has some type of proverbial wheelchair that is challenging for them. I began to look at my situation a little bit differently.

I began to think of this as, *Well, what if you were able to get over this? What if you were able to be successful despite this?* Because that's what I really wanted. I felt like this disability had robbed me of being successful. How was I going to be successful in this situation? I couldn't see how, but I began to think, *What if all these things you want to accomplish – the job, the independence, all of that – what if you were able to accomplish that despite your circumstances? Think about what that would do for your life, how it would change it. What would that do for other people in your life? How would that change the way you feel? Would that make life worth living?*

And for me the answer was, *wow. That would be a beautiful thing. That would impact a lot of people. That could really make a difference for me and the way I feel about myself and about my circumstances.* I began to pursue that. I began to say, "Okay. You know what? I have this wheelchair, I have this disability. I'm going to figure out with my mind how I can be successful. Even though my arms and legs are injured, I'm going to figure out how I can be successful despite this."

That started me on this journey. It didn't happen overnight, but I kept trying. I kept working with it. I started looking for ways that

I could strengthen myself. I kept going back to the doctors, asking, "Is there anything that you can do for me? What can I do?" I went through multiple iterations of physical therapy, with my family supporting me and praying for me and moving me; they were not giving up on my life. They were trying to figure out, *how can I make this work? How can we bring healing to Rodney?*

It took 18 years for me to start walking again. Some people say I healed myself, some people say that God healed me. Some say it was the determination and the longevity of my treatment. I think it was a combination of all of that. But the point that I love to get across to people is that, regardless of your circumstances, whatever you want in life, whatever you want to be in life, you can do it. If you're stuck, you can get unstuck. When you're going after your challenge, goal, or dream, you're going to meet resistance. Things are going to pop up. Things are going to happen. It's how you respond to those things that make the difference in your life, your final destination.

Where you finally end up all depends on your response to what shows up in your life. A lot of times, we come up with excuses or blame others. A lot of times, we give up just because it seems too hard and those are not the proper responses. Given the situation that I've been in, I see where people are paralyzed and they're paralyzed by their emotions. They're paralyzed in their minds and in their hearts. Because when things show up, when things get hard, I believe that if you want to progress through them, you need to change your perspective on the thing that's happened in your life. You may feel that it's stopping you, it's preventing you from moving forward, but it could be the very thing that propels you, strengthens you, the very thing that exposes the areas in your life that need work, that need your attention, that may be a little bit weak.

Now this thing that showed up, that seems so detrimental, so debilitating to your life, is actually a blessing and a gift. That's how I chose to live my life; I use this as a gift. One thing that Bob talks about is harvesting the good; it's the Law of Polarity. For every good, there's a bad; for every up, there's a down. So, whatever is showing up in your life, it's important that you harvest the good. I think about a farmer whenever I think about this Law. When a farmer is harvesting, it doesn't mean there are no weeds in the area where he's harvesting.

But he's not focused on the weeds. He's after the goodness, the things that he can use, which can bring joy, gifts, and abundance to this life. He forgets about the weeds and only harvests the good. He could have a field of weeds, but there's still some good in there. The weeds are growing right alongside the good stuff, but that doesn't mean you harvest the weeds. You harvest the good.

Whatever's showing up in your life, there's something good to be had from it. I made the decision to look at this situation, this disability, this paralysis, and say, what is the good? And the good is that, as I overcome paralysis, I strengthened myself. I became an example for others and I can actually show others how to get over their paralysis, how to go from being stuck to living a life of joy, how to go from being restricted to being free, physically, emotionally, spiritually, and financially. Whatever it is, you can have that.

Where do you draw all this power from? Tell me about the process of standing up again.

Rodney: I got hurt in 1993. August 26th was the date of my injury. It took about a year for me to just stand up on my feet on my own and, even then, that was with assistance. I couldn't stand by myself.

After one year, you were already on your feet?

Rodney: Not so much, but my family would not let me sit in that wheelchair. They would stand me up and I wouldn't let myself do it. I would go to my therapist and say, "I want to stand up." They would put me on this board, it was like a standing board, and they would strap me in and tilt the board up, to get the blood circulating through my legs and try to get the brain to understand weight bearing, muscular support, and nerve response.

I really couldn't stand on my own, but in my mind, I was standing. Even after I got out of the hospital some four months later, I would just have my mom or my dad stand me up. They would hold me up and they would try to let me go, and I would fall. We just kept doing things like that and before you know it, I was able to stand. I wasn't able to stand for very long, but I was able to stand.

It's like the Wright brothers. They stayed in the air the first time for 11 seconds or something like that. A lot of people said that was a success. My 11 seconds of standing, for me, were a success. I built upon that. But it was 18 years before I could walk without needing my wheelchair.

Incredible! I read in your book, Get Up! I Can't. I Will. I Did... Here's How!, *that you always did more than the rest; if other people walked for five minutes, you walked for 10 minutes. Other people were in the same situation as you, but nobody put in the kind of effort that you did. That's why you got the results.*

Rodney: There were many times where I had the attitude that I was going to walk again or die trying. That's pretty much what it was. I demonstrated that through my work ethic. The physical therapist would put electrodes on my body to get my muscles to move. They would shock me. They would put this electrode on my arm and it would make my hand open and close. Then they would put it on my leg and it would make my leg extend and then contract. I would keep doing little stuff like that, all day. I'd go back to my room and if there was a little twitch – this is where this all started. It wasn't a full movement. It was a little twitch in my leg, arm, toe or in my finger. I wanted to move so badly that I would go in my room, after physical therapy, and I would make that little bitty twitch. This required enhanced concentration. I would twitch it until I couldn't twitch anymore. I kept doing that over and over. That really started a snowball effect. I got into the habit of doing that and, 18 years later, I was walking and I felt confident enough that I didn't need the wheelchair anymore.

How long can you walk for, as of today?

Rodney: I can walk as long as the average person. When I go to amusement parks, which I don't do often anymore, I might use a wheelchair there because the park is so big. I don't walk fast, I'm a little slower than the average person. But other than that, I feel like I don't have any limitations as to how far I can walk. I can walk as far as I want to. I barely use my wheelchair at all anymore. I don't take it with me wherever I go. I just use my crutches and that's it.

How is your hand?

Rodney: I can hold some things. I have to hold my crutches. I can grab my phone. I can write. I can type. But I don't have the dexterity that I would like. I'm still working on that. My motor function is limited as a result of the injury, but that's okay because I'm still functional. I still need assistance with certain things, but it's nowhere near what it was when I got hurt. I couldn't wave my hand. I couldn't stand up. I couldn't even have held myself up in this chair. I would have fallen over. The return of the functionality and the mobility that I have is miraculous. I think it all stems back to having that change in my mindset. That really changed it all for me, because without that, I would have given up. I could have given up in year five, or in year ten, year twelve; after 18 years, it finally happened. I don't know anyone who continued to fight that long. I'm very proud to be here, because I'm proud that I lasted. It was tough. You hear people talk about pushing through, doing it until the end. It sounds great, but for a lot of people, that's not their reality. They can't last that long. They try, but they end up giving in. I can say that with so much conviction because I've lived that. Hold on, keep trying, stay focused on what you want and do not give up. Just get the fact that it may take a long time out of your mind, because it really doesn't matter. Now, living the life that I live, having the functionality and the mobility that I have, was it worth the 18 years? Absolutely. If I had given up too early, I would never have been able to bear the idea that if I had just persisted, I could have had everything that I have now. It would be like to be three feet away from hitting pay dirt and stop digging. We have to keep going.

In your book, you wrote, "Don't just do it for you, do it for those that need to see you do it." I love it so much because you also did it for your father, mother, sister, and all of us. You were an example for the people surrounding you.

Rodney: I feel like this was given to me is a gift and I truly view it like that. I feel like we all have something about us that we can offer. That's something I will challenge people about. What is your offering to the world? I thought my offering was going to be football player, because that's what I enjoyed doing, I was good at it and I loved entertaining people out there on the field. But that wasn't my offering. And I thought I didn't have an offering after this happened to me. I felt like I was useless, like I had no purpose.

Now, I understand. I have raised my level of consciousness and I understand that this is my offering. I believe everyone has that offering to give. I believe that, whatever your passion is, whatever gets you up in the morning and makes you want to just go after it, that's your offering to the world. That's what you have, and I believe it's important for you to pursue it and to cultivate it to a point where you can be an example to as many people in this world as possible, because they need it.

You think about some of the inventions that have been made – the things that we enjoy in life, simple things like a car. Imagine if Henry T. Ford didn't invent the car. Imagine if the Wright brothers didn't invent the plane. Imagine if someone hadn't invented the light bulb or the system that we are using to communicate across the country right now. We wouldn't enjoy those things. There are a lot of people who are not living their passion, who are not living their dream and in those circumstances those people and the rest of us lose out. That means that out of all the things that we are enjoying, there's probably a deficit of what we could enjoy if everyone was pursuing their purpose.

My offering just so happened to involve being in a wheelchair and overcoming paralysis; what that looks like and how that can support you and your dream, that's my service to you, so you can bring forward your offering to make a difference in the world.

I love that chapter in that book, because I truly believe that it has been the driving force for me. It's not only about me. The part about me is very small, compared to the purpose behind service to everyone else in the world, to those that are willing to listen, to those that need to understand how to get out of their situation. That can be life-changing for someone and it has been for several people that have read the book and have had encounters with me. But if I had not made that decision, I couldn't have had this interview and couldn't have had the impact that I have had on the world. It just wouldn't have happened.

People are not going to be blessed by you if you give up. If you don't bring this forward, you're going to leave a deficit in your life and in the world. We have a short time here and, while we're here, we have to give of ourselves to the highest capacity possible, to bring forth life in some degree, for the sustainment and edification of life. That's what I believe our purpose is. By reading this book and watching the videos, you can increase your life, because you expand

230

your understanding, maybe achieve a higher consciousness, and become inspired to move forward. This book that you're writing can improve someone else's life. Whatever it is that they want to do, whatever offering they have, they bring that forward and it adds to someone else's life. Now, we start changing the world, one person at a time.

The money and the fame is great, but you can't take that with you. You have to leave that behind. But, someone can pick up this book or watch this video and listen to it 20, 30, 50 years from now, and the information will still be relevant. No one's going to care how much money you made in 50 years. Who cares about that? You want to live life to the fullest and abundantly while you're here, but there's a bigger legacy that you can leave. You need money so that you can bring forth your offering as much as possible, so that you make the biggest difference in the world. That's the purpose of money. It's not just for you to be selfish and grab it for yourself, purely doing things for yourself. I need money so that I can serve more people. The more money I have, the more people I can serve and get this message out.

Who gave you this inspiration to continue and not to give up?

Rodney: Passion for people. In the moment, I understood that this is something I could use to impact the world; it became a purpose for me, a driving force.

Was there a person that was your inspiration?

Rodney: There wasn't anything a single person could do for me or really do to help me. I was inspired to walk again because I wanted to walk again, and I had this purpose behind it.

My family supported me. They supported that vision. We began to see the impact as I began to heal and improve. We saw how that affected people, so we continued to push that. When I met Bob, I was out of the wheelchair. I was satisfied that I made it and I was walking, that's what I put my focus on, but I wasn't fully satisfied with my functionality, movement, and mobility. My focus was never really on running, although I still desire that. I thought that if I could walk, that alone would be huge.

Then Bob said, "We can get you out of those canes." He raised my consciousness even higher. He was looking at this from a whole new perspective; nothing broken, nothing missing. He inspired me to reach even higher. It's always been a desire of mine, but it's become more of a desire after meeting Bob.

When did you first come across Bob Proctor's material and what was your situation in life at that time?

Rodney: When I was growing up, my mom always had preaching on in the background in our house. If the TV was on, there was probably somebody preaching. If we weren't home listening to preaching, we were at church listening to preaching. I was always filling my head up with good material, good information. But I wanted more. I was always searching for something. I wanted to be healed more and to do more.

In 2012, I ran across the book *The Secret*. It was right after I started walking. That's how I met Bob and that's how I came across this material. For some reason, just after I started studying the material, I got an email from Bob about the *Science of Getting Rich* seminar that he was holding in Dallas.

I thought about what it would be like to go see him, because he was the one who made the most impact on me during the movie *The Secret*. When he said things, I thought, That's it. That's what I'm talking about. That's what I'm feeling. And the way he explained things, they resonated with me, more than any of what the other interviewees said. His message was kind of spot on for me. I wanted to go and meet this gentleman. I wanted to go hear him live. I went to his seminar and a friend there, someone that I met while they were sitting at my table, introduced me to Bob. She knew Bob personally. I met him and Peggy McColl. They found out about my story and both of them encouraged me to put it out there to the world. Less than a year later, I was an international best-selling author.

What has happened from that moment and what did you start doing differently to change your results?

Rodney: I realized that the success that I was experiencing was a result of the way I was thinking. I'm very clear on this now as a result of studying Bob's material. I was an 'unconscious competent', as he calls it. What I do differently now is that I consciously, deliberately, and purposefully use my mind to create the success and the experience that I want to create in life. I have become more tuned to the vibration that I'm on, the frequency, and how to change them. Also, I learned to listen to that little voice, those spiritual thoughts, that connection that you have with your spirit. I live my life very tuned in now, not only hearing but listening.

Listening involves acting so that you can hear something, but if you don't do it, you really don't listen. When you listen, you take action on what you heard. That has been a change and, as a result, I'm building a business around this message and around what has happened to me. I've literally flipped this accident and this trauma on its head. I use this as a means to show people how to overcome the challenges in life, how to get unstuck. I don't accept too many excuses, if any, because there are none. We are all a product of what we have been thinking and if we want to change, we have to change our thinking in order to get a different result. By the Law of Perpetual Transmutation, we can do that.

Everything is made of energy. We're made of energy. There's one source. We're connected to the source. We have an intelligence. There's faculties that we have and we can use them in order to create the life that we want. That's what I've been doing.

What paradigms did you discover that you need to change?

Rodney: When I got into this industry with writing and speaking, I had overcome being in a wheelchair, but I still had a level of limitation, physically, that you could see. Anyone can look at me and say, "Oh he has crutches. His mobility is limited. He has a challenge." That forced me to look at myself as less adequate than someone else or not good enough. I would get on stage and feel people were going to look at me and look at my disability, and they're going to judge me.

That was a paradigm that I had to get over, that I wasn't good enough. That I was not qualified. Now, I know that I'm absolutely qualified. You can see me and you can see my life, you can see the challenges that I've overcome. It was huge for me to realize that and now I want to do it as big as I can; not for the fame or the money, but because I don't want this holding me down in any way. I want to get this point across to as many people as I can.

It doesn't matter what your circumstance is, it doesn't matter what it looks like. All that matters is the level of intensity that you're willing to hold in your mind toward the goal that you want to accomplish in your life, toward your dream. That's what really matters, because when you do that, hold that level of concentration, align your emotions and your behavior behind that, you can do anything in this world.

How long did it take you to start seeing results?

Rodney: After meeting Bob, in less than twelve months I was an international bestseller. I couldn't believe it, so I had to do it again, just to make sure. I did it three times. I saw results immediately after meeting Bob and it was because of getting involved with someone who was of that same mindset. I have to give credit to Peggy McColl, because she really helped me to see that I could do this. That was a pivotal time in my life; the title of 'bestselling author' is mine for the rest of my life and it has allowed me the credibility to start my business, to speak to people, to coach and mentor people. I have a new life now. My whole life has changed.

What were the most difficult moment and the best moment in the process?

Rodney: One of the most difficult things for me was changing that self-identity that says, I'm not good enough. It was difficult and that takes time. That's not something that happens overnight. It takes work to change that identity. A lot of people don't feel like they need to do that. They think, *Oh, I'm fine the way I am.* But I knew that it was limiting me. I knew that the self-image of me was not lining up with the me that I could be, the me that can help millions of people, the me that can speak all over the world. I had to see myself there. I had to get that, resonate with that, and then start living that.

We have these goals and dreams and we say, "When I get there, this is what I want to do." You can start now. You just may not be doing it as massively as you want to do it, but you start where you stand, being the person that you want to be. Nothing stops you from doing that. That's a paradigm shift, because we feel like we have to do this, this, and that before we can be all we can, but the truth is that all we have is right now. That's it. Yesterday is gone, tomorrow is not promised. All we have is now. So, if you want to be a superstar, start feeling like a superstar and doing the things that a superstar does right now. Be that person.

Stop trying to do and just be. Be present with that, that's who you are. I'm an author, I'm a mentor, whether I'm doing it with one person or ten thousand. You're an artist whether you have one person buying your art or millions of people buying your art. You're still an artist. Be an artist and work on your craft every single day. I feel like that's the most powerful thing and it trips people up, because they feel like they have to do this before they can be that. Be, and as you be, you do.

You already talked about two Laws but when you hear the words "Universal Laws", what do they mean to you?

Rodney: Universal Laws are a mindset, a toolbox. It's how we play, if you will, with the power of God, with the universe. These are our basketballs, our toys and tools. These Laws really govern how to live an abundant life. If you can get these Laws down, understand them and apply them to your life, you don't need anything else. You can go through life and live an abundant life. These Laws can help you with every encounter or every experience that can come up in your life. It really can.

Do you want to talk about one more specific Law?

Rodney: We can talk about the Law of Relativity. I can talk about this all day. By the Law of Relativity, nothing's big or small until you compare it to something else. And the reason why I love talking about this one is because it has had an impact on my life. My experience was big and traumatizing and debilitating. But then I realized, it's not bigger than me, because now I understand my purpose and my place in the universe and what it is that I'm assigned to do. In my opinion, it's not really big at all.

Things that show up in our lives, if we're not careful, we begin to make them look like giants to us when they're just things. We create stories around the thing and then we believe in them. We make up stuff and then we believe in this stuff, and that governs our lives. I'm talking about things that happened when we were kids that we haven't dealt with yet. It could have been abuse, it could have been rape, it could have been neglect, negligence, and all kinds of stuff that shows up, and it causes us to behave as adults in a certain way that's not serving us. You feel that it was too big and you don't know how else to deal with it because it's so big. But it's never bigger than you. Someone else is probably dealing with something that's a little bit more challenging. Why compare it? Why give it a size? It's noting if you don't compare it to anything. It just is.

Can you tell me your story about one specific goal that you managed to accomplish?

Rodney: Outside of walking again, I have to say, starting this business, mentoring and speaking was a goal I accomplished. That has been a goal that I have been able to accomplish that I feel is very life-changing and very fulfilling for me at the same time, because I'm able to see the difference that I can make in the lives of other people. Whether it's through a book, something that I say, a speaking engagement, or a mentoring session, I love that. And that's something that drove me when I was flat on my back and couldn't move. To be here now, doing that, is very fulfilling and rewarding for me.

What were you prepared to give up, to sacrifice, to arrive at your goal?

Rodney: It's funny that you say that because at one point in time, I felt like I didn't have anything, and so I was willing to give up everything in order to accomplish the goal. You have to be very careful there. I think your passion is very, very important. But we don't want to lose ourselves in it to the point that we're forsaking people. There are sacrifices that we have to make and I was willing to make the necessary sacrifices without losing my sanity.

I feel like sometimes, if we're not willing to make the necessary sacrifices, or if we're doing it for the wrong reason, we can lose ourselves in trying to chase money, success, and fame. So, there is a balance, and there is a level of understanding that we have to apply to ourselves whenever we are going after those dreams, because we don't want it to break up families. We want to do things in harmony with the universe. But if it was anything that wasn't serving me, that wasn't serving my purpose, I was willing to give that up. One thing that helped me stay focused and stay aligned was asking myself, is this thing serving me or serving my purpose? If it's not serving my purpose, it's highly likely I'm not going to partake in that.

What is the one key lesson you can give to everyone who wants to reach his goal?

There is a sentence from your book that I like so much "Tired? Do it anyway."

Rodney: Do it anyway. It goes hand in hand with not giving up on your dream. Bob talks about when you see all the graves in the graveyard and you're saddened by the fact that those people lived their lives and now they're gone, they're not here with us to share their lives with us. But what's more important is the fact that most people don't fulfill their passion, they don't fulfill their dream during their lifetime. Now, that dream is gone, that dream is dead because the person is gone. The person whom that dream was given to is not here with us anymore. So that dream didn't come to pass. That passion was never fulfilled and that offering was never given to the world.

Think about your life, and think about the idea that when that life is over, nobody else will give your offering to the world. That's a very personal gut-check***. I can give you tools to get over it and motivate you to keep moving forward, and I could show you four or five things that you could do to stay on top. But I want you to feel this from a personal level. Do you want to live your life not having provided your offering, not having served, and not having given back?

Life is a gift. And then it gives you a gift: your passion. And the best thing that you can do is give that back. You can make all the money in the world, but if you're not making a difference, what is the good of life?

If you really want to do something great in this life, the best thing that you can do is give of yourself, to cultivate your gift and give it to as many people as you can, because that's going to be your greatest reward. That's going to reward you spiritually, financially, emotionally, and intellectually, because you're going to grow through that process. You get everything through that. That would be my advice to you, to live your life with passion. Cultivate your passion. Give it everything that you've got, because that will pay you back ten-fold in ways you can't believe.

What is your next goal?

Rodney: My next goal is to transform as many lives as possible. I'm planning on doing live events and group coaching, and the purpose of all of that is to make a difference. I want to give of my gift so that people can get rid of excuses.

It is not so much that I want to get on people; I don't want to make them feel bad. But, I truly believe that we make excuses for ourselves and that's one of the things that drives me forward. A lot of people don't feel like they can do it. It's okay for that person to do it, or that celebrity to have it, or for Bob to be the great speaker that he is, but they never can see themselves doing something of that magnitude. The goal, for me, is to do something so great that it inspires people to say, "You know what? If that guy has given everything that he's had to deal with things in his life, and he's accomplished something like that, wow. What am I doing?"

I want to turn this on its head, because I believe that everyone is great, but not everyone lives into their greatness. My goal is to get people to live into their greatness.

What would you like to accomplish in your life before you leave it?

Rodney: I would like to be one of the top speakers in the world. I want to transform the lives of millions of people. I would like to see people who have physical disabilities be more active in their community. I really believe that people who may have a physical challenge are a gift to us. A lot of times, we view them as lesser or inadequate somehow. I would like to see more people with disabilities doing more things like public speaking or being leaders, because these people deal with some of the most challenging things, compared with any of us. I would like to see them raise their level of consciousness and be advocates for that so they can get healing and also send a message to other people who have emotional, physical or intellectual challenges.

We all have challenges. That's what life is. Life is an accumulation of experiences; some good, some bad. That's what it is. But, I feel that if we can help each other through those experiences, by giving, serving and providing the lessons learned from those experiences, we can make the world a better place.

If you had to choose one sentence that has a lot of meaning for you, what would it be?

Rodney: It would be from Thomas Troward: "My mind is a center of Divine operation. The Divine operation is always for expansion and fuller expression."

Do you have something more to add before we finish?

Rodney: I feel that one of the things that holds people down and stops people from really reaching their dream is resistance. I plan to do a seminar on resistance, because resistance is like procrastination; it's a thief. When resistance shows up in people's lives, it causes them to quit, or they get fearful and uncomfortable. My philosophy is that resistance is just part of the process. Don't be discouraged by resistance. Don't be discouraged by something that shows up, that seems like it's against you and is stopping you. Rise above that resistance. Be resilient, grow. Understand that it is the process and sometimes you're not ready for the thing that you want just yet, even though you want it and it seems like these things are against you. That's part of the process to get you to a point where you are ready to take that on, handle that, and be responsible with it. That's all part of the process. That's all resistance is.

You have to be willing to do that in order to get to the other side. It's as if you want to climb a mountain, you want to see what it's like to get to the top of that mountain, you have to be willing to travel the road between the bottom of the mountain to the top of the mountain, and that's not always a straight line. There are dips and curves and all kinds of experiences between the bottom and the top. But that doesn't mean that you can't get there; you just have to be willing to go through that. If you are willing to go through that, using these Universal Laws that we've talked about, with the right mindset you can experience that view at the top.

Rodney: When we see someone that has a physical challenge, we label them disabled. Let's look at that word; what does that mean?

Incapable of moving, that's what it means. That's what paralyzed means. But disabled means unable, not able to do whatever it is that you set out to do. You don't have to have a physical challenge in order to be disabled. There's a lot of able-bodied disabled people walking around. It's all about thinking. It's raising your level of consciousness to reach that concept.

There are people in the world who need to learn how to get unstuck, how to move away from the wheelchair in their minds. I am honored to be an example, an advocate, and an inspiration to those around me.

About Rodney Flowers

Rodney is the founder and president of Inspirational Endeavors, LLC, and the author of three successful books. After a traumatic high school football injury in 1993, he was bound to the confines of his wheelchair. Although Rodney was told his recovery prognosis was unfavorable, he knew he would turn things around, make an impact on the world, and walk again. With self-determination and faith in his ability to persevere, he did!

Contact Rodney at:
http://www.rodneyflowers.com
rodney@rodneyflowers.com

* The National Football League (NFL) is a professional American football league consisting of 32 teams, divided equally between the National Football Conference (NFC) and the American Football Conference (AFC). The NFL is one of the four major professional sports leagues in North America and the highest professional level of American football in the world.

** Christopher D'Olier Reeve (1952–2004) was an American actor, film director, producer, screenwriter, author, activist, and sportsman. He is best known for his motion picture portrayal of the classic DC comic book superhero, Superman, beginning with the acclaimed Superman (1978), for which he won a BAFTA.

On May 27, 1995, Reeve became a quadriplegic after being thrown from a horse during an equestrian competition in Culpeper, Virginia. He was confined to a wheelchair and required a portable ventilator for the rest of his life. He lobbied on behalf of people with spinal cord injuries and for human embryonic stem cell research, founding the Christopher Reeve Foundation and co-founding the Reeve-Irvine Research Center.
Source: Wikipedia

***A gut-check is a test of willpower, courage, fortitude, etc. Rarely does it involve any physical strength or skill, instead being an almost entirely mental challenge. The term was first heard in the US Army, but has spread through usage amongst veterans.
Source: The Urban Dictionary

* Bonus Story *

Fight or Flight

Josh Thomas

Josh Thomas is the brother of Austin Thomas (see Chapter 11). He tells the Thomas brothers' story from his perspective and recounts his heroic struggle to break free from a lifestyle of drink and drugs. Josh is a service plumber who lives in California. He managed to transform his life and, today, he helps others with dependency issues. His goal is to help one million people become sober and live the lifestyle of their dreams.

Can you, please, start by introducing yourself?

Josh: My name is Josh Thomas and I am the CEO and co-founder of the Power Within Institute. I've lived in California my entire life. I was born in Orange County and I grew up in a really poverty-stricken neighborhood. It was the lowest of lows. Every day was fight or flight. We didn't know any better. There were a lot of paradigms that were transmitted from generation to generation. My dad raised his six brothers and sisters until he moved out and started a family; there was my dad, me, my brother, and my mom. We moved up here to Bakersfield and we've been living here ever since.

Growing up, every night was a party. I saw my parents drink, smoke marijuana, and use different drugs. I saw fights every night. I grew up in that lifestyle. That's all I knew.

I continued to fight my way through life. It started in junior high and went all the way through high school. Once I finished school, I did the same thing.

Why were you in and out of jail?

Josh: I got into a lot of fights in the neighborhood. It was nonstop. Someone walking down the street would say the wrong thing. I would say something back, hop the fence, and start fighting. I've been stabbed a few times. I attacked people with weapons. I've been jumped by several gang members. That neighborhood was really tough and it's still that way today.

I first went to jail when I was 18. I've been in and out of jail several times, for fighting and alcohol-related stuff.

Jail was the worst – it's not a fun place to be. It's really the downfall of a lot of people, because once they start living that lifestyle – in and out of jail – they become institutionalized.

I lost my first marriage over this. It tore my world apart. Then, in 2003, my dad died of cancer. In one month, I lost my wife, my dad, and my job. I hit rock bottom, until I learned that you have to either get busy living or get busy dying.

I knew that this wasn't the life for me. I had to pick myself up, put the pieces together, and move forward. I had to get straight. As Johnny Cash would say, I had to walk the line and that's what I've been doing ever since. I finally broke free from that cycle at around 30 years old.

Today, do you have any connection with the people in that neighborhood?

Josh: No. I don't see them anymore. It's rare. I live in a better part of town. When I do, I act like I don't see them. I turn my head and keep walking. I don't associate with that group anymore. When I'm around that part of town, I get a really bad vibe and I know I have to leave. I do service work in that town as a service plumber. I do my job quickly – in and out. I don't talk to anybody. When I'm working, I can still see fights down the street. I can hear yelling and sirens going by. It's a really bad neighborhood.

When did you first come across Bob Proctor's material and what situation were you in with your life?

Josh: I came across Bob's material in 2011. I was talking with my brother in my garage about tithing; I was telling him how I pay tithes and that I'm taken care of. He said, "That sounds like The Law of Attraction." I said, "What's that?" He sent me a link to a video of *The Secret*.

Watching it, I kept seeing a man in a white suit; something about him really resonated with me. I have pretty good intuition. I thought, that man knows what he's talking about. I searched for Bob Proctor and I entered my details on his website. After a phone call with the organization, I signed up for the year-long coaching program.

At this time, I had just started my plumbing company. It's called Thomas Plumbing and Affordable Drain Service. I've been doing service plumbing for about 20 years. I started fresh out of high school. It's just something I picked up; I knew it was something that I could do. I worked for several people – I would lose jobs because of fighting and jail time and my bad paradigms – but I stuck with it until I started my own company.

I left a job in which I was making $160,000 a year to, literally, nothing. I had $15,000 savings in my bank account. I took that and started my business.

This material came at the right time. I had two weeks to pay my rent, my child support, and my vehicle payments; I didn't know what I was going to do. Once I started reading this material, there was a snowball effect. One thing led to another. After that, I took the *Thinking Into Results* program and I became a *TIR* consultant.

I've been going strong since 2011. I started out with just myself in the garage. Now, I have an office, five employees, and four work trucks. It gave me the financial freedom to do what I want to do.

At first, I made about $40,000 a year. When I started taking Bob's coaching program, my business really took off. I went from $40,000 one year to $175,000 the next year to $375,000 the year after that. Last year, we broke $1.2 million. It was all because I kept looking at my goal card. That's all I did. I went about my day, reading the goal card as often as I could. The goal card is powerful because it puts us in the present tense and brings the goal forward from the future to now. The business got better, my life got better, and I'm doing excellently now.

I've got a beautiful four-bedroom, two-bathroom home. I don't have to rent. I have nice vehicles, a travel trailer, a booming business, and a loving wife. I'm raising a family – I have a 23-year-old daughter and a 14-year-old boy – and I'm doing what I love to do.

What happened from that moment and what did you start doing differently to change your results?

Josh: I dug into the material – what Bob teaches and what he tells you to do. That was hard for me at first because it was a change of paradigm. Why have I got to read this, do this, and write this down? But, I thought, the guy knows what he's talking about. So, I listened to what he said. I read the recommended books. I did the exercises in the *TIR* program. I read the goal card and became emotionally involved with my goal.

Arash from the Proctor Gallagher Institute sent me my first goal card. He said, "I want you to take 15 minutes in the morning and 15 minutes at night, and throughout the day – as much as you can. Visualize and read this card. See what you will do with the money that you're going to get." That's what I did. That's what got me to where I am.

I have goal cards. I get up every morning and write my gratitude list, which is very powerful. I recommend completing a gratitude list; whenever you're having a bad week, write down 10 things that you're grateful for.

People see me doing well and they ask me, what do I need to do? What's going to make my life better? I hand them a gratitude list and they look at me like I'm funny. I say, "You asked, so here you go. Give it a shot." The ones that stick with it come back and say, "Thank you. That was very powerful and my life has changed." That's what it's for. Writing is very powerful.

When did you do the TIR?

Josh: I did the TIR in 2013. I didn't have a coach. I'm very strong-willed. I did it myself. In fact, I went through the program five times myself. I did the videos and the workbook. I made time for it. At the time, I didn't know who to go to for help. I hold myself accountable. If I want something badly enough, I'll get it.

What paradigms did you discover that you needed to change?

Josh: I needed to change my limited way of thinking. I was taught that rich people were rude, mean, selfish people. I wondered why they lived better lives than I did.

The drinking and partying – that was another big paradigm I needed to change. That was a really hard one to kick. I realize now that it's just thinking in reverse, when you go down that route. I've lived that lifestyle – I've already paid for that.

Another one was being a loving person. I always had to be the tough guy. I always had to be the one to watch out for. But that would just land me back in jail. I didn't want to live that life anymore.

I also began to write. When I was a kid, my stepfather used to make us write book reports. If it wasn't good enough, he would shred it up right in front of us and tell us to start again. I got writing – the language and punctuation – down to a pretty good tee. Once I left that house, I never wrote again unless I had to – maybe invoices for work. I knew I had to start writing stuff down, because that's what Bob said to do.

At the beginning of the coaching program, he says, "I'm going to tell you what to do and if you don't do it, I'll stop helping you and you won't get a refund." So, I started writing everything down.

Where did you find your power and how did you manage to get out of the bad neighborhood?

Josh: After my divorce, I attracted a certain lady into my life. She was the one who helped me get back on my feet and move out. She was the one who looked me dead in the eye and said, "If you stay here, you're going to die. You won't see your kids. Your kids will be raised without a dad and you won't have me in your life, because I can't stay here." I knew right then that she was right. I couldn't let that happen. Today, she's my wife. We've been married for 14 years. She's the one who helped me get out. At first, I didn't want to leave. I was comfortable there. That was where I grew up.

We upped and moved to the northwest side of town and we've been there ever since. I got away from all the drama, the trouble, the drugs, the drinking, the partying, and the fighting. I haven't looked back since.

How long did it take you to start seeing results?

Josh: I saw results almost overnight, especially when I did the TIR program and Bob explained what to do with the goal card. When I first started my plumbing business, I wasn't getting any work. I was out there talking to people, – old clients and restaurants – but nothing was coming in. Then I wrote my goal down and started reading that card over and over. Whether I was in the bathroom or at a stoplight or in a restaurant, I would read it. And one day it just started. The phones started ringing. Jobs booked up.

It took off like a firecracker, like a rocket. I had so much work coming in, I had to turn people down. That wasn't typical of me; I was brought up not to turn down work. If you turn down work, that means you're not willing to work. I was flooded with work.

How much time did you dedicate to learning the material each day?

Josh: Even to this day, I study for about four hours. When I first started, I'd get up about four o'clock in the morning and study until eight when it was time to start work. I'd put in another two hours when I got home. At the time, it was six hours a day, because I was so intrigued.

Did you read the same chapter in the TIR?

Josh: I read the same thing over and over and over. The constant spaced repetition of the ideas really helped me tune into what I was seeking. I'm an early bird. When I first realized that what I was writing down was coming into my life, it was like a light bulb. I read

Bob's recommended reading, *Think and Grow Rich*. Every day – even at night when I'm lying in bed – I read a chapter.

What were the most difficult and the best moments in the process?

Josh: The most difficult moment was when I doubted if it was real – I had to try to believe in it. That was difficult for me to accept, because it challenged my paradigm and changed my whole logic, my whole belief. Even as I did what he was telling me to do, I had doubt. Throughout my years in the plumbing service, there have been ups and downs. When I had my downs, I would get frustrated with myself. I would stop studying, or at least not study as much as normal. That brought me down.

My best time was hitting that $1.2 million mark this past year. I'm able to travel the world. I've been to a lot of places in the past two years. I've been to the Caribbean several times. I've visited the Virgin Islands, Mexico, Canada, and Hawaii. We're working on Alaska next. I'm enjoying good times because I created a thriving plumbing company which has allowed me to do what I love to do.

I remember Arash asking me, "What do you want?" I said, "I want to travel the world." He asked, "Why aren't you doing it?" I answered that I didn't have any money. He asked, "What do you need money for?" I thought, where is this guy going with this?

He said, "You don't need the money till you make a decision to do it." I thought that was kind of odd. I didn't expect this answer from anybody. It threw me off. Now, I understand the concept. As soon as you make a decision, it's yours. The trips I've taken in the past two years have been my 'ups'.

When you hear the words "Universal Laws", what do they mean to you?

Josh: The Universal Laws are my way of life. Understanding these Laws was a turning point in my life, especially when it came to the Law of Attraction.

It really hit home with me when I went to *The Invisible Side of Success* event with Bob Proctor and Mary Morrissey. You need to understand and work in harmony with these laws.

Can you talk about the effect of one specific Law on your life?

Josh: One of my favorite Laws is the Law of Cause and Effect: what you put out into the universe, you get back. Without even knowing this at the time, I can see that I was getting back what I put out.

When I started studying the material, I realized that if I envisioned wanting $175,000 a year, it would come back. This applies to the way you treat people or talk to them.

Sometimes, you can de-escalate a situation with the Law of Cause and Effect. You learn to respond and not react. This gives me calmness of mind. I know if I talk to a certain person a certain way, I'm going to get that in return.

Once, I hadn't heard from a customer in a long time. I thought, I'd sure like to hear from Paul. Two hours later, I got a phone call from Paul. I thought, this is real!

I started to play with it. I thought, I haven't heard from my uncle Jason, who lives up north, in a while. Sure enough, two days later, he sent me a text message. "Hey nephew, how are you doing?" I thought, this is awesome. Now it's become part of my daily life. When I do my gratitude list and write things that I'm thankful for, I know that by doing that I'm going to get more things to be grateful for.

Another Law that has made an impact on me is The Law of Vibration. By understanding my emotions and their vibrations, I'm starting to notice what I'm attracting into my life. If I'm having a bad day, I know that if I keep focusing on those bad things, I'm going to get more of those bad things. I learned how to switch it. I had to. I'll stop what I'm doing. I'll put on a piece of music. Or I'll look at my kids' pictures and my wife's, and think of a good memory. That automatically reverses my thinking and the vibration I'm in. It improves my day.

Can you tell me about one specific goal that you managed to accomplish?

Josh: In my plumbing business, I never expected to make a million dollars. As I was studying this material, I wrote down "I am so happy and grateful now that Thomas Plumbing is earning over a million dollars a year". I wrote that goal two years ago and I reached it.

When I first started going to Bob's seminars, I noticed a lot of people sitting up front. I always sat in the back. I didn't talk to anybody at first; I was shy. I watched everybody and I noticed there was a certain group up front that Bob kept talking to. I wanted to be around Bob, so I wanted to sit up front too.

Of course, you have to pay a VIP price to sit up front, but I knew I wanted to be around those people. I was drawn to their energy – the way they were. I made it a goal. I told myself, I'm going to be sitting up front at one of those tables. One day, I was heading to Mammoth Mountain on vacation with my wife and my brother called me. He said that two spots were open at a VIP table at a discounted rate. He said, "Are you in?" I said, without any hesitance, "Sure". When I did that, I knew it was going to be a good seminar. Bob kept coming to the table. I thought, I'm with people I want to be around. I'm up here with all the heavy hitters who Bob talks to. That was one of my goals.

Now I'll pay VIP no matter what. I don't care what the cost is. I get to hang around with all those people. I met a lot of great people that weekend and it really changed my life. It was an eye-opener. That was the energy I was looking for.

What were you prepared to give up or to sacrifice to arrive at your goal?

Josh: I was prepared to put in a lot of time and to be away from my family. Being a service plumber is a lifestyle. It's not an eight-to-five job. You don't get to wake up and say, "I'll be home at five." I would sometimes work 24 hours straight. One time, I worked 35 hours straight. I work in homes and commercial buildings where there are water leaks and you have to dig up the concrete.

Most plumbers say they are open 24 hours a day. That's normal. All plumbers are. I have a slogan on the side of my truck saying: "I'm open 23/7." People ask, "Do you need an hour for sleep?" I say, "No, I need an hour for lunch."

I missed a lot of birthday parties, Christmases, and vacations to do what I had to do to reach this goal.

I also gave up friends. They're just not on my level anymore. I don't say that in a mean way. I'm on a different frequency. I had to leave a lot of them and even some of my family members behind, because they are all still stuck in the old paradigms we grew up with. I had to move on. I was lonely at times, but I knew that I would persevere. I knew I would succeed.

What is the one key lesson that you can give to anyone who wants to reach their goal?

Josh: Write your goals down in the present tense. At first, it was hard for me to understand and believe, but I knew if other people were doing it and achieving their goals, that was what I had to do. Write down your goals, become emotionally involved with them, get into the visualization process, and dig deep. Becoming emotionally involved with that goal is one of the lessons I can tell anybody to do. Becoming emotionally involved will set you up in that vibration; once you're in that vibration, you're going to attract what you're in harmonious vibration with. If you're in a good vibration which matches the vibration of what you're seeking, it will come to you. You just have to be patient. Sometimes it doesn't happen right away.

What is your next goal?

Josh: My next goal is to help over one million people become sober and live the lifestyle of their dreams. My brother and I are working on *Think and Grow Sober*. That's very important, because I know that if I came from such a background and I changed my life with this material, others can do the same.

Thirty-three percent of the world's population has a problem with alcohol and they're scared to admit it. If they can come forth and learn this material, it'll change them for the better.

How are you going to approach these people?

Josh: Thank God for technology! We just have to take action. Action is key to succeeding in anything. We're getting out there – especially with Facebook and social media – and letting people know. We've joined different groups, such as sobriety groups or recovery groups. We talk with people and let them know that we're here if they need help. Some people tell us we're crazy, which is okay. We've always been a bit crazy! We've also met a lot of great people who have a lot of contacts.

What would you like to accomplish in your life before you leave it?

Josh: I would like to sit down and make videos with Bob and work with him on our programs. His persona and the way he puts things will help change the world for the better. He has that attraction for people. He's a busy man, but I know that if I write my goal down and read it again and again, every day, it'll come to fruition.

If you had to choose one sentence that has a lot of meaning for you, what would it be?

Josh: The problem is not who you think you are, it's who you think you're not. I was the bad guy, the tough guy, the alcoholic. We become what we think about. In the past, all we would think about was when's our next drink? When's the next fight? We had this type of thinking because we didn't know any better.

I write down my goal in the present tense and I read it every day, bringing it forward into my life. Writing is power; it gave me the power to change my beliefs and to change my life for the better.

About Josh Thomas

Josh Thomas is the CEO and co-founder of Thomas Plumbing & Affordable Drain Service, the CEO and co-founder of the Power Within Institute, and co-author with his brother of *Success by Design: Blueprint for a Prosperous Life.*

Contact Josh at:
jtpowerwithin@gmail.com
https://powerwithininstitute.com
https://thomasplumbingservice.com

About the Author

Free Spirit: Inbal Hillel

Inbal Hillel is an Israeli businesswoman, mother, and partner who lives in Costa Del Sol, Spain, with her beautiful family.

Photography and travel are a part of her soul and her daily life includes taking time out to enjoy design, vintage items, yoga, self-growth practice, nature, and being with friends. Inbal has already traveled to 30 countries since she began her journey in 1995, and she plans to keep on collecting adventures and stories as she travels.

She speaks three languages and lives her life at full power with courage, keeping fear out of the game, and following her own truth.

Hillel's company, Multinational Kid S.L., helps children as young as four months old, all over the world, to achieve their potential and become multilingual.

In her other business, Inbal Hillel Photography, she lights up people's beauty by capturing them in their most natural moments.

Since she was a teenager, Inbal's awareness and understanding of her personal power within created a passion for growth that saw her devouring self-help material from the best mentors in the field.

Through her diligence in studying and applying the material, Inbal devised a successful formula.

Alive with excitement, she felt a sense of duty to share her knowledge in gratitude to those from whom she learned.

In her personal journey, it was inevitable that Inbal would meet other aspirants thirsty for success. From her desire to share, Inbal has persuaded fifteen more inspirational successes to share their stories and methodologies, along with her own, in this landmark book, "15 Stories, One Bob."

Contact Inbal at:
www.inbalhillel.com
Inbal@inbalhillel.com

Services Available

Now you can benefit from other exceptional services provided by the author. Contact Inbal Hillel to find out more:

Inbal@inbalhillel.com

Follow me on Facebook:
https://www.facebook.com/inbal.hillel.photographer

Your own unique video package

Enjoy the full unedited video recordings of all the interviews in this book. Experience first-hand the pleasure and excitement of the interviewees as they tell Inbal their personal stories of transformation.

Extraordinary Photography

Discover special places and unique moments captured by Inbal Hillel as she travels all over the world with her camera.

Teach your child other languages

Help your child become multilingual and to read in different languages using award-winning software which requires only five minutes' practice per day from the comfort of your home.

The value of teaching your child when they are young

Learn from Bob Proctor why it is important to start teaching your child at an early age, and how the mind and the subconscious mind work.

View the interview with Bob Proctor here:

http://bit.ly/2x0EiVw

www.ingramcontent.com/pod-product-compliance
Lightning Source LLC
Chambersburg PA
CBHW051818090426
42736CB00011B/1539

9 781988 071695